Rosemary

With love

from

Mummie.

Xmas 1945.

GARDENS IN AMERICA

AMERICANS ARE PERFECTLY ENCHANTING TO MEET INSIDE
THE GARDEN GATE

GARDENS IN AMERICA

BY
MARION CRAN

ILLUSTRATED

HERBERT JENKINS LIMITED
3 YORK STREET ST. JAMES'S
LONDON S.W.1 ✿ ✿ ✿

CONTENTS

INTRODUCTION

THIS book is not likely to be read by Americans because it is in no sense a record of the famous and worth-while gardens of an enormous country; nor is it a text-book; it is only, indeed, the travel diary of a garden-lover.

If I have made an unexpected picture for some of my fellow-countrymen who have laboured under my own misapprehensions about American gardens, I have fulfilled a task.

Americans declare, both severally and in chorus, that the British gardens are the loveliest in the world. They insist on it; they harp on it. They are eager to learn from us, and modest about their own achievements in horticulture, so that one is thoroughly misled—at least, I know I was; I really believed ours were the best.

I never suspected that (in this matter, at any rate) they suffer from a passionate and child-like humility. I know it now—it took eight months of time and twenty thousand miles of travel to learn.

I know now that it is all nonsense about our English gardens being "best." There is no "best" about it. American gardens are just as splendid, and as piteous, as aggravating and as precious, as maddening and as marvellous . . . and as healing as ours. Gardens are, in fact, the same over there as here.

There arises from them, as from our own, the essential fragrance of the national heart.

The films show America to us as a land full of crooks and gangsters, and "it" and night-clubs; the newspapers show us America as a Shylock snatching its pound of flesh

GARDENS IN AMERICA

CHAPTER I

THE CALL

IT was in 1920 that the man misled me. He said there were "no gardens" in America.

I was seeing the country for the first time; seeing it in the unfortunate manner common to a large number of Europeans, a manner highly resented by the Americans themselves;—that is to say, I was spending a month in New York. I was hospitably entertained by English friends in a pretty flat, high up in the air in Park Avenue by 56th Street.

It was early January, and the frozen-into-stone appearance of everything so wrought upon my peace of mind that I began—perverse and inopportune—to think about gardens; the very last thing any sensible Easterner thinks about in the bleak New Year. I tried to get some American gardening books, to cheer me up, but could not find any, though I must say Lewis Hind was kindness itself, taking me to picture galleries, museums, art galleries and such poor substitutes for the living flesh of flowers.

I sat humped in a very easy chair, surrounded by radiators and all the dreadful comforts of matter, remembering my garden in Surrey . . . how I had made it . . . how people insisted on calling it "old-world" . . . I longed, with a sickness, to be back in the shrill but kindly air of the misty Island with knees upon the ground and a trowel in hand.

was so sensible and dry to the feet, that it took my eye at once; he had made an avenue of brick pedestals and had set pots of flowers upon them all the way up; the whole humble effort at beauty was infinitely touching; inspired by it I made haste to buy up some old paving stones and make tiled paths. I knew no better than to buy the old "pitchings", being cheap, and then found each long narrow stone had to be placed in the ground like a nail, lengthways downwards, only a small surface showing. The effect was lovely enough—like an old cobbled street —but the work of laying the stones was very slow.

Refreshed by the pretty effect of this hard work, I then essayed a much greater thing. I found the steep slope of the field drained every scrap of moisture away, so conceived the idea of terracing and making a sunk garden below, where the rain and dew might linger on a flat surface and keep some life in the sandy soil. This gigantic effort took many weeks of digging to transform the slope into levels, and after that a great deal of learning and prying and questioning to find out how to build steps and walls. The only paid labour was that of the old man who taught us how to mix cement with sand and water and bits of scrap iron.

I hunted restlessly for a garden book while I was prisoned in New York "seeing America" in that long ago year of 1920 . . . thinking constantly of my own garden over the sea. It had been a shaggy hillside when I first came to it; now it had grown into a lovely and romantic garden, full of sweetness and charm, where I had learned many a priceless lesson. One was patience. Cities make a bewilderment of the fevered day, but in the long, strange silences of tilth we learn to lean on a larger rhythm.

And another thing I learned was the true pleasure of hospitality, for a garden charms the sweetest note into the voices of friendship.

I know exactly what I want when I ask for a "garden book" . . . I want something quite local; I want to be taken into the very heart of some particular garden and to share the fun of it on the printed page with the person who has made it and loves it best,—I want to catch the rays of that personality, spending itself on the passing flowers, reflected back from a written word. I want warm, breathing human books such as Gertrude Jekyll writes, or Sir Herbert Maxwell or Alfred Austin. But I did not seem able to find any such in New York and I discussed this sad blot with Lewis Hind, my host, who pondered awhile about it, and then said:

"Ask B. He ought to know."

"B," it appeared, was the American manager of a very well-known firm of British literary agents; and I thought he sounded a hopeful sort of person.

". . . and you must go alone, Marion; I can't take you because I have an appointment. The sooner you get used to the traffic the better. It's quite simple."

I peered down into the cauldron of noise, appalled;—all the traffic in those tunnels of streets went "the wrong way" and bewildered me to death. I felt I would as soon walk along the underground-railway track, or fling myself under the first car and get it over. But Lewis shamed me into going; he was quite right of course; I was a perfect nuisance having to be taken everywhere . . . but nothing then or ever has made me like the streets of New York . . . the nightmare of that journey to B's office remains still! With nerves pulped to receive any impression I found myself at last sitting in front of Mr. B the literary agent and besought him to tell me of some American garden books,—he promptly assured me there were no gardens in America; and therefore no books.

When I vented surprise he waxed positive and slammed his hand on the desk with vigour.

There were no gardens, he said; none at all. Americans did not care for them and the climate made them impossible anyway. As a faint whimper of doubt still curled round my tongue, he even grew wrathful in his emphasis.

At last he convinced me;—and labouring under that belief I set forth to the Cape of Good Hope to write a book a false position . . . *were* there any gardens in America? At last, peering over the marble balcony on the fateful night, I saw a regal woman come sweeping up the great staircase carrying our bouquet with an air both sweet and stately; I felt enormously relieved, and also certain that if Mrs. Samuel Sloan represented them, the gardens of her country must be worth seeing. We all enjoyed her immensely. She gave most of us our first glimpse into America's lovely world of flowers; and played the winning part of an ambassador probably better than she knew.

Her bright gleam remained for some time practically my only illumination except for stray American visitors whom I met now and again; they babbled rather humbly of their own gardens while they revelled in the beauty of our famous English parks and pleasaunces. They were too keen on learning from us to render any very distinct educational service to our woeful ignorance of their own land,—though by reason of rather gloomy beginnings some of the personalities of those Americans bit deep into memory; etched in clear light and shade . . . one of them was that of a tall dark-eyed Californian with a very pretty wife and young daughter, who had taken tickets for an English tour arranged in aid of the Queen Alexandra Fund for Nurses.

I had been asked to conduct parties round gardens in this good cause and found myself considerably mortified during the adventure because it happened quite often that we had to put up at very dreadful inns,—and by that I mean the dead-alive hostelries of this England. Houses without central heating, with one bath (if any), with appalling coffee, frowsty menus and unspeakably slow, dull service. With all their enthusiasm for gardens, I often found the patience of my pilgrims wearing very thin. On one such occasion, after a long tiring day rumbling in a motor-coach down lovely curly lanes hung with may blossom, turning into one old historic garden after another, we ended up in a provincial town with a rather worse inn than usual. The pretty lady complained loud and bitterly. I was about to snap, being no angel, when the tall husband led me aside and spoke with such sweet sincerity of how tired she was, and how sorry she would be to-morrow, that friction was averted. He took her back to London where the Savoy was more to her liking and the next time I saw him he was walking, with other pilgrims, through my own garden, the little dark-eyed daughter holding his hand.

He had come to ask if I would join them all at the Savoy for dinner and cabaret, next evening. It was the last thing I wanted to do! I had escaped at last from days on the dusty roads, from strangers and strange gardens. I had no wish in the world but to sit under my own old quince tree and hear the nightingales when summer dusk fell on the wooded hills. I did not want to toil off to London, and dress up, and go into the fashionable throng where I am entirely foreign (though I must admit, never bored, for people are very amusing to watch). . . . However, this quiet guileful creature persuaded me that the most generous thing I could do was to accept his hospitality. And I went. I struggled into elegant raiment,—cursing softly under my breath:

"Whatever's the good? They have plenty of resources without me. I don't even know what the fellow's profession is. And I shall have to drink sweet champagne or sparkling burgundy or something disgusting."

For it was well fixed in my mind and with ample reason that Americans do not know their way about a wine list since prohibition worked its wicked will on the States.

While we were getting chatty over iced melon I learned that my host knew many Californian nurserymen. That was interesting; I began at once to try and find out something about American gardens; but he became obstinately modest and would only talk of English ones. I could not learn a thing; absent-mindedly I took up a glass of golden wine, which was not champagne, and was about to gulp when a heavenly fragrance crept out, and fixed all my attention. I put the glass down and caught the dark eyes quietly observing me.

"Don't tell me I have found an American who *knows?*"

she her city chains. It was a book to read; and re-read.
Night after night in the old English house I would read
myself to sleep with it; what was "shad-bush" and what
did "hickory" look like? The elms I pictured of course in
the form of our shaggy, rather shapeless English elms with
heavy Dundreary whiskers up their trunks. What was
"Joe-pye weed" like? She wrote so vividly that I could
smell the ferny woodland scents of their forest. I lived in
their joy of the bird-life, the stories of their animals. I
felt the thrill of buying their land, building the house and
working it out through the years to a sanctuary for all wild
things. I certainly walked in that American garden, till
sometimes I wondered if the writer could not feel an eager
heart meeting her now and again at the turn of a path. I
wished I could find more American garden books, intimate
and local like that one.

It must have been about this time that young Michael
Rimmerley began being a nuisance to me. I had known
the boy for long and long; and never more of him than
that he was a husky lad with broad shoulders and an oddly
assorted passion for dogs and trains. Michael and his
puff-puffs! Once let him stay in a house with a spare
attic or lumber-room and he would start building like a
beaver; tunnels, tracks, signal-boxes, stations (with flower-
beds on them to scale, Heaven help us!) gradients and all
the rest of it . . . a fearful and wonderful railway system
with miles of rail would suddenly appear round the walls
of the room, with expresses, goods trains, red and green
signals and noise complete, puffing along. I believe he
blew cigarette smoke into the stomachs of his engines; they
certainly belched out white stuff like steam. He would
come down to stay week-ends in my garden in Kent and
terrify me by surveying the field and orchard with trains
and tracks on his tongue; a "wonderful system" he could
work out, he thought. But in odd moments between he was
very good to Jock, the self-willed, highly-bred little Dandy
Dinmont;—and he was very obliging about books.

Now I never lend books, because to me they are very

precious; precious as people; but I gratefully read and faithfully return any lent to me.

And Michael lent me books.

One was called the *Raven*; after reading it the State of Texas became to me all glory and a beacon; that which had hitherto been nothing but a hard and clacking word, leaped forth into a brilliant entity because of Sam Houston —the *Raven*—lover, statesman, dreamer;—Texas, the Lone Star State . . . I was all aglow.

And then Michael lent me a book called *Father Mississippi* which started a dreadful longing to see that wide, muddy, turbulent river,—and to tread the high grass banks they called "levees." To see the old plantations which Mark Twain and *Show-boat* had already sketched in my imagination.

Now and again Michael would sit in my garden and talk of stuff called "dogwood"; and of a place where there were in America, seven miles of red roses by the roadside; and of the cherry bloom at Washington . . . his young face full of longing. I began to realise that there must be a great country to be learned; that there was a lot one ought to know about America. . . .

Time went on; I kept on learning new things. Tales drifted to England of lilac at Rochester (New York), of the marvels of the Arnold Arboretum, of azaleas in a phosphate-bearing country, of pansies growing wild on the hills, and of some magnolia garden somewhere . . . I pricked up my ears at each of these comely little noises of hidden sweetnesses in that land "where there were no gardens."

Then in 1929 we English garden lovers became suddenly aware of an invasion; the English Speaking Union had bethought itself to invite delegates of the Garden Club of America representing every State, to visit England; and here they were among us; lively particles; exciting visitors.

They loved our bluebell woods, our old gardens of yew and box, our lanes hung thick with fragrant hawthorn. They found their feet among our flowers, charmed us with

their happy enthusiasm and startled us with their keen and
real flower knowledge. There was no longer any question
about gardens in America! That untrustworthy fellow B
had lied in his teeth and utterly misled me all the years ago;
they existed,—but still for us in a nebulous mist of fancy.
Did they have gardens like ours, we wondered, or were
they very different? Did they grow roses like us? . . .
daffodils, tulips, primroses, herbaceous borders, rock plants
and the like?

We really learned more from their exclamations than
from any actual descriptive conversations . . . every now
and again one or other would say "Have you any dogwood?"
seeming to miss some precious familiar of the Spring. And
another time, surveying the south wall of my old house
powdered blue with the pale fluffy balls of ceanothus
papillosus, I heard to my astonishment, "it grows wild all
over the hills of the West." Ceanothus, that precious
wall-shrub, wild? I had never so dreamed of it.

They exclaimed in a real envy at our holly trees and
hedges, and sniffed luxuriantly "how *fragrant* your pink
may is!" In short, by their flattering appreciation, they
roused in us all a keen desire to know what the gardens
of their own land were like; and it was borne in on me
that I, for one, must lay the insistent ghost. Whatever
the cost of time and trouble I must face the toils of travel
by road and sea to discover for myself what it was all about
—and what American gardens were really like.

Here then, is the story of how they looked to me through
my English eyes; it would have taken years to see them all
and see them properly; that is to say, with the thoughtful
attention one enjoys giving to every garden, great or small.
It is nice to approach with respect that which is, or should
be, so intimate an expression of the heart. I was only able
to spare eight months but during that time I travelled
industriously and made a fairly representative survey of a
great bewildering splendid country. I missed the roses of
Oregon and did not get to the gardens of the Middle West;
I only passed through Wisconsin; so my mortal feet have

not touched the paths of "Wychwood," nor my mortal eyes beheld that unknown garden friend; yet she and her garden are mine; possessed and treasured long before I breathed her native airs and passed by her country.

I saw the Spanish gardens of California, the date gardens of the desert, the lovely forlorn lost gardens of the South, the azaleas, cypress swamps and wistaria of South Carolina; —the historic gardens of Virginia; I learned the incomparable grace of the American elms, the green avenues and cherry blossom of stately Washington, the dogwood in Pennsylvania where I discovered in a gulping second how lovely England is because suddenly I saw curly roads and hedges once again . . . I touched the splendours of Long Island and Newport, the gardens of the North Shore and New England, coming to rest at last in the enchanted woods of Maine. A long and lonely journey covering thousands of miles by motor, ship and rail; exhilarating; sweet with kindness, and rich with beauty beyond any I had ever dreamed.

CHAPTER II

UPHOLSTERED GARDENS

IT is easy enough to say I did all that; but it took a great deal of arranging; because I am not one of those lucky writers who find the way smoothed, to the heart's desire, by private means. All I do and all I have has to be wrung from the point of a slow little pen.

There came a day when I surveyed the (somewhat shaggy) remains of a cheque for a serial story and announced to my publishers that I could write them a book on American gardens.

"Whatever for? There aren't any," they said.

But I knew better by now. I poured scorn on this vile calumny and spent a long time telling them of the slow steps of my own enlightenment. . . .

"Well! who wants to know about American ones even if they have any?" they asked.

"I do," I said, "and if I do, a lot of people do. I am just like everyone else. I am the Ignorant, who goes out to learn; and I write for the ignorant who like to learn. It's my own particular public I am thinking about. I feel sure they will be amused."

"They may be like Queen Victoria and say 'We are not amused,'" said Herbert Jenkins Ltd., thoughtfully.

But I had the bit between my teeth. . . . I had the pressure of many things behind that they did not wot of. . . . Sam Houston, the Mississippi,—shad-bush (what was shad-bush?),—ceanothus on the hills . . . wild . . .

By the time I had secured a (return) passage and was ready to face the salt sea-water, I realised that I was as usual flinging myself into a strange land with my heart

firmly imbedded in a green garden in the Weald. When
the wanderlust is upon me I forget the dreadful moment
of farewell that waits. On a bitter January in 1930 the
great roof of old hand-made tiles withdrew itself into a
frosty mist,—I said good-bye to the "ruin" * and realised,
with a sick pang, that I should not see my daffodils.
That was a dreadful business! I had been waylaid at the
last daffodil show by the marvels of Tenedos, Beersheba,
Mystic, Mitylene and other expensive beauties and spent
a great deal of money indulging the beloved garden with
a planting of aristocratic bulbs.

And here was the year of their first bloom, with me
going to America. If I had thought of it in time, nothing
would have induced me to leave them.

I sat on the spacious deck of the comfortable old *Baltic*,
rolling solemnly through a wintry ocean and pondered on
the flesh of the daffodil beauty I should miss. The thought
of them became an active pain . . . there was Fairy Snow,
the winged Leedsii of an exquisite delicacy; it has a vivid
emerald eye at the centre of its pure white flower,—I had
put it in a group alone where it would grow rapidly to a
large clump, being a great increaser; and not too far away,
among the peonies with their bronze and carmine shoots,
were the great gleaming flowers of Irish Pearl with its big
frilled crown . . . Mitylene, with her strong wide creamy
crown; the purity of Lady Sackville, so tall and strong,—
Raeburn and Mystic, those perfect snow-white narcissi,
each with an eye of apple green, rimmed with red, like a
wonderful bit of lacquer; white trumpets of St. Dorothea
and Snowdrift and warm peachy crowns of Stateliness;
beside the fiery confusions of Sunrise, Gallipoli, Slieve
Donard, Prince Fushimi and Spanish Flag . . . I should
miss them all. . . .

The Statue of Liberty sighted us, and we were met by
the usual embarrassing questions. Were we drunkards or
epileptics, lunatics or gaol-birds? Did we desire to blow
up the Constitution of the United States? How much

* See *The Story of my Ruin.*

money had we? Where were we going? How long did
we mean to stay in America? A sweet greeting.

The hostess, to whose hospitable apartment in Park
Avenue I was about to repair, had asked me to bring out
a parcel for her; and the first emotion, therefore, which I
suffered on landing was a slap from the "prohibition" laws;
the customs stalwarts pried into the package which I had
so faithfully carried across the sea and displayed three
bottles of a colourless liquid. I found I was suspect of
carrying gin about! And branded in the eyes of all
(American) fellow-travellers who stood by smiling. The
English ones being able to get the stuff at home if and
when they wanted it, did not carry it about or imagine
that I should want to do so. It was some time before I
realised the dark suspicion under which I laboured; and
blackened the case against myself by protesting loudly
when they threatened to knock the heads off the bottles
because I was so long trying to unscrew the silver-gilt tops.

I was quite sure my friend would not want her bottles
broken; I laboured virtuously to undo them; registering
afresh my regard for tariffs, customs barriers of nations and
labels of race . . . man-made, artificial miseries which our
children will look back upon with astonishment.

The irascible official was at last able to plunge a bulbous
nose towards three open necks and receive the intimate
blast of some elegant toilet preparation. He dismissed
me with disgust; and I was shot forth into the city of
New York; I was vetted fit for the society of the Free.

Nothing will ever make me like New York; it would be
easier to like an armadillo. But there were lovely happen-
ings; the very first sight I saw on entering my friend's
front door with her "gin" bottles in my arms, was a great
basket of daffodils sent to greet me by Pete and Lucia
Norfolk, the dark-eyed Californian and his pretty wife . . .
and there were my sea-change friends to find again.

They were the first New Englanders whom I had ever
met, with time to know them well (and therefore to love).
We had shared a strange journey years before in a German

prize-of-war, captured in Peru in which we breasted the
Trade Winds and drew up after an exciting month amid
strange companions, to feel the warm, indolent welcome of
Cape Town. They agree with me still that that journey had
a glamour and a quality no other had on any other sea . . .
the crew was mutinous, there was a fire in the hold half-way
across the ocean, the scuppers were plugged, the cylinders
had been dynamited; we stopped one night of full moon in
the tropical seas to bury one of the crew; we were never by
any means sure that the engines would not give out . . .
and we had but just come out of the shadows of the Great
War. The bones of our souls ached still;—we were men
spent and thankful for the isolation of the seas. We were
happy; suspended in a moment of Peace. It was a journey
to faerie lands forlorn . . . not of this world. . . .

Under the blazing sunsets we talked of England and of
America. Mrs. Robins, it seemed, was of Boston and he
was of Connecticut . . . I mentioned one day that a far-
off Dudley had been Governor of Massachusetts and that
my father's heraldic beast was the same lion "erased or"
. . . our motto also "nec gladio nec arcu." And then it
transpired that she had Winthrop blood, and that the
Dudleys and Winthrops had intermarried. So I hung a
fairy lamp of kinship on the frail filament of that far-away
loving . . . and made a place in my heart for the first
American woman I ever deeply admired. Sometimes we
would talk of gardens and she described a bare rock at
a place called Stamford, Connecticut, where they had a
country house built on a saddle of rock well out in the sea;
she tried to grow flowers there, she said.

It sounded a difficult job. I would talk of my sandy
garden in Surrey; I had not then turned to the clay of Kent;
and now I was about to see her garden at last. . . .

There was Dr. Norwood to meet, the poet-preacher
of St. Bartholomew's, who made a whole long evening
pass like a breath of summer on the flying beauty of his
words. There was Michael to make long noses at . . . the
nuisance! . . .

"Yah! I've got here, bother you; now what about this Mississippi and all the other bits and pieces . . ."

Michael grinned.

"You'll have to see the Grand Canyon, and the azaleas in South Carolina before you leave."

"I won't have any more of your awful soul disturbing," I said. "Azaleas! I've seen Ghent. Azaleas indeed! . . . and as to your epic in erosion I don't want it; I know South Africa; your Canyon is only an enlarged donga."

"Well, I will show you a bit of New York," he said.

And so he did. The roads of Westchester county . . . and the Hudson . . . and George Barnard's birds of Paradise under the shadow of the Lincoln that he brought to life in stone. . . . I liked George Barnard with his fine head and grey hair; the lovely old face was like George Meredith's, only warmer; we talked of Edward Carpenter; of Lee; of Nature. Tom Marshall, Michael's cousin, was with us, fresh from sailing round the world in the *Chance*.

And Michael took me to the Roxy Cinema-house, and Haarlem and the Metropolitan Opera with Gigli singing . . . and the Great Central oyster-bar and many other things young Michael showed me; till at last the ancient sickness of my soul came down again strong and heavy and I clamoured to be taken somewhere near a garden . . . away from the terrible city. He made faces as at some nit-wit, and consulted his mother's friends.

"Please!" I said. "O please take me, I shall not be disappointed—I shall be very happy to see even the shape of a garden here. I can imagine the flowers that will be there later on, if only I can see the places where they grow."

People looked dubious. It was early February, and New York was iron-bound in frost; the only flowers to be seen were the highly expensive cut blooms in florist's windows, and no one could quite understand this passionate desire to be taken to a garden in mid-winter, where there would be nothing but bare sticks and brown grass.

They did not know how the blinding beauty, the remorseless stress and splendour of their unreal terrific city wounds the nature-lover; how the peace of my mind was bleeding away and nothing but the sight of some growing things— of even a few leafless sticks of sleeping shrubs and flowers, with their roots in the eternal safety of the dear common earth—could heal it. I longed to look on a garden as the wayfarer longs for cold water on a dusty road at red noon. The desire must have had a fantastic quality, uttered as it was in an apartment high up over the roaring avenues of streets amid towering skyscrapers; but nothing, it seems, is impossible to ask in the city that is itself an impossible dream. Suddenly it was arranged; and I was whisked off to see some gardens along the most surprising roads.

Americans are an exceedingly thorough people; once they decide a thing has to be done, they do it very well; we in England are only slowly waking to the uglification of our countryside by bleak new roads, vulgar dwellings and hideous signboards, and in our usual way we are leaving anxious, good-hearted amateurs to tinker with the problem.

Observe an English village, now that it is released from feudal control. The death duties and war taxation have set them free for good or bad. Good we hope. But "Lordship" came of old stock and knew his trust; he kept up repairs on the broad acres, farms, and holdings; and he built his gates and palings of good strong oak; he did nothing scamped or shoddy. When houses were restored or new ones built the work was done with taste, so that it should not clash with the character and period of the old village. His estate was to him a vast garden, and it was his pleasure to see it kept beautifully in order. His tenants used "Lordship's" picturesque wells and pumps, the Village Hall he built for them, the playgrounds and the greens; they accepted dowdy, if useful, Christmas presents of red flannel petticoats and coal; there were certain social events thrown in during the year; they knew exactly what to expect from him and his. True they did not think much for themselves or in any way express themselves; they were more or less the creatures of the greater soul which brooded them, and which kept the countryside in a state of orderly grandeur. But if they were stagnant, the land was quick with beauty; weeds were abhorred; the fields were clean; rubbish was an impropriety kept out of sight; the woods and greens were planted and preserved, wild flowers flourished and peace reigned.

The old order has changed; there are new men and manners. Taxation necessitated the sale of the estate; another bought the property who was of a different order of mind. He was a "business man." He cut down the towering trees and sold the timber; dales where nightingales had sung for generations knew them no more; he stripped the woods and then sold the mansion for a commercial enterprise, and left the place.

The farms and houses and small holdings, thereupon, came into the possession of lesser fry; and timidly at first and then more boldly the freed village personalities began to express themselves; and they made a dreadful mess of their works! Their freedom none will deplore for a moment—but the crudities are hard to bear, until a better Thought prevails. Choice sites, sacred in the former days, were bought for building; a hideous medley of architectural styles broke out everywhere; disorderly ways crept in; the farmers, having paid off the imported hop-pickers, cast loads of rubbish close by the open roadway; tins, broken crocks, bones, boots,—all the obscene garbage and refuse of a collection of people housed under elementary sanitary conditions.

The hop-pickers, poor souls, went back to their mean streets, gaily decked with sprays of hops and "posies" begged from kindly gardens, or trails of honeysuckle from the hedges that had sheltered their raucous courting. But the unsightly memorial of their junketings lay for every eye to see, revolting and shameless in the lanes where formerly "lords and ladies" grew at cuckoo time, and "milkmaids" unfolded their dainty lilac smocks before the cool-eyed primroses. Advertisements in rabid lettering and colour began to show like leprosy on the face of the lovely old village which before had worn so sweetly its ancient dignity; . . . a petrol-pump,—roofs of tarred felt, of corrugated iron—abhorred material!—tawdry hen-houses which were but ramshackle contrivances of sacking, wire netting and (again) corrugated iron, . . . held in place with stones and bricks. Formless ugly makeshifts; lazy work.

Busybodies began to appear who must meddle and make things worse—the War Memorial must be scrubbed, forsooth, because the bronze figure on it had made the stone plinth green! So the softly weathering grey was duly washed away and the exquisite shimmer beneath it stared out in rude contrast to the suddenly whitened stone. The allotment holders must have a toolshed, so another corrugated erection must be placed in the most conspicuous position possible. Townspeople coming down in their motor cars and charabancs to picnic by the thinned woodlands must needs pick the wild flowers, not even keeping those they picked but strewing the dainty native daffodils, frail wind flowers and starry primroses dead and dying along the roadways as they walked. What is true of one village is true of hundreds; everywhere an orgy of bad taste and of greed prevails.

England, that "gem set in the silver sea" is lovely enough and dear enough, to make the thing an agony. A secret pride, a deep unspoken joy in the land of our birth is threatened.

The newly freed must be taught the place which beauty takes in the life of the community, and respect the desire for it in others, if themselves devoid; beauty, which is the essential need of every decent and sensitive soul, as vital to soul's health as the air we breathe is to the body's health.

In moments of spiritual courage one pictures a time when the "lords and ladies" smile courtly farewell to the days of privilege in the lanes and hedgerows, and the ethereal lilac-kirtled "milkmaids" grow sweetly beside them unplucked; admired of all. A day when all folk, common folk and grand folk, rich folk and poor folk, will learn in the rich democracy of nature the lost way back to harmony.

But in America they have taken hold of things with

vigour. The State has bought the land bordering on its great new roads so that no houses can be seen for a quarter of a mile on either side; building is absolutely prohibited there, and the effect is that of travelling through endless parks and woodlands. It requires some effort of imagination to realise that one is really passing all the time, through ugly towns; they are out of sight behind the trees and shrubs and grassy spaces, beyond the sylvan lakes and rocky dells of those great inspired roadways.

It was exhilarating to discover this fine road-sense in the New World; to spin down the great wide straightnesses. Mannered, efficient, commercialised nature as it all was, still there was a sniff of the "lusty pal" about me once more;—I revived and became chatty at seeing every bare tree whizz by . . . and my heart sang for the sight of a garden gate again.

We were away to Porchester to see Mrs. Henry Mallory's garden, and the designer of it,—Mary Rutherford Jay,— was beside me. It was a very exciting moment to me, as we stepped into that pretty place,—in my own body and blood and bones I knew at last, touched, saw, and walked within an American garden! It framed a vista to the sea; the surround-hedge looked like yew, but was hemlock, very neatly kept and darkly green; the shape of a lily-pond showed clear in a brown lawn that would be emerald in due season; there were some tall clean-looking shrubs beside it. . . .

"Those are white and pink dogwoods," I was told.

Dogwoods! These dogwoods . . . I tingled to realise that I should see them some day, at last, in bloom and learn what all this American passion for the things was about. The shape was pretty,—with the upward purity in outline of a candelabra.

I could see the idea of the garden design very well as I looked round; the pergola was made of chestnut wood, ample and restful, with flared-up cross-pieces telling the visitor that Miss Jay had been in Japan. But like New York itself (which is not so much a city as the sketch of one, dreamed by a god in his sleep and dropped to earth before he had wakened up enough to see what he was doing), so this garden was not so much a garden as a place of sheeted shapes. It was like some sculptor's studio; most unexpected.

It is not easy to describe to English eyes the curious effect of seeing everything wrapped carefully in hay and sacking—"put to bed" for the hard winter—nor to explain the queer sympathetic pity which mixed itself with warm admiration as I looked round, realising the courage such gardening needs.

A glimmer of understanding came my way for the ancient lie which had misled me for so long . . . it might be quite possible for people to think that there were no gardens in America if they judged the whole country by New York in winter time . . . but he was a silly, as well as a mischievous man; he had no right to be so positive in blackening America to a traveller.

I knew now that there must be many and very wonderful gardens, since the spirit was strong enough in Americans for all this packing-case effort every winter. It must need real spirit to face blistering winters, and scorching summers; unflagging energy and spirit.

I stood a long time by the neat hemlock hedge, stroking those flat graceful green growths while I made a sun of my eyes and woke the slumbering flowers up to a mirage of spring. I could see that it would be a lovely place, with its rose-arboured seats, fine peony borders and hosts of bulbs—scillas, crocuses, muscari, tulips, daffodils; all the enchanting race in every form and colour.

I did not meet Mrs. Mallory. I never saw her flowers in bloom; but her garden remains to me for all my life a magical spot, a place of illumination . . . and also, though she did not know it, a place of healing, for it made me well again of my city sickness.

Frozen, bandaged, swathed-up, desolate though it was, the deathless charm was still to be felt. The seal of living hands was there ministering to the living earth;—the sense

for dancing, theatricals, art exhibitions, entertainments, etc.;
it has three restaurants, gardens of fountains and flowers,
four fine roof-gardens and solaria, spacious lounges and
beautiful sitting-rooms in every period for every mood—
a richly found library—a gymnasium with every gadget
even unto rowing machines; a swimming pool of dazzling
flame tiles and blue water, like the Midi;—meeting-rooms,
dressing-rooms, laundries, infirmary, to say nothing of
1,250 bedrooms, each with its private bath and individual
enchanting scheme of decoration. The A.W.A. is an
Association of self-supporting women, every member in it
a worker . . . "therefore a builder, a creator," said Miss
Morgan, with that brilliant glance of hers.

She is the President of the A.W.A. and Mrs. Vanderbilt,
delicately beautiful, one of the Board of Governors. I
wished we women who work so hard for our living had
such a club in London; just such a club! As spacious, as
beautiful, as reasonable . . . an E.W.A. . . . . why not?

It was the day after I saw the A.W.A. that I went to a
christening-party and wanted a baby. He was the loveliest
black-eyed creature, of purely friendly aspect; most engaging; he went to my head having never had a son,—and I
had ideas of foundling hospitals, or something, where I
could get one for a pet. A tall leathery-faced Westerner
was interested in the idea, and said he knew all about
foundlings; but there was nothing very practical except that
he took my tea-cup away and led me to a thing he called
"apple-jack." One meets peculiar drinks in a prohibition
country; this stuff was new to me; quite palatable; a sort of
apple brandy. There was a lot of it, and I did not know it
was strong. . . . .

Trotting home, much exhilarated, on the arm of the
leather-jacket, who was all smiles, I found a wire from
Pete and Lucia bidding me come to California without
delay; they wanted to show me their spring.

I had to do some business first; I must sell some articles
or I should travel with carking care upon my brow! I
was "bought" without much delay, by the Scotch editor

of a well-known paper, for a new paper; the contract would just suffice to pay the expenses of my venture to America, I found,—which was pleasant,—it did not leave any over and it cut me out of any other magazines. But I was content.

I embraced Michael with fervour at the station a few days later; I had an enormous ticket fluttering in my hand . . . yards of it . . . and on bits were written such words as meant the Grand Canyon, the Mississippi, the "azaleas" and seven miles of red roses by a roadside.

I was going to lay his many ghosts.

CHAPTER III

INTO CALIFORNIA

CROSSING the St. Louis River that divides Wisconsin from Minnesota I felt sad at seeing Wisconsin pass out of sight . . . all because of that book *Wychwood* with which I had lived intensely, night after night, far away in Kent; the old house stilled to deep repose . . . everything asleep but my heart, which roved a garden and grew intimate with Wisconsin. It looked a bare State as I saw it now from a train window,—barren grasses and leafless scrub with snow lying thin and crisp under a cloudless sky. It was hard to believe the cardinal bird came there to build at Wychwood in summer; but Mrs. Hutchinson has told the tale with verity in every word.

How can American publishers say any garden book is "too local"! That is all it should be if it is to hypnotise you out of Place and Time and do the "magic carpet" trick for you. English publishers know that.

You go into Cleveland, Ohio, through garbage heaps; banks of rubbish; old tins and shoddy, like a dustman's cart.

I changed at Chicago; and was glad to get out of it. I was going to steal a week-end in Vancouver on my way to California. There was a sister I longed to see again; a war-widow; she and I had been dumplings together in the old nursery full of lively boys and girls; we had loved each other and had been friends all our days . . . a merry dear. . . .

At sunset and in the dawn Vancouver is ringed with mountains of rose and gold against the blue. Crisp airs blow down the boulevards from snow-peaks, sweetly

44

scented with aromatic breath of pine and cedar; gulls wheel overhead crying a tale of the sea, and of ships that bring the cargoes of distant lands to a city spread in beauty on mountain slopes.

It was ten years since I had seen it last and Alice, then a new made widow;—it was twenty years since I saw Vancouver first,—and the spell of it stays.

The years have not changed its loveliness, nor its big-hearted spacious charm. They have, however, greatly increased the beauty of the gardens, for the spirit of planting is now wide awake both in civic and private minds. The boulevarding is seriously regarded, even to an Act which decrees that house-owners must keep their boulevards in order, lest the Park Commission do it for them and charge it up against the property! Chestnuts and silver birch are the favourite trees, with avenues of maple and poplar and mountain ash here and there, these last for various reasons being regarded unfavourably.

Now mountain ash berries have a shining glory of their own. "Those bright red bunches would surely look very effective against the mountains and the sea," I asked, sorrowfully; for I do like rowan jelly, and am enamoured of the fruit which makes it.

The berries, it appeared, were the trouble; they make a slippery mess in the streets. The gorgeous maples with their incomparable autumn pomp of colour are too vigorous: —their roots heave up paving-stones and pipes, disarranging the hard-won civic amenities; but the blot on the poplar escutcheon I failed to discover.

I expanded and grew healthy in all the pores of my soul in that garden-lovely place, where people are still near enough to pioneer days of stress and struggle to have quick hearts. Material comforts and the hardness of riches have not yet spoiled British Columbia. I was among my own kind, very happy and gay; the worn face of my sister all asparkle; our hands clasped once more;—her spoilt young son, a handsome lad, driving us both mad with incessant jazz on the wireless.

I met some keen gardeners;—one of the lively spirits on the Parks Commission, and for years President of the Greater Vancouver Horticultural Society, is its founder, Mr. Fyffe-Smith. Their garden at Southpines looks on to the Fraser River over the Gulf of Georgia, through tall pillars of native cedar framing a beautiful distance. Thuja plicata, like the yellow maples, Douglas firs, maples, and dogwood are other natives there. Outcrops of stone upon the green lawns, set with heather, tell the nature of the soil which I admired in frank envy, gloomily remembering my sticky, heavy clay at home.

This dark, gritty, peaty stuff of theirs is far kinder to work; and the whole place being full of water-springs, it does not dry out in summer. One spring is piped from the lawn to a charming stone bird pool in a hollow, where robins and humming birds make their tiny hanging nests in the trailing vines and clematis.

The way iris gracilipes grows in that garden makes one want to pull oneself up by the roots and come over to British Columbia to grow it! Its mauve orchid-like flowers carpet the joyful ground in June.

"I give away cartloads of it," said Mr. Fyffe-Smith, as I peered down incredulously, "and look how this little oriental poppy grows. We call it Columbia. It came out of a sailing ship where an old sea captain had it growing in a tin can in his cabin; it is a clear bright pink of a different colour from any other that we know."

Columbia had evidently found a home to its taste, wherever it came from and whatever its colour.

"I am not sure that it will not be almost a weed soon," said his wife, dubiously, "but it is a lovely poppy."

I could imagine the foundling flying its crinkled pink silk against the blue of their delphiniums, campanulas, and Dutch and English bulbous irises; it must be one of those "weeds" no garden would be without; like sweet alyssum, or mary-buds, or Siberian wallflowers.

The rose-garden, dressed up in neat garments of dried bracken-fern, proclaimed a harder winter than we know in England. The plants were beautifully grown, for my host proved to be a keen rosarian. He pointed out the stalwart canes of a robust climbing rose, saying that Mme. Edouard Herriott was one of the best climbers he knew: —a tip which I pass on to English readers, for I do not believe we have yet apprehended the value of this good free-blooming rose under that form.

"The lithospermum looks dead," said Mrs. Fyffe-Smith anxiously, and I was about to inspect the brittle brown foliage of that "heavenly blue" rock plant with her, when a cry of vexation from her husband called her back to the border. A net had come adrift and he was in a great taking. The garden was spotted all over with small tents of netting because of the pheasants that come into the garden and eat the lily and tulip bulbs. They dig them out with their sharp beaks and peck out the heart of the bulbs. Wherever you go on the Pacific Coast, you will find nets spread to protect the bulbs from these robbers. "English pheasants," they say severely; but the pheasant is not a native of our British Isles. It is the bird of Phasis and has only been kept abundant in England for the last sixteen centuries by constant preservation and protection; it seems to me it flourished with a far greater vigour in this Britain beyond-the-seas! It is a real garden pest, eating the shoots of delphiniums and pyrethrums, too, I was told. The nets over liliums speciosum, auratum, regale, and tigrinum gave an odd appearance to the long herbaceous border where some varieties of campanula grow nine feet high. Near by, the great "king's spears" the eremuri, sent up their enormous shafts of asphodel, with cacti, sedums, and saxifrages scrambling at their feet.

We stayed by a broad scape of the Japanese Kæmpferi irises to observe the weeping form of a cherry tree.

"It makes a fairy pink veil, to see the irises through," said my hostess, who is the tree-lover and tree-planter of the garden, "behind that gnarled wistaria, which comes beautifully into the picture."

And then I noticed they had a wistaria grown as a

shrub; a knotted, twisted, fantastic piece of decoration—
the form in which we, in England, all too seldom see it;
being given over to the plant in its climbing incarnation.

The "joy-beds" were brim full of heuchera, potentilla,
auricula, kaffir lilies, aubretia, broom, hepaticas, primula-
marginata and such familiar friends. Daffodils, King
Arthur and Van Waverens Giant, thrust up among phlox
and delphiniums; large beds of peonies, massed blue and
pink hydrangeas and astilbes edged with pulmonaria and
trollius led at last to the wild fern-garden where the bright
indigenous vine-maples grow with trilliums, crocuses, bluebells, snowdrops, aconites and the blue forget-me-not.

"I knew we would have an early spring this year," said
the daughter of the house. "If the ground-hog comes
out of his hole on the second of February and does not see
his own shadow we have spring straight away; but if he
sees his own shadow he gets frightened and goes back to
his hole, and we have winter for six more weeks."

I was greatly interested in this piece of old Indian lore.
"Now I will carefully watch the hedgehogs when I go
home; there are some in my garden," I said. But the
"ground-hog" it seems, is a marmot, and that timid prophet
does not grow in the fields of Kent.

Mr. Fyffe-Smith took me to see Mrs. Roger's garden
at Shannon, planted on a magnificent scale over the views
which are the birthright and glory of British Columbia.
Among her wide borders and green lawns, under the
shadowy cedars and on her sunny terraces, I listened entranced to the old, old music in the voice of a gardener,
the note of longing for something not there! For she told
me of a mysterious wonder, "the cup of gold," a marvel
beyond compare; a huge golden cup, a great bowl of a
flower; there was nothing so wonderful in the world, she
declared, longing to have it over her pergolas as they do
in the warm suns of California.

Truly the language of the garden is the same the whole
world over; to step into a garden with its pretty grumbles
anywhere on the round globe is to step over the threshold

of home. That beguiling enthusiast, Dr. Cheeseman at Field, has his particular groan likewise. He longs for a lark to sing while he toils over his difficult soil in the Rockies!

"The hedges of England," he said lamenting. It made one homesick to hear him, remembering the tangle of wild roses and honeysuckle, the primroses and wild violets in the Homeland. He motors miles and miles through the Rocky Mountains to get river soil in sacks to put into pockets of the implacable rocks; *somehow* he will make himself a garden; possessed of our common passion he works, indomitable and obstinate.

The wayward habits of spruce puzzled him considerably . . . there was one that grew . . .

"I lifted them all so carefully in the fall, with a big ball of soil," he said in a soft voice as if he were talking to himself, "and then when they died I tried again in the spring. I tried watering and not watering; I tried different soils; I tried everything. I had no one to tell me, but I meant to find out their secret."

At the end of an arduous day, disheartened by many failures, he put one little spruce in quickly and carelessly, and that was the one that grew.

"And I still do not know why," he said reflectively, the handsome head of his collie dog thrust into his hand. He looked away to the peaks of the great snow-capped mountains and fell into a dream. I did not move or speak. . . . I waited to hear some more of his garden stories . . . but all he said, in a monotone, as if he said it often, was—

"I wish larks would live here and sing overhead."

Every day I could spare in Vancouver I wanted to give to the dear companion of nursery days in our father's house, —of girlhood—of lifelong friendship unspoiled by time, and tragedy, and distance, and the accusing parting hands of children. But I had to spare one day for Vancouver Island, where I met some gardeners who knew my books and wanted me to write one about Canadian gardens. I was very complacent.

D

"All right," I said, "I'll put them in this next book."
But they were very upset.

"You must not muddle us up with the United States;
we are quite separate.   We want a *Canadian* garden book
all to ourselves."

And so, of course, they must have one to themselves
. . . some day.

After that they tried to break my heart with their dogwood.   The word began to rouse queer reactions.   I had
had it hammered into my ears so often.   There was no
escape, their faces grew solemn with a sort of spiritual
ecstacy, "the dogwoods!"   It was not out yet, . . . but
they sang the saga of the shrub, their Cornus Nutalli,
till it almost bloomed for me upon the sound of their
words—their vivid ardent words; they breathed out a
blossoming into the crisp chill February air!

I began to realise I had strayed into a land of poets
(a dreadful thing to happen to any traveller), for poets
are lovers with tongues of fire when they talk of that of
which they love.   They make a music to stir the heart;
they create a longing.

Away in green fields of England was a garden to which,
as a man's to a wife, my vows were spoken, where my
duty lay; an ancient wife worn with centuries, hoary with
moss and lichen, sagging with time; a garden I loved and
to which I was honourably linked.   Yet here was this
young lovely British Columbia twining herself about my
heart, whispering of new gardens to be made . . .   I began
to understand the temptations of married men. . . .

The dogwood was not in bloom, heaven be praised: for
to see it is evidently to give up all peace of the heart.   I
saw again its straight clear wood, the graceful purity of
its "candelabra" habit of growth, the distinguishing two
leaves at the tip—all but the bloom and that has a siren
voice.   It calls from the primal woods and forests with a
great sound, and marks its victims so that they never cease
to long to live where it grows, and watch spring by spring
for its wide white flowers to open on the dark wood.

My fellow-gardeners in the far-off Island on the Pacific
Coast speak with the authentic voice of romance. They
have tenderness, they know how to love, they have fought
the wild and know how to be lonely in a distant land. They
have still the hearts of children; of visionaries; and they
speak a language which is full of song.

There was a rare wistful beauty in their eager enthusiasm, in the unspoilt child-like love they have, one and
all, for the beauty of flowers, and they made of every
moment a pleasure. They spoke of many delights,—of
the shooting stars that love wet meadows and look like
delicate wild cyclamen.

"They are dodecatheons, you know," said Mrs. Palmer
becoming botanically minded . . . "and they have a sweet
perfume."

They talked of cloud-berries in the June peat bogs which
are strange delicious little raspberries; of potentilla anserina
feathering the ground in silver leaf and golden flower, an
intelligent plant adapting itself, with great good nature,
to most varied conditions and rushing with concentrated
vigour into any that seem better, as most of us know to
our cost.

They called primula farinosa "mealy primrose"—a good
name for the delicately-powdered exquisite; they wanted
to show me the "bluebells" which are really a kind of
borage being Mertensia paniculata—I had often observed
struggling specimens of Mertensia Virginica in England
but could have, I knew, little idea of what it must mean
in the woods of Virginia;—or what this western form
could be like seen as bushes on mountain slopes bathed in
mist. They grew lyrical again over carpets of fragrant
twin-flower, the lovely little trailing honeysuckle Linnæa
borealis;—and then I found we were among dogwoods
again; they began to tell of the beautiful woodland carpets
of bunchberry; starry white in spring and heavy with
coral fruits in autumn. "Cornus canadensis" this one
is. I began to get dogwood indigestion.

Of all the Vancouver gardens, Mrs. Buchart's is the

largest and the best known. It is planned round the
central feature of a great disused quarry where alpines
grow in profusion and water has been skilfully used with
flowering shrubs and specimen trees. Everyone in British
Columbia, speaking of rock-gardens, will come to a pause
in time and say—

"You've seen the Buchart garden?" and then direct the
rest of the conversation to suit your yea or nay. The
avenue of approach to it is under standard red hawthorns
of melodious contour, round and richly full as a singer's
throat. Roses, lawns, fern dells and the majestic quarry
gleaming with its coloured draperies of bloom make up
the fairy tale—"like the garden of the Sleeping Beauty
when she woke and it burst into bloom," as they express
it who know it best.

It must be nice to plant things in Vancouver Island
where the soil is rich and growth abundant. The large
tracks of unexplored land away up in the interior give one
a pleasant sensation of plenty of room, of adventure still
to be had, of wonders yet to find. That precious call of
the dear unknown is hard to find on the round earth these
globe-trotting, over-populated days!

Strawberries and bulbs grew gloriously in Victoria; it
is quite likely that Vancouver Island will become the
Holland of the Pacific in the matter of bulb supplies, some
day, when the present tariff restrictions are removed in
the United States. The day will come, of course, when
distribution will be properly organised all over the world;
when the parasitic middleman will be closely watched, or
done away with; when the best goods of the world will
fetch the best price all over the world; when the attrition
of competition in international free trading will give a
zest to workmanship which it lacks under the coddled,
hot-house, enfeebling airs of Protection . . . the day will
come when our children will remember in amazement the
time-wasting irritation and expensive corruption of frontier
Customs . . . when they will travel swiftly and comfortably
and the goods of the world will wash freely round the world;

when false values will not be made by restricting output to keep up prices.

Loganberries make a standard crop in Vancouver Island; they are grown with an interesting cultural trick, for the canes are left trailing on the ground all through the winter to save them from frost. They are tied up to supports and made tidy again only in the spring; all the old wood is cut out in autumn. Very excellent wine from logan- berries is made in Victoria, for which the demand is so great that they can never mature it for more than two years!

The most lively and persistent shrub about the Island appears to be a yellow broom (not to be confused with the pricklesome gorse), which has taken hold of the country with passionate glee. A few seeds were brought over years ago and scattered, by somebody who liked broom, with surprising results, for the pretty stuff now seeds itself recklessly and turns each hillside into a sheet of gold. I looked at it with rapture as we drove along to find Mrs. Biggerstaff Wilson's garden, while my host muttered darkly, bending over the steering-wheel—

"I'll give you something to love it for presently."

He did not seem to care so much for the riotous happy- go-lucky broom as I did; and I wondered what he had got up his sleeve for "presently."

Mrs. Biggerstaff Wilson's garden is a lesson in how to grow winter heathers and purple daphne mezereum together for warm broad colour and rich perfume; early iris reticulata and species of crocuses sent up sharp shafts of blue against her banks of rose and purple. The place is planned with a nice sense of proportion as well as colour; one felt that a sensitive and thoughtful spirit worked sweetly there.

"I have so much to learn," she said softly, looking down on the rosy erica bells; and grew quite confused when I said she had been teaching me something—for I had never thought of growing the purple daphne with ericas carnea and darleyensis before. I do not know why, except per- haps that I have always preferred the ivory spikes of the white daphne mezereum and grown that variety only. Now that I have seen the bright harmony in her garden the purple one will grow for me in Kent beside my winter heather!

She asked me some questions about flowering shrubs, and the next thing we knew was that an English nursery-man's catalogue had materialised out of her study, and we had our eyes glued to those enticing pages heedless of time, while my host made faint gestures towards the car, uttering sounds about dinner and such vile matters. We were lost in ethereal dreams of Prunus cerasus bleiriana, Pyrus lemoinée, Syringa reflexa and other delights; his hospitable anxieties were spluttering in some dim and distant star. We bent closer to the book and trod the paths of wonder, regardless.

She told me the tale of the Victorian lavender. A man came to settle in the Island at Metchosin who had lived in China, and learned to observe things in that contempla-tive land; it seemed to him that the English lavender he grew (lavandula vera) was particularly fragrant, so he sent a sample to England. A cable came back asking for his entire crop, because it was richer in the fine essential oils than any other!

The war came along then and spoiled the development of what would have become a charming flower-industry in the Island. But a lady not to be beaten has now set up a still; and makes very good lavender water at Metchosin. She planted a quarter of an acre at first, and had a hard time with her still, because at that time British Columbia suffered from the prohibition illusion. (It quickly re-covered, and the liquor trade is very sensibly handled in Canada.) I was given a flash of Metchosin lavender water and sniffed it thankfully afterwards, over thousand of miles of desert, hill, and ocean, for it is a very delicious perfume.

I listened to the tale much enchanted. I have always wanted to grow flowers for a scent distillery. Visions of a halcyon life on Vancouver Island, far from the madding

crowd, in a pretty labour-saving house set among acres of
lavender, floated through my mind . . . with woods at the
back where dogwood grew. . . .

"Where can I see a davidia tree?" said Mrs. Palmer,
and I had no idea in the world, unless she could come to
Kew and see it fluttering its little white handkerchiefs
among the boughs.

I promised to hunt for it in my travels and let her know
all about the rare peculiar tree if ever I found one; I might
see one perhaps in California, the golden land of fruits
and flowers and immense treasures of oil and energy. The
land of great populations, great cities, great riches. She
thanked me with an air of one receiving a kindness. She
was quite sure I would not forget. And of course when
I saw her perfect faith and shining gratitude I knew I was
committed to hunting for a davidia tree on her side of the
Atlantic if it cost me my life. It would be like robbing a
child's money-box to betray that heartfelt "Thank you!"
I fell into dreams, wondering whether the people of California would know the grandeur of simplicity as these do
here in Victoria, whether they would love the incorruptible
earth, with its living grace, or whether material prosperity
had made them utterly sophisticated and cynical.

At this juncture I heard further and more peremptory
clamours from my patient host, and we bundled into the
car to see Mr. Croft Bennett's Quadra gardens, and meet
for all too fleeting a moment the charm of his rare smile
among the alpines he grows with a scholar's skill.

In the darkening hour we drove back to the pretty
garden of bulbs and shrubs where Mrs. Howell had spread
the board for her garden friends; and right merrily we
talked, for Mr. Howell's obscure "presently" proved to
be a warm insidious golden wine made out of broom
blossom!

The "week-end" I had plotted to steal in Vancouver
spread itself out into ten days . . . and suddenly the
azaleas began to worry me, I knew I must go on my way,
or those azaleas would be out before I got to them.

I found myself at the station saying good-bye and good-bye to the worn face that smiled as it had always smiled on me. . . . We had made merry the night before at a French restaurant of the underworld,—trying to recapture in innocent British Columbia the Bohemian gaddings of our youthful days . . . student days, . . . press days, . . . in London, Paris, Milan, Berlin. . . . We had curry and clams and baba-au-rhum and café "avec," . . . two longshoremen, a soldier's widow and a writer-woman . . . we talked a lot and grew homesick for the faces (and the prices) and the pace of long ago . . . indulging ourselves in memory . . . one of the mature delicious joys denied to callous youth. . . .

I stumbled into the train ruefully . . . Vancouver had been an indulgence . . . I must leave it and get on with my job . . . its soft names rang in my mind. . . . Kitsilano, Lulu Island, Coquitlam, Nanaimo, Siwash Rock, Burrard River Inlet, Burnaby, Kerrisdale, each name a music to make a picture in the heart.

I was rudely shaken out of sentiment by the exasperation of the system of train travel in U.S.A. You are jolly well punished for travelling in that country. My large, magnificent ticket, yards of it fluttering every time I had laboriously to dig it out, written all over with magical names to teach me the beauties of America had cost a terrifying sum in New York, but that apparently only gave me permission to look at the train. From Vancouver to San Francisco I had to pluck out of my trembling hands 12s. extra to get on the train, £2 extra to sleep on it and 6s. for a "parlour car"; I fluttered the first-class ticket unavailingly and said I did not want a sleeper; I was an old traveller and could bear anything; but it appeared that I was not allowed to travel without a sleeper on that train. "It was an Express."

I said of course it was an "Express." Was it likely I'd want a slow one?

"All right," they said, "you must pay for it."

"In England," said I, "we do not penalise the worker

like this; we are democratic. You can go third-class on the fastest express; and I have a first-class ticket here."

The man flicked it contemptuously.

"No good on this train! and look at the size of your country, anyway. You can go anywhere in a baby-buggy; and fall off the edge too, if you don't look out."

A vision flashed across me of the fells of Cumberland, the purple hills of Scotland, the deep moist lanes of Devonshire and Ireland, the craggy pastures of Wales; . . . the flat rich fens of Lincoln, the silver Norfolk Broads, the murmuring pines of Surrey, the rolling chalk downs of Sussex and the fruitful Kentish weald . . . what does size matter . . . the whole miracle of life will revolve for one in a yard or two of earth . . . *size!* . . . I paid the man in silence. I do not care for the American train ramp.

In this expensive and impolite vehicle I passed Portland, Oregon, the city of roses, in the night; and by morning the full excitement broke . . . I was going to see the gardens of America at last . . . in flower . . . I was "on ma' journey now," as Paul Robeson sings in his rich voice . . . we were climbing the hills of California where the white peak of Mount Shasta rose, under skies as blue as Cape Town. It was exciting to have breakfast in the Southern Pacific Car with the country unfolding like a book before my eyes; the marks of man were here in the hills,—placer mines by water sluices,—old log cabins, where rounded stones tell the story of washed ground and the trail of the gold miner is marked along the Sacramento Valley. I went and sat on the open platform at the end of the train and watched the hills slip by.

The warm sunshine soaked into my skin like water into blotting-paper,—and the call of lonely places rang out sudden and clear; I wanted to stay in the hills and forget people with their selfish and confusing thought . . . Soon there will be no lonely places . . . the earth is a little place; it can only support five thousand million humans—we have now two thousand millions; in 2031 there will be standing room only. I basked in the sun and pictured these healing desolate places in another thirty or forty years . . . parcelled out into city lots, . . . with comfortable plumbing; and prams full of more babies. . . .

At Endicott there were buds of almond blossom; at Redding I found mistletoe on oak trees,—as well as on apple, willow and black poplar . . . I had begun to think the Druid stories were a myth . . . that oak never grew the sacred bush . . . though I had found it to my surprise on pines in the Black Forest of Germany . . . but here it was, sure enough. Mistletoe on oaks! Presently there were olives and oranges . . .

The sun went lower in the sky . . . I began to shiver; the expensive train had given me a lovely day and now I was nearing San Francisco.

I had flung myself upon this journey to the Pacific on the thin paper of a wired invitation; I expected to meet the dark eyes and the pretty blue ones smiling a welcome; they had wired me to meet them at the Clift Hotel; I had not the foggiest notion of what kind of place that meant; suppose something had happened to keep them and they were not there?

I stepped into the taxi and uttered Clift Hotel with a lively sense of adventure. Pete Norfolk had said several times in England that he wanted "to show me California" . . . I was sure they meant to do something kind,—but suppose they were not there . . .

They were waiting for me;—and my room was full of flowers.

CHAPTER IV

A GARDENER BY THE GOLDEN GATE

THOSE mimosas! It seemed absurd to look for gardens here where the whole place was a garden. Bushes of erica melanthera, the richest and softest of all the heathers, wide drifts of primula malacoides, and bowers of Japanese double peach in full bloom make the streets outside San Francisco look like a Chelsea Flower Show.

I blinked my happy bewildered eyes.

These things come out of greenhouses in England, and here they belong to the everyday world; actually out in the streets; in the open; in all their delicacy of colour and form! And growing more luxuriantly than we ever see them in Britain.

The mimosa spread wild boughs everywhere, grey leaves tufted with their honey and gold. Acacias they called them; acacia mollissima, latifolia, Baileyana, dealbata. I found myself looking round for that broad-leafed acacia podalyræfolia, which makes a distinct cord of its own in the melody of trees, with its enormous yellow fluffy balls and glaucus cactus-like leaves. There were avenues of eucalyptus globulus with satin-white trunks and foliage of a queer majesty; live oaks, and Brazilian conifers.

The sun poured down; the benignant sun of spring in California; it emphasised the poignant drawing of Monterey cypress against the sun-washed creamy houses. But, for all that warm clear brilliance, mists come out of the sea every now and again; they cling, cool and kind, about the city of the Golden Gate, tempering the heat; soft clouds of mist, that move about the hills and lie in the

59

valleys, refreshing all living things, the green of the leaves
and the rose-leaf skins of the children.

I found myself contemplating Pete and Lucia now
and again with a faint wonder. I had no way of judging
values in America, but it seemed to me as if they must
be spending a very great deal on my entertainment; there
have been certain adventures of my own when I have
become reckless in the sacred cause of hospitality, too
happy in the company of some precious guest to count
the day of reckoning ahead;—I did not wish to incon-
venience them . . . or impair presently their peace of
mind!—It was difficult to know what to do. Perhaps
all Americans entertained in this style, and had four
Cadillac cars and two chauffeurs who were wonderful
drivers and never let one put foot to ground.

"You are not a prince in disguise?" I said to Pete once.

"No," he said soberly, "I am a squab-farmer."

I wondered if perhaps he could let me do a spot of
work when we came to his farm;—something to help . . .

The only way I ever learn geography is by going to
places, I always believed that Los Angeles was a suburb
of San Francisco; this misapprehension upset my garden-
viewing considerably, because it was told me by the
Garden Club of America in New York (I believed) that
San Francisco had no Garden Club but Los Angeles had.
I discovered too late that the reverse was the case. Under
the belief that there was no Garden Club to approach in
San Francisco,—and that I could presently drive out to
Los Angeles and ask the president to put me in touch
with its representative gardens—I met Pete's question:—

"Now what do you want to see?" instead of with—

"Please take me to the president of the Garden Club,"
—with an odd request.

I said I wanted to see something of the beginnings of
gardens in California. And he, whose one idea was to
give the traveller what she wanted (and quite ignorant of
my Garden Club confusion), set about taking me to places
I would not otherwise have seen. So though I missed

A Roof Garden in San Francisco

Mrs. W. B. Bourn's great well-placed oaks and her series of enclosed gardens at San Mateo, and Mrs. Hunter's lilies under the redwoods at Burlingame—and Mrs. Lawrence Scott's and Mrs. William H. Croker's gardens and only heard of them later from Mrs. William C. Van Antwerp at Pebble Beach when we sat on Mrs. Tobin Clark's loggia looking out on to the rough foreshore with grey skeleton Monterey cypresses fantastically flung against the sky . . . although I missed all these I gained something different but to me most precious,—the touch of the hand of a lost gardener by the Golden Gate.

The wish I expressed to Pete was born of a little book.

Among my treasures is an inconsiderable volume entitled *Scharman's Journey Overland to California*, printed privately by Mr. Scharman's son. It contains the personal story of the pioneer's journey from New York to the Californian goldfields in 1849, with his wife, a three-year-old daughter and two young sons—his entire family. He wrote it in 1852 on his return to the East. It was the pioneer's granddaughter who gave me the book in a stately apartment in New York and I loved to read it, and realise the comparison between America then, and now. Looking at the beautiful gardens around San Francisco, the fertile valleys full of richest commercial orchards, at the pageant of almond, peach and prune blossom I cannot but remember how he says in his book:

"California will never be agriculturally prosperous because the places suitable for farming are very few and far between—at present it is only a land of vice and gruesomeness."

With all his sense and courage that young forty-niner hated and feared California. One cannot wonder; it cost him his wife and little daughter—both died on the desperate journey.

Wherever we drove, out to parks, to the Golden Gate, to houses, we went along roads set with gardens. The hilly streets of San Francisco reminded me of Madeira and so did the flowers and gay bright blossoming trees;

as I looked at them Scharman's words came back—and came back. I wanted to see something of the beginnings of what is now so settled a beauty, and established a prosperity in this "land of vice and gruesomeness."

So one day I stood with Mrs. Horace Jenkins, a white-haired, pink-cheeked, dark-eyed sprite of a woman, an "old-timer" who made poetry out of her garden for us. Not only were her flowers lovely, spread under the bright sunshine, but the story of her struggles, her failures and successes made a little saga as she unconsciously unfolded it.

The site looked an unpromising place for a garden when she and her "sweetheart" chose to perch their home where the dunes of San Francisco end at the Pacific; wind-whipped, hungry, inhospitable; she has flowers now tumbling down to the sea brim, where the wide blue ocean curls white upon the sands; artemesias and mesembryanthemums and such frolics; above them is her succulent garden, every rock and every paving stone selected, carried and laid by her "sweetheart" and herself.

I did not meet "sweetheart," but he abounded in the conversation; she only used the word husband once, and that was obliquely, when we passed a veteran aloe. Poising like a humming bird near it for a second she sipped the honey of a thought,

"One gets to love old things, husbands and things, . . ."

And then she passed on to the ledges and rocks, where the lily-pond gleams white with its snow lantern and its goldfish, and high overhead the tea-house looks over the garden.

Against the fence hung a grey curtain of the climbing mesembryanthemum verruculatum with its rosy blooms about to break, so easy to grow that one felt it could start anybody making a garden picture; a carpet of buttercup-oxalis, sweet alyssum and grape-hyacinths led to the treasures of her rocks; cacti, agaves, opuntias, sedums, stapelias, echeverias, sempervivums and the rest.

"Look at the dogwood," she cried, ". . . if I had limbs like that I would not care if I bloomed or not."

Dogwood? Dogwood? I pricked my ears . . . but no entrancing blossom could I see.

Pete caught my glance of hope.

"No! no luck: its not Cornus Florida or Cornus Nutalli! This has lovely wood but only an unfortunate creamy green flower."

We pored over a rare striped agave and she mourned in a sorrowful motherly voice, "He's only had one baby"; a low birth-rate! She had looked for a nice prolific troop of young striped agaves and the fellow had only had one. However, bunches of green "baby toes" were plentiful enough; and also the long white hairs of "old men"; baby "old men," hoary in their youth.

I paused by some lovely rosettes with a silvery patine and ruddy points to learn that echeveria farinacea is native to San Francisco, and I marvelled at the great yellow flowers of her sempervivum holochrysum.

"These succulents are very bewildering, their names are growing laborious," I complained.

"You would be confused enough if you went to Mr. Orpet's place," she laughed. "He has some eight hundred kinds of cacti; genera, species and forms, and I can't keep pace with those words anyway; there are at least twenty genera split from mesembryanthemum! The botanists are crazy, drunk with syllables. They must all go back to mesembryanthemum in the end; they'll have to! But succulents are really lovely things to grow; they are so atmospheric. They don't want manure; air is enough for them. They love to live."

We left the botanists to their tongue-twisting of the cacti while we stepped lightly over "Johnny-jump-ups" and "Baby-blue-eyes"; and I learned that the lovely name of their wild godetia is "Farewell-to-Spring."

By a bush of Pride of Madeira, that blue echium I have admired in its own bright island at times on journeys to South Africa, she looked around her garden affectionately.

"It was all a sandiness when we came, a few wild lupins

catch the real history of him from the voices and records
of the living, while yet his essence lingers among men.

Mrs. Oakleigh Thorne said a very true thing to me in
Santa Barbara:

"The Californians should be keeping their records and
writing garden history now, or much that is wonderful
and interesting of the early days will be lost."

I wish they would.

Write it accurately, with knowledge and sympathy, trace
the history of the taming of the arid, forbidding, difficult
country, which so sorely tried the heart of Scharman, Mrs.
Liebman's stalwart pioneer grandfather; trace the tales of
lost garden-lovers and tillers of the soil so that men like
this well-beloved dead Abraham may be read of in the
land they served.

There must be many more; I would like to know more
of Ozro Howard, the naturalist, who collected the birds,
plants, reeds, relics, etc., of the Death Valley Exhibition
which was shown in New York and in London and is
now (I believe) at Kew. It was he who knew where to
find the native succulents of the desert in the haunted
stricken places; he loved the birds so much that he would
utterly forget the rattlesnake at his feet to get a look into
a bird's nest. He was a naturalist and a poet who fell in
the race, and died, and did not win to glory.

I want to know more of Mrs. Rowntree who roams
the Californian hills with a Ford and burro and sleeping-
bag, collecting seeds of the wild flowers all over the west;
a seed-gipsy, a lover of the wild lands; a comely, delightful, small, keen, gentlewoman, who tore the heart out of
me with longing to "leave all and follow"—to listen again
to the silence of the hills—to touch the heaven of loneliness with nature, where through the "slit of the senses" one
gets a fleeting glimpse of the four-dimensional body. . . .

I want to know more of Judge Silent who loved and
helped flowers in California; of Francis E. Lester's experiments in rose stocks and his researches on the old roses
of the Pacific Region. He and I stood together among

Johnny-jump-ups—(viola pedunculata) and fairy shooting stars, while he showed me his collection of rose species, and talked of the sport from old Veilchenblau, he uses for budding; a nice stock with smooth clean wood.   I want to know more of Mr. Hugh Evan's garden life. There was a lady with a large "place" kept by many gardeners at Beverley Hills who said to me of him, "That fellow has a lot of junk," and when I visited his garden at Santa Monica I found it a treasury of beautiful and rare plants!   Mr. Evans loves South African flowers and bulbs; he is, so far, the only man who has flowered a protea in California; not very successfully, as he will be the first to admit, but he flowered it.   I wonder why proteas are hard to grow there?   I can see the rainbow wonder of them at the Cape, still in my dreams.

I want to know the inward story of Edward Howard who travels the wildest places in the tropics and collected the rare palms for Mr. Doheny in his great glass house where I saw first that absurd climbing palm with stems that grow thicker at the tip—coral stems dotted thickly with small green marbles—rambling in a fantastic fury and ending in a tuft of green palm-leaf.

I want to know more of those plant-men Howards. . . . . Paul the nurseryman, traveller and eager enthusiast, and his sister, who knows all the wild flowers, Fred the rosarian, who bred the Los Angeles and Wm. F. Dreer and Mrs. W. C. Egan roses; it was he who made the first cross between amaryllis and crinum (that Amacrinum Howardi won him a silver cup).   Fred Howard has represented America as judge at the Bagatelle Trial Gardens of Paris, where they try roses from all over the world. I want to know more of the Howards' father, who had no respect for trespass signs, but would take the whole herd of his children trailing through anyone's garden—his "menagerie" went anywhere where they could see new plants!

There is so much—so much—in that wonderful, incredibly lovely California to know; so many silent men of San Francisco;—also that we were going to take it "quietly," and stay at Pebble Beach, Santa Maria and Santa Barbara on the way down to Green Valleys Ranch, Pete's country home, where they purposed to spend a week-end before we went to Los Angeles.

In so short a time I had grown to love San Francisco! There is in it an untamed heart . . . the hall-mark of men; —I enjoyed my early morning scrambles up and down the steep hilly streets,—I loved the soft sea fogs, the sparkling noon sun; old Abraham's untidy nursery garden and the "sweetheart's" wife and succulents at "the end of the Trail". The splendid civic centre with its Opera House and Courts of Justice was beautiful; a marvellous square, white and stately, set in green shrubs with golden doors. I could admire their splendours with all my might but there was something else,—something Vancouver has,— a shadow behind the bright prosperous eyes,—a memory of hardship, of loss; they have known the insecurity of all but love. . . .

I was aware of Harry's observant eye watching me in the mirror over his driving-wheel as we spun down the State Highway, between the clean silver trunks of huge eucalyptus trees,—straight tall gleaming pillars support-ing a green roof. Long afterwards he told me he watched to see if I was "nervous." That was funny;—I have been driven by the maddest assortment of drivers in the strangest vehicles in rough forgotten places all over the world. That his superb driving on that perfect road should make me nervous was indeed a jest!

We passed ponds of goldfish, so many that I became suspicious and asked questions to learn that they have goldfish "hatcheries" in California as we in Europe have trout hatcheries,—in Hampshire and the German Black Forest, etc. At Palo Alto we went to Stanford University and I asked about a property called Casa la Bomba sup-posed to have existed some fifty years ago, if the stories of a wicked old adventurer were to be believed. I was curious to learn what truth there was in his highly-coloured

tales;—but no one had ever heard of him. He posed
as a playwright, a very dishonest and disgusting person,
treacherous to everybody—including all his wives. In
the days of my ignorance I thought he was a typical
Californian!

Besides goldfish hatcheries there were squab farms,
"rabbiteries" and silver-black fox farms all along the way;
for miles on either side stretched the famous prune orchards
of the Santa Clara Valley,—apricot, peach and cherry
orchards, beautifully kept over their carpets of cloth-of-
gold mustard;—and at Saratoga, which lies under the
wooded hills we found Cherokee roses in bloom.

Pete was busy consulting his watch,—"there was time
to see the Scanavena garden," so off we went to it, whatever it was,—and soon we were high on a hillside with
two eager-hearts in the land of their desire.

Four years ago the garden was a dog trail without even
a cow-path; Pete was faithfully observing my request to
see the beginnings of gardens! On twenty-two acres of
rough hillside, there are now paths of oranges and lemons,
camellias, tree ferns, daphne odorata (the maddening sweet
thing), roses, fuchsias, rare acacias, rhododendrons, . . . and
Dr. Scanavena said he had fruited mango. I love that
fruit; it tastes like a pinewood smells; I looked about with
a hopeful mango-ish expression but a glitter in Pete's
eye makes me wonder if perhaps the Doctor's mango was
like those passion fruits that sometimes ripen after a tremendous lot of coddling and fuss in England—and taste
frightful.

The Barberton daisies in that garden were a marvel;
gerberas they call them,—but I have been in the Northern
Transvaal and prefer their home-town name. Mrs.
Scanavena came out of the woods, with nice earthy hands
and a perfect gardener's scowl. That hatred of "visitors"
that I know so well had her by the throat. I was in
absolute sympathy . . . we had interrupted her planting;
we were a nuisance . . . in three minutes she had for-
given us and was laughing out of her bright dark eyes

CHAPTER V

THE SMOKE OF THE HILLS

ALL I knew of Carmel and Pebble Beach had been gained precariously from a book called *The Valley of the Moon*, by one Jack London.

This place as it materialised in the dawn before my astonished eyes was not in the least like the picture patched together in my mind from that entertaining book; I set forth for an early morning walk along a coast-line, rocky as Cornwall and far more vivid in colour, to find all sorts of entertainments. Accustomed to see James Carter's solemn presentment of carefully-grown hothouse cinerarias in England at Chelsea Flower Show every year I was much taken aback to find this, the most lovely groundsel, positively boiling out of Mrs. Dan Murphy's garden on the roadside in a bewildering confusion of size and colour . . . it was as if a bit of the Chelsea tent had escaped . . . no cypress hedge apparently could restrain the cinerarias' passionate growth.

An orange datura hung its wide bells over them . . . the morning light shone on large bushes of echium . . . blue spikes rayed with soft mauve-pink, translucent in the sun; early shadows lay dense and black on emerald grass and among them, under the pine trees, looking out to the sparkling sea, was a log house; rough and simple as if a poet lived there close to nature, among the violets and moon daisies . . . a sense of great beauty stole out of that little house . . . later I was to meet the lovely daughter whose studio it is. . . . I trotted back to our bungalow to find Pete and Lucia deep in a huge mail and ready for anything. There were some letters for me, one from

74

my faithful maid at home with snapshots of the cats and
Jock the Dandy Dinmont terrier in the garden. Jock
looked a bit solitary sitting by himself observing the cats
at play. I gulped down a lump of homesickness. There
was another letter from an American in England telling
me to be careful whatever else I missed "not to miss magnolia in early April." Well! I couldn't be bothered with
any more appointments. I had one with the azaleas at
Charleston in early April . . . and another with cherry
blossom in Washington, and another with apple bloom in
the Shenandoah Valley, and again the lilacs at Boston
where I hoped I might perhaps catch a glimpse of, or
even have a word with, Dr. Wilson of the Arnold Arboretum . . . yes, and what about the Mississippi, too? . . .
I could not take on any magnolias. . . . I dismissed the
letter. . . .

Presently we went to see Mrs. Tobin Clark's rockery,
and sat in the courtyard with her while she told us about
it;—the sea-spray and poor soil make gardening difficult,
but seeing that it was then only two years old it was a
very nice one. There were some fine young rose trees in
a sort of wire prison because they had to be protected from
deer. I was looking around me, happy in the sunshine
and the sound of her pleasant voice, watching the sea
tumble on to the foreshore piled with great grey boulders
between which grew the ancient Monterey cypresses in
their native habitat,—when she said something to make
me come to attention with a jerk. . . .

"The tree doctors want to cut the dead wood off them,
but I won't hear of it." . . .

You never know when you will hear the voice of poetry
. . . it sings out of people unconsciously,—they are the
reeds through which the music blows; music borne on
the wind of the wild heart . . . that bloweth where it
listeth . . . you never know when you will hear it.

What Mrs. Clark said was a word of pure poetry. She
loved the grey skeletons rough drawn against her wild
seas; she had no place for tree doctors with saws and

from the common world by wild beasts,—to approach
whom the courage of everybody was vastly tried. Mr.
Hearst has made himself into a fairy story.

We ascended marble stairs, passed the plash of fountains
among marble limbs of naiads, trod wide terraces of marble
hung with roses; I glanced up at the familiar sky to catch
the sense of a common world in this staggering Arabian
Nights place . . . but the mist had blotted out the stars!
. . . In one spot a cluster gleamed; and to that my eyes
clung. . . .

"The Pleiades have changed their shape here," I said
at last, faintly.

The escort smiled.

"Those are the lights on the castle towers."

Later I heard how guests tell stories of arriving at San
Simeon at a late hour; and, losing their way in those twin
towers, wander up and down for hours in the night looking for their bedroom (each with its bath-room).

The "Castle" itself is an amazing palace of treasures,
where Mr. Hearst entertains his week-end guests, looking over the green plains that roll down from green hills
to the sea; that is to say they were green as I saw them,
in spring after the rains. Later I believe they are golden
brown,—sun-burned,—and Californians have told me they
like that colour best.

There were a great many people in the house-party,
some famous for beauty, some for rank and some for wit.
All attractive. There was a lavish, gay simplicity in the
entertainment, but of course it was the simplicity of the
sophisticated and the aware; so I did not expect to meet
the voice of Pan there.

Yet I heard the pipes for a fleeting memorable second,
—at the misty hour of dawn among marble naiads and
nymphs, on one of the terraces.

A watchman passed by, curious, I suspect, to know what
I was about at that odd hour. Together we bent over
the rose and mauve wings of a large dead butterfly.

"Have you noticed the daffodils?" he asked, lifting an

eager old face. "They are clean and strong in this cool morning mist. They do not often stand up well in our hot climate; but the pansies do. *They* hold their heads up! O! the mettle that is in them!"

Of all the splendours of that magnificent establishment with its lavish entertainment and many guests, that is the moment I remember best. The "mettle" of the pansies! A new word, a poet's word.

It was during the long drives round Carmel and Pebble Beach that the sentence which I heard spoken by Americans beside my old house in Kent came leaping to sudden life. "It grows wild on the hills in the West."

Lucia said to me, smiling, "Our wild lilacs will be out for you," and I thought of course of syringa, the lilac family. When I cried out at the pale blue smoke like the smoke of a wood-fire, upon the hills, I was surprised to hear them call it "lilac." I had never seen such blue lilac. . . . When the car was stopped and we got out to walk among it the smoke of the hills was ceanothus!

It grows wild on the mountains of the Pacific Coast. Thysiflorus is the commonest variety; there is a savage abundance of it everywhere . . . on the chaparral-covered slopes, on the sea-edge, or among redwoods, with a long florescence like the pretty hybrid form we call Gloire de Versailles.

The ceanothus I myself prefer to grow is C. papillosus, —I have regarded that charming shrub, with its aromatic smell as more of a wall climber than a sturdy, self-supporting semi-tree. . . . I looked upon it with profound amazement now growing all over the place in a solid jungle of blue.

Mrs. Rowntree at Carmel Highlands showed me more in her "garden of holes" as she called it (referring to the pot-holes and gopher-holes). She has gardened in England and New Jersey, in Northern and now in Southern, California; each with its own flora. She told me there were about sixty species of ceanothus, one with a leaf like a holly, but they are often difficult to identify and the botanists' obtained from plants grown under cultivation. Mrs. Rowntree does all the collecting, personally; taking care never to exhaust a stand of native plants, and she makes a point of scattering seed in flowerless places.

"In the course of collecting," she said, "we use every means to rescue wild-flower seed from real estate and agricultural developments, cattle, and insects. We are working in co-operation with the conservation societies, our motive being to preserve the natural flora of the Pacific Coast."

"I shall get a burro and put him on a trailer at the back on my next seed-hunt," said the gipsy-lady thoughtfully, "there are always places where the car can't go,— and I must take the seed-bags and sleeping-bag along. They are too heavy to carry."

I wonder if she has her burro by this time? . . .

In Carmel Highlands I saw Mrs. Harris's intimate garden, sweet with bird song.

"It looks so like home," I mused; and then found she is an English officer's wife.

Not far away Miss Pilkin's garden slopes to the sea very sweetly. "Here is the first moraine in an American rock-garden; wouldn't Mrs. Beebe Wilder love that?"

I glanced at the alpine garden, so familiar a feature of gardens in England; envying them the fun of newness.

"Who is Mrs. Beebe Wilder?" I asked.

"Hush! She is *God* in America in rock-gardens."

At Carmel Mrs. Sidney Fish has a "garden enclosed" with four beds, very simple. A dial pencils the illusion of hours in a sun-stricken place, there is a sun-court outside its heavy doors, monastically studded with nails, where gazanias, calla lilies, and a small pool make a mocking bow at the idea of a garden.

"It was only made a year ago," she said; "we call the Ranch 'Pescado'; it is a lot of fun. That is the joy of the West; one can make new things."

We sat quietly, looking at the great rounded hills billowing away on every side, where the cattle love to lie on the roads in Recamier attitudes at night-time, utterly undisturbed by the car's headlights, which have to honk-honk to be allowed to pass.

"One feels rather an ass planting things when the wild flowers are so lovely all over the hills," she said.

I looked at her, beautiful, young, aware; uttering an unforgettable word.

I had come to her Ranch expecting to find a vast conventional garden invaded by a hurly-burly of Press men, cars and people, because Lindbergh had been gliding there that morning;—but the tall lord of the air had gone. I found instead the sun, and silence and a few distinguished guests. There were strawberry jars by the door; "Stuyvie steals the berries!" (young Stuyvesant, aged eight, in a big sombrero, looked a trifle conscious). There were Scotch terriers, a borzoi; Mr. Fish, brown and lean and laughing on a piebald horse; and this brilliant young hostess with her wise, rare flower sense.

I was to meet the same Pan-pipe again in my travels through America; sounded in many ways; a simple, passionate feeling for flowers. In Texas they love their "blue-bonnets," the wild lupins of the plains; in California their "Johnny-jump-ups" and "shooting stars"; in Oregon their "fairy-bells" or "golden-drops," their blue Ithuriel's spear and "crimson firecrackers" (brodiaeas, these two); in Sierra Nevada they have their "Lanterns-of-the-fairies"; shining satin-white globes that dance in shady places. There are blue "Virginian cowslips" in the woods near Richmond; rosy "lamb-kill" in Rhode Island; "bunchberries" in Maine. In every part of the continent I found these intimate affectionate names; and also men and women who loved to show the flowers to me.

Sometimes I found a soft perversion of names. To one Western woman the honey-scented, pretty alyssum was "sweet elysium!" So she would call it whenever she looked down on it, rubbing its little white heads against her feet; and another set forth, when "good-bye" was near, to pick me a bunch of her "Johnny-quills" because though! That was a happy memory to take from Monterey.

He is the Chairman of the "Committee on old roses" of the Pacific regional rose conference, a division of the American Rose Society. A small man with a shrewd kind face, that suddenly grew remote and sensitive at the word "Penrith"—(I had been lecturing there a few days before I sailed for New York and the name cropped up). He comes from the Lake District so the name made him homesick. Mr. Lester is a very interesting rosarian,—he grows ecæ and many other species, pteracantha, moyesii and so on. . . .

I had a moment of fun when he was very much confused. He had not, I think, caught my name when Pete said it; anyway we came in time to a place where copper-bronze shoots were thick with bud.

"Marion Cran, a new rose raised by Samuel McGredy," he said briefly.

I walked beside him a step or two and then said—

"Do you like me?"

His dismayed bewilderment at this searching thrust was exquisite. He faltered in his stride, glanced at me timidly, rallied his forces and said with gallantry:

"Very much." . . .

And then Pete explained. Much too soon. I was enjoying myself.

Once at Sevenoaks in England I had such another moment, when Mr. Baker, President of the Iris Society was taking a party round his beautiful garden to see his new seedlings.

Caged in wattle was a tall, pink flower of most voluptuous grace.

"That is Houri, out of Marion Cran," explained our host far too deep in iris pedigrees to have the least notion of the outer world, manifest in various smirks at his elbow.

"And who is the father of my child?"—I said at last, —interested. . . .

His face, absorbed, withdrawn, full of iris-history, turned

to me;—it fell league on league to the workaday world, touched the circle of smiles gathered all round; snatched vainly at memory, and then, the courtier hidden in every male, rushed up to save him.

"O! Imperator," he said wildly.

Mr. Lester did not think much of American gardeners . . . he likes the slow old country methods.

"They are always in a hurry," he said, "and want a garden in a year. They won't wait for things to grow."

And that, of course, is true in many, many cases. But I have also known it true in England.

Americans do like to get effects in a hurry. The exploit which stands out in my mind in all their gardening is the transplanting of very large trees. Where we in England, like to plant a seed and watch it grow for us in the slow majesty of nature's rhythms, enjoying our shrubs and trees from their infancy, living with them as they grow, these people prefer to "ball and burlap," and get immediate effects; they will not wait as we do in Europe for an acorn to sprout. I cannot say in how many gardens I have stood under wide spreading boughs of great trees, newly planted and held in place by wire stays. They seem to have mastered the art of transplanting anything of any size to any distance. Marvellous mechanics these American gardeners! Somehow they always make me a little uncomfortable, accustomed as I am to the other tradition. I do not know that there is any sense in feeling like that; it is something like my grandmother's attitude towards electric light I fancy. "Flying in the face of Providence," she called it. Too quick, too easy! I wonder if the trees mind . . . if they live as long . . . they certainly seem happy enough in a couple of years in most cases, after that major operation.

We lunched at Pop Ern'st's.

It is a wooden shack on the sea-shore where you get abalones and sea-food from the Bay of Monterey, cooked by Pop, a wonderful old dear of about three hundred pounds in weight, with bright brown eyes under his red fez and a white moustache and a white apron over his splendid paunch.

Gulls, those birds of the tramp royal, who cry the wanderlust back into my blood at the most inauspicious moments just when I think I am going to settle down and grow peonies and roses in Kent for ever . . . the gulls wheeled and cried round our sun-hot backs. . . .

A pelican sat on a row-boat watching us cynically. . . .

"Whoever saw a human mother vulning?" says he.

Whoever did?

Blue and white fishing-boats ride in the Bay, the hills around were dark with cypress green . . . Pop came and told me how to cook squabs.

"Baste them with red-currant jelly and butter . . . and cook them on a spit," he said.

Lucia and I went down to choose abalone shells,—rich in their lustre-lining of mother-o'-pearl . . . we clambered into the car, filled with much good food.

"I am getting to love this country," I said.

"We'll show you California," they said; "wait until you see our poppies."

I wondered what their poppies were; having seen their "lilac."

CHAPTER VI

POPPIES AND REDWOODS

WE left Carmel, that place of artists, after lunch at the Blue Bird, and on we went, spinning down El Camino Real . . . the Highway of the King.

There is beauty left even to American "efficiency," in the mere music of these old Spanish names. . . .

Hour after hour the great amazing country whirled by; we passed under miles of eucalyptus avenues, and fragrant golden mimosa; saw thousands of acres of sugar beet by the foothills of Solidad; and kept on passing "hot dog" stands (whatever they are), "barbecues," where apparently the hungry motorist may find fowls, piglets and other beasts roasted whole on spits ("beak to tail," one surmises, is the idea imbedded in that word); twisted native sycamores leaning, friendly, to the ground thick white mottled trunks which never rear themselves straight up.

In the deep blue of the February sky a tiny luminous cloud over a distant hill took on a significance; could clouds ever rain in this golden land? . . . small homesteads, bowered in pink peach-bloom, on hills of powder-blue ceanothus had a quality of utterly unreal loveliness. They had crept out of picture postcards, they were of the stuff of books and fairy tales! Impossibly, absurdly beautiful. There were walnut orchards, pepper trees, huge tracts of lima beans, camphor trees, and grevilleas.

Lucia and I were nodding a wee, lulled by Harry's marvellous smooth driving and the bright whirling landscape; but suddenly Pete woke us out of any such vile thought of rest.

"Look at the poppies," he cried.

Away to the left was a gamboge stain on the land,—a mile or two of gamboge at the foot of the hills. . . . Poppies? . . . The car turned off the highway and off we went to the coloured place. Everything looks close in that clear dry air, as in Africa; but it is not close if you try to get there. When we reached the poppies they were what we so clumsily call "eschscholtzias," I don't know why, for they are Californian poppies; they belong to the order Papaveraceæ; their graceful, glaucous, fern-like leaves and satin shining cups are little like most other kinds, but poppies they are and most attractive. The calyx forms a hood which is pushed off over the bud as the petals expand, —absurd little merry dunce's caps which I had watched often enough in my gardens at home, where I had sometimes been annoyed with the gay orange flowers for seeding themselves here and there, about the place, year after year, as if it belonged to them.

"Poppy and mandragora" . . . the words belong to each other in their heavy sleepy rhythm because of Shakespeare's immortal line, "Not poppy not mandragora nor all the drowsy syrups of the world." . . .

The mandrake, the true mandragora, is a nearly stemless perennial herb, with milky blue and purple shaded bell-shaped flowers borne in clusters among the tufted leaves. It is a native of the Mediterranean, and one of the most interesting of folk-lore plants. The roots are thick and fleshy, spindled and forked; sometimes they take on a remarkable resemblance to the human form. Those are the treasured roots used in love potions; the plant itself is frequently called the love-apple. When roots are violently pulled from the ground, they are said to shriek as if a body were in pain.

I have heard tomatoes called love-apples. I do not know which is the true love-fruit, but they both belong to the same order, the Solanaceæ.

The old herbals give eerie drawings of the mandrake root and branch, shaped like a most unhappy-looking man with long hair and leaves and fruit growing from his head; not at all the sort of wight one would associate with love-spells.

The chief beauty of mandragora is vested in the rich sonorous name; it is not a genus beloved in gardens; but the poppy, its eternal associate, is quite a different matter.

Now here is a race to please the world; poet and mater-ialist, artist and tradesman alike, and to make a grateful call upon the intelligence and affection of a good gardener.

Poppies grow in many forms and many colours; as annuals, biennials and perennials; in fine fragments of petalage, delicate as crumpled silk; in great heads of the same texture or in tangled mops of baby ribbon; they may be flaming scarlet or all the shades from pale to deepest of purple, pink, white, yellow, orange, and now we have them at last in the clearest, truest azure blue.

The botanist will call them papaver, and some mecon-opsis—which means poppy-like—but they all belong to the Papaveraceæ and papaver stands for poppy, which is the name by which the happy Ignorant knows the lot.

There was a time when every fashionable drawing-room rang to the strains of a song called "The Garden of Sleep." Clement Scott went to Cromer one year, and saw the chalk cliffs ablaze with the flaming scarlet corn-poppies which are the envy of every American who comes to Europe, and for a long time many of us regarded "poppies" only in the light of those brilliant sun-loving chalk-loving flowers, "papaver Rheas."

Nowadays we have enlarged our apprehension of their possibilities, for we grow in our gardens the dainty Shirley poppies in all their pretty variations.

The tall stately annual poppy which has large crowded double flowers of "baby-ribbon," is the opium poppy notorious in commerce, precious in medicine. It is the one that gives us handsome heads of seed, and has an un-mistakable glaucous foliage; the same soft colour as these Californian poppies upon which in their millions my ravished eye now rested.

Oriental poppies are perennials, and very easy to propagate by root division; they are those great hairy-leaved plants with enormous flowers of dazzling clarity and very often a black centre, which catch every eye in the herbaceous border; like the blue poppies and the Iceland poppy, they like to be grown in a shady border. The most amazing colour is perhaps Mrs. Stobart, an indescribably clear cherry-rose. The pink orientals make a handsome clump in a border and their colour usually accommodates itself to the general scheme more happily than does that of the scarlet flower.

The dear little Iceland poppies never grow very tall, but of all the race none is more beautiful than meconopsis Baileyi, which likes to find itself in leaf-mould in shady places. I have seen drifts of the stately plants, with the pure blue crumpled silk petals round their golden crowns, growing gloriously in Miss Jekyll's famous Surrey garden; and also fine plantings carrying hopeful seed-pods in Mrs. Kemmis's wood and water-garden near Beaulieu.

These rare blue poppies are not difficult to grow, if they are given the conditions of soil and shade which they prefer. I must admit I never saw any really well-grown plants of the blue meconopsis Baileyi in America;—there must be some somewhere; but I always happened to see very mournful struggling ones. There was nothing like that in these ramping orange cups here at our feet! I did not stand up and deliver any dissertation on papaveraceæ, or mandragora either. I fell on my knees and put my hands among them. Exquisite, satin fine! Pete was going quite mad like a school-boy, running among the flowers, picking white, cream, or double sports where he came across them.—Lucia looked on indulgently, forgiving the maniacs.

Harry was hard at work grinding the cinema handle,—to make a flowery picture for the archives of holiday; their memory album.

The poppies grew among fragrant sage-bush,—and a Californian horned toad came to join the party. A shy, pretty fellow, with loose grey scales like a snake,—a tail,—and a

DEEPSET IN SHADY TREES—THE WISTFUL, FLOWERY INN OF
SANTA MARIA

ring of small horns round his head. He ran away quickly over the loose gritty sand, a beautiful bit of grey life among the grey poppy leaves;—something between a chameleon and a lizard.

The poppies went to Pete's head. Lucia was full of practical sensible notions, about dinner and the inn to which we were bound. But what did inns or dinner matter now,—his feet were among the poppies in nature's own garden; Pete felt free. . . . He did not want to go back to the high road.

"I have always wanted to see the Pinnacles;—let us go now;—we may never be so near again."

And so off we went to one of California's National Monuments of which I remember best the difficult rough road and clear brilliant views on the way to it . . . I could hardly believe I was not in South Africa trapesing over the veld again. . . .

When we came back, a good deal later, weary and content, and passed the poppies they were all closing; a mile or more of wild Californian poppies shutting their golden cups tidily for the night. They looked like yellow crocuses, their small parasols rolled tight in points of gold among the fragrant sage-bush.

We sniffed sorrowfully at Paso Robles, where they have mud-baths and sulphur-springs; breathed the clear sifted air of almond orchards, where "smudge-pots" filled with heavy oil are on guard every few yards to make a protective veil of smoke in case of frost.

Mile after mile raced by—

Under the lids of our eyes hung the heavy sunshine; we tired of the whirling whorls of dust; of the spinning country; of the endless fertile valleys; of the heat. Hunger began to gnaw. It was then that we stepped from the dusty highway into a spacious house, deep-set in shady trees—the Santa Maria Inn.

Life is full of surprises. I never thought that I should find such an inn in America! There it stood, in a celestial shade of trees, withdrawn from the glare of the road—

the wistful flowery inn; the most unusual Santa Maria Inn!

And what was it after all? Cool bedrooms with their own cool bathrooms, an excellent dinner, a smiling host. I have had those before in other lands and not fallen in love with my house of refreshment. But here was a difference. . . .

In a land of flowers this is the Inn of Flowers. Mr. McCoy loves them and has made that passion the appealing note of his business; so he grows acres of a very well-organised "picking garden," and he fills every table, every room with the loveliest flowers. On any day of the year one may go to that inn and find it full of blossoms and never a faded one. It is a woman's job to arrange them daily, in bowls of glass, china, copper, pewter, brass and basket-ware. He has made a collection of fine old pitchers and vessels in all these materials to carry the beloved flowers. Fresh, brilliant, fragrant, they leap to the weary eye as one comes in off the travelled road; an unforgettable welcome. It did not surprise me to know that 60,000 people pass through that inn in a year.

Out of the cool flowery rooms we sped again at morn under wide camphor trees and lemon scented verbena; over the Santa Inez River and the Gaviota Pass to Santa Barbara. . . .

Pete began to change as we went;—he had been quiet and observant in England, and in Northern California;—now he sat up and chatted a lot, he seemed to grow bigger; his dark eyes flashed; he crowded the beauties of the country into aching words . . . he was flapping his wings—this was his country, he was crowing on his own roost—and I watched him spell-bound. He was as proud as proud. And he had reason. It was a glorious land.

"We will lunch at the Samarkand," he said; "but we will see Orpet's nursery first; and then you will see Santa Barbara mountain-girdled, island-guarded, as they say."

Avenues of acacia floribunda, the ever-blooming mimosa;

of Lombardy poplars, tall and massive;—of orange flowering grevillea, and miles of walnut orchard . . . a line of kelps strung along the sea . . . oil derricks all along the shore. . . .

At the Samarkand there is a "mirror pool" in the Persian garden, where one can pass enchanted hours before the moving shadow story of the garden. There are no lilies or plants to disturb the mirror surface, nothing grows in the water;—nothing but a darting goldfish breaks the limpid emptiness of the blue pool; in it hang pergolas upside down, roofed with bougainvillea, terraces, roofs, windows, balconies, cypresses, riotous purple petunias and orange calendulas, all a Dulac picture in the unsubstantial element. We had "cocktails" of pure tomato juice; a most sickly contrivance, but then I have never really liked the sweetish, oniony taste of tomato—I think Lucia enjoyed it;—we made merry over it, and sat in the sun at one of the coloured tables overlooking the hills. There are "cottages" for guests all round the formal court; and, beyond another lily-pool, the archery grounds.

I shall not readily forget Mr. Orpet and his nursery; he gave up his post as head of the Parks in Santa Barbara, to run his own nursery within easy reach of that Nice of the West; where he specialises in cacti.

He was born in Cirencester in Gloucestershire and worked in Cheshire and Hampshire before he came out to America. He looked at me with twinkling eyes, "Fifty years of gardening, Mrs. Cran, and never a week without a job!" He looks about forty-five and says he is seventy, but it is hard to believe . . . fifty maybe . . . he is the youngest "seventy" I ever saw in my life!

The nursery is full of interesting precious things. He has over eight hundred kinds of cacti there;—genera, species and forms. I pottered round in the blazing February sun wishing I knew more about succulents and could bring Mrs. Dudley Ryder to collect treasures there, for her beloved garden at Beaulieu.

We call succulents ice-plants, sedums, prickly pears and

houseleeks at home in England where only a few forms
grow comfortably in our cool wet climate, on rockeries and
roofs.

The variations in hot, arid countries are most entertaining; the creatures have habits; they are brimful of ideas,
and flourish on air, it would seem; certainly they ask a
frugal diet, a frail foothold. Out of their forbidding,
obstinate, antagonistic bodies suddenly spring the most
surprising flowers! Tender astonishing lovely flowers;
. . . you never know where you are with cacti.

I enjoyed looking at them, feeling their strangeness;
their humorous, twisted personalities, rough-hewn by
adversity. . . . In pans of fine sand, plants were increased
by the thrifty method of putting a lot of fleshy little leaves
on the sand and letting them do the rest for themselves.
They turn up their toes at first and then think better of it
and grow whiskers. At last a tiny rosette comes over the
whiskers and Mr. Orpet has a new plant.

There were scores of pans containing thousands of
strikings, seedlings, etc., for he was busy increasing a
precious collection of kalanchoes from Texas,—attractive
creatures with their spoon-shaped leaves.

There were kalanchoe Aliciæ, K. tubifolia, K. beharensis
among them, and K. mucronatum with its shell-shaped
scallops of silver velvet, crinkle-edged. Mesembryanthemum Schwantesii has limy incrustations, and M. speciosum
(which comes true from seed) has a gorgeous fringe of red
orange round a black collar and white eye, the characteristic fleshy foliage has a sheen like sparkling velvet. He
told me he had M. Alstonii with its flowers of blazing red
in bloom all the year round; he grew it first from seed sent
by Marloth, the S. African botanist. He has, too, the
strange opuntia papyracantha, in which the spines turn to
paper; one of the rarest of the prickly pears.

Euphorbia bupleurifolia, the pineapple succulent, is well
named, but I found it hard to associate it with its gorgeous
relation, the flaming pointsettia, and even harder, that other
euphorbia "grandicornis" with its milky spikes on the

thick green flesh; a vicious cactus-thing, with milk in the spikes!

I preferred the amusing succulents which pretended they are stones, like lithops Leslei, the protective "stone-face"; or the wily mesembryanthemum-pseudo-truncatellum which hides (with enormous success) in a pot of stones. The African dumplings, conophytum wiggettæ, are most amusing in their deceitful appetising appearance, like the best apple dumplings, and so is the alligator succulent, echidnopis dammaniana; an alarming miniature monster!

Of the aloe pienaarii, he had at the time I was there only two plants, direct from the Cape; but plenty of the German rush, equisetum, which is the best possible file; all the clarinet players use that rough-skinned marestail to whittle their reeds.

It looks a good deal like the handsome, smooth mares-tail, equisetum maximum, which grows in my Kentish ponds at home; and which I never suspected for a moment of having a relative in Germany with so different a hide; or that I was destined to discover it in distant California.

Argyroderma testiculare I found to be a silver-skinned testicle affair and admired its *savoir faire*; growing placidly between the old men cacti (cephalocereus senilis) with their long white beards, and fenestraria rhopatophyllum, the toddling little bunches of "baby-toes."

Outside the cactus houses, full of the rare new and only cacti of this astonishing collection I found other treasures. There was a Himalayan gigantea rose from Mr. Sturtevant's old original stock; the great white platters of bloom are out all the summer, smelling their sweetest at eventide. An interesting Texan plant is sophora secundiflora, a shrubby darker blue imitation of wistaria; Mr. Orpet is tenderly inclined towards that shrub, believing it will serve the gardens well; and he is also very fond of the beautiful clematis cirrhosa, an absolutely evergreen and everblooming clematis. It is a lovely climber, of C. montana leaf and habit. I wish I could grow it in England; it has fluffy "old man's beard" seeds; only they are pure glossy white, instead of the grey

fluff of our native English clematis; the constant white
flowers of cirrhosa show through and under this pearly
mist; it is truly a lovely plant.

The white broom they grow in Californian gardens is
genista monospermum, but here in this nursery of many
treasures is an improved form of it. The garden-lovers
prettily call it their "bridal veil";—it is a fine new introduction, genista Filipes, with a dainty, yet full-flowered,
spray; the bush looks like a fountain of snow and is very
sweetly scented.

It was blooming, when I saw it, near the dense orange
flowers of thunbergia Gibsoni, and not far away were the
staggering coral sprays of the hesper aloe. That western
aloe is native to Texas and Arizona; Mr. Orpet had the
first plants in Santa Barbara, some ten years ago; it is very
beautiful, with its striking silvery aloe-leaves from which
hang filmy white threads, and the long strong flower
branches set with tremendous graceful coral sprays. Cantua
buxifolia was out, with its drooping bells of pink; and then
suddenly I lost myself in a transport of memory . . . for
I saw hundreds and hundreds of gladiolus tristis growing
like weeds, sprawling and spreading everywhere in full
bloom! . . . In an instant I was back among the mountains of Africa; tasting again the hour in which I first
brushed a gladiolus growing wild . . .

Mr. Orpet was smiling at me. "They like it here, don't
they?"

He said they grow wild in Mrs. Elwood Cooper's ranch.
It was she who brought the first bulbs into California; his
own he worked up from an original planting of twenty-four
bulbs, specialising in his own strain which is a pure yellow
with no streaking.

I said "good-bye" regretfully, passing pink and white
sweet-scented oleanders from Honolulu as I left and handsome bushes of dombeya cayeuxii, with flowers like huge
pink hydrangeas. . . .

There is a great craze for gardens of succulents now in
the West, started originally by one of that vital Howard

family of plantsmen, Ozro Howard. No one had thought of collecting the odd whimsical plants of arid desert and sun-baked rock, much less making pets of them and putting them into gardens until he so enthused a wealthy woman of the West that she put her enthusiasm, money and social weight on the side of cacti and made them fashionable, so fashionable that they are now protected by the Government from "collectors" who were despoiling the wild; and killing most of what they dug up by unsuitable treatment in unsuitable soils. For her excellent share in the succulent "boom" she has now received a loud, not to say noisy, "thank you" from the Royal Horticultural Society of London.

I had looked forward a great deal to reaching Santa Barbara because of Mrs. Oakleigh Thorne. Among the members of the Garden Club of America who came over to England and won so much affection from everyone they met, certain faces and personalities had engraved themselves deeply upon my memory from our short meetings. I am ashamed to say how rarely people do impress themselves upon my memory; I remember flowers better. But these charming and very different women made each an imprint.

After Pete had taken us to the Biltmore Hotel and housed us in princely apartments, causing me some qualms at his extravagance, I rang up Mrs. Oakleigh Thorne, therefore, and heard her pleasant voice again. She was very kind, —would come the next day and take me to gardens; then we would see her own garden; lunch, and set forth to see more.

"There is no end to the energy of these people," thought I. But I did not know then that even Americans can drive up to the edge of their energy and over it!

I spent the evening looking over Mrs. Gardiner Hammond's place with poor Mr. Armstrong, the head gardener, who gave me the same feeling dear old Honess did in Lady St. Cyr's garden. In both cases the owner was away so the heart of the garden was gone;—and it was but a wounded place, lovely, but desolate because the mistress, whose smile was to each of these good men their exceeding great reward, was no longer there. The familiar of the beautiful plants was away . . . only strangers came now and again . . . the pleasant sound of happy guests had vanished and their laughing feet upon the grass. . . . I do not know anything more forlorn than a good gardener in a forsaken garden.

This one had many beautiful things in it,—there was a golden fruited solanum with purple flowers amid velvet leaves blooming at the same time,—a shrub like buddleia that wants pruning hard;—the Belle of Portugal rose, a hybrid from the Himalayas, makes a great hedge and Kennedya comptoniana was so full that we had to go up to a loft in order to see it spread below us in a great cushion of blue spikes, next to a sheet of rose bougainvillea. It is a climber very like Hardenbergia, I thought;—and the purple spikes reminded me of our own tufted vetch in the hedgerows. In a green garden apart, set with blue statices, blue echium, blue agapanthus and white arum lilies was the grave of Miss Salt:—on the sea-shore sheets of the cream-coloured native mesembryanthemum covered the sand and made their frolics round the guest's empty bathing-boxes, . . . a silent bowling green, a desolate boat-house. . . .

There were hedges of the glossy green pittosporum undulatum in flower; it was a revelation to me to see that amiable shrub, it is good for hedge work and to grow as trees, thrives in sun or shade and any soil, is a good ground cover, North or South, all along the coast; among the crinkled-edged glossy leaves are borne bracts of fragrant cream-coloured flowers.

I set forth very gay and festive with Mrs. Oakleigh Thorne next morning, and had a great time with her, so witty and wise among the gardens; I did not know the poor lady was fighting with an impending cold and staving off the overdue hour when she must go to bed, and rest it out of her system. She never let me guess it at all.

We saw Mr. Knapp's "Arcady," nobly planned between

The Swimming Pool in Mrs. Oakleigh Thorne's Garden at
Santa Barbara, California

the mountains and the sea, with a splendid lawn spread before
a majestic view, tier on tier of mountains, great live oaks and
green grass . . . "It looks like Italy and England mixed,"
I said; and they told me it was the largest lawn in Montecito
where water is scarce and gardening therefore a great luxury.
It was, I could see, a garden of great riches; but it was more
than that. It was a loved and lived-in place.

Here I touched (and did not know it) the desire of Mrs.
Roger's soul away in Vancouver.

"That is Solandra guttata from Mexico" I was told;
—and glanced at the handsome foliage without much
interest. The ugly name meant nothing and rather put
me off.

"It has a wonderful flower . . ." Mr. Munro went on,
hopefully;—waiting to catch a gleam; but if he had said
it was Copa d'Oro,—the "cup of gold,"—I should have
thrilled . . . and lingered entranced.

I found daccha, the "lion's tail," growing in the yellow
garden,—and was much interested in that. I know it wild
in wayside ditches in Africa where the natives are forbidden
to touch it. They eat it or smoke it or something; it is an
aphrodisiac apparently, for it is supposed to make them
run about and rape white women. I have seen it tidy and
elegantly flowered at the Vincent Square Shows in London,
labelled full-coldly, leonotis leonorus, not looking at all
like the handsome ragged outcast of Africa, with its whorls
of bright orange blossom always full of ants. The flower
arrangement is very like that of phlomis fructicosa, the
Jerusalem sage, which grows by my study wondow.

There were royal strelitzia reginæ holding up their bird-
of-Paradise heads; pomegranates, bougainvillea, alstromeria,
cannas, delphiniums, campanulas, great pillars of eucalyptus,
lotus, daphne odora, echiums . . . a great rose-garden
beyond a blue garden.

The bathing-place was like a Greek temple and debouched
into the water garden which ran in a series of cascades
from heads of differing design, (from a ram and a devil to
a lovely lady,) into stone troughs to a fountain and thence

down the hillside in a long runnel of stone to a grotto; there is a weeping pittosporum by a pool.

Arcady is very noble;—I have seen great gardens in many parts of the world, but not always to enjoy. This one was not only magnificent in its breath of treatment but also heart-beguiling. I was suddenly reminded of the man, who told me there were no gardens in America. How silly people are . . . I looked about rather helplessly. I knew I should never be able to tell English gardeners a tithe of this reeling wonder . . . it was too much . . . and suddenly I saw some polyanthus blooming at my feet! That was a great relief . . . though they were few and evidently precious in that soil and climate they linked my swoon with Kent, and restored my courage. How they must be blooming now in that misty England-Isle! Mrs. Oakleigh Thorne, sympathetic and sensitive, saw my reaction to the bunch-primroses. She smiled.

"They take you home."

They did indeed. I could see them pushing through the thick covering of decaying leaves which I prefer to have over them in my garden, obstinately obeying the rule I read in the hedgerows; and not the rule of the text-books which tells us to remove the dead leaves that autumn strews about their roots, because (they say) these make a hiding-place for slugs which eat up so many of the early primrose flowers.

Now the book of the lanes tells us how all the primulas enjoy their blanket of dead leaves; the embossed and fretted leaves of the plants push through the dead brown drift of last year's oak, ash, beech and thorn more crisply green, and with a stronger and more comfortable growth than ever they do in places that have been swept and garnished of this, their natural, food. So I, for one, am never given to cleaning them away. I have, instead, distasteful and back-aching slug hunts, with a basin of very strong salt water as a lethal chamber.

The polyanthus in Mr. Knapp's Arcady took me out of Illusion for a moment: out of the illusions of Time, of distance, which make such a confusion for us every day through the muffling veils of matter.

Mrs. John J. Mitchell has a small house and large garden, that happy combination; also the largest wistaria in America. It was on a stone house, and that was carefully taken down, and a pergola built to carry it; it measured three hundred feet.

In her garden again there was a stairway of waters that ran singing down a hillside. The Villa D'Este effect is much in vogue in California where water is precious. Some day they mean to irrigate the whole of Arizona, New Mexico and Southern California from the Colorado River. . . .

Mrs. Mitchell was Lolita Armour of Chicago, too pretty a name to forget; her garden of terraces and cypress vistas goes down the hillside to a Japanese garden, and in her garden I found a feeling for topiary.

Going round gardens is ten times as interesting if you go with the owner who loves it. I had a joyful time at Las Tejas with Mrs. Oakleigh Thorne of which I can give but the poorest reflection. I was, as usual, carrying my note-book, and was constantly stopping to take notes. That was not to be endured, said Mrs. Thorne, so a secretary came forth and did "dog's body" for me. But alas, when I came to study the beautifully clear typescript sent along to the Biltmore a day or two later, I could not make the notes fit with my memory at all. My own clumsy, untidy, rapid scribbles mean far, far more; a word here and there and the whole scene is reconstructed.

I have no idea what the difference is, but somehow my own jumble makes a clear path for memory . . . and this tidy, elegant manuscript was meaningless. I could not decipher the tale it told. I learned once more, as so often in life, that the longest way round is the shortest way home . . . that one has to do the job oneself and get on with it. But it was a heavenly rest to listen . . . and not to write; for Mrs. Oakleigh Thorne's radiant enthusiasm overrode the malaise of her cold so that one never sus-

pected it,—and every step of the way was a new illumination.

The garden is only eleven years old; she surveyed it and
laid it out herself.

"The Californian garden is supposed to be on dress
parade all the year round," she said, "but we have to rest
sometimes!" In the spring they get colour from annuals;
nemesias, stocks, snap-dragons, etc., and then come the
bulbs; Barberton daisies (gerberas) live for ever and bloom
the year round,—and so does the pretty little rose-purple
lantana, a great friend to the garden that has no insect pests
and accommodates itself everywhere.

I admired it much, as I did later on the sand verbena in
the desert; I must have a leaning to that colour for I like
the catch-fly, lychnis viscaria, too, and fireweed. But my
hostess did not like the little lantana.

Suddenly she began to suffer from shyness as we walked:
"You have such wonderful flowers in England," she
said. "We are only beginning here". . . and then she went
on with a rush of courage—"I don't care *what* my garden
is! It is what it is to me!"

All the rest of the time we walked in her tended and
lovely place I kept thinking of the humanity of that sudden
humbleness, that sudden courage.

"We can't grow hollies," she said lamenting; "they are
my favourite shrub; the nearest I can get is our Californian
holly, toyon (photinia arbutifolia). I planted five hundred
last year."

I looked at the toyon; it was something like holly;
but what astonished me was that anyone should so greatly
long to grow our prickly shrub.

It has truly, as she said, a clean washed look, with its
bright enamelled leaf and sealing-wax red berries . . . but
still!

It grows down the lanes near me and I have never troubled
to put one single plant of it in the garden. I made up my
mind I would now. One. Just to remember her. . . .

Camellias must face north here or else grow in the shade

of the oaks; they do well in her acid soil,—and she was
full of glee because she had just acquired a trainload of peat
moss soil for them from Holland. . . . I remembered
Sark, Swinburne's Garden of Cymodoce, where I first saw
the red and white camellias flashing, long, long ago,—
they grow in the sun there;—and I was not then a gardener,
I did not see what soil they liked. Only adored the flat
waxen platters of flower-flesh among the laurel-like leaves.

Las Tejas garden is two miles from the sea on the foot-
hill of a mountain; it is Italian in feeling, richly architected
in green with a beautifully restrained use of stone and
marble; the stairway of ivy goes right up the hill-slope,
leading the eye through grey-green of Italian cypresses,
ruddy bronze eugenia, and gleams of pale gold on Japanese
box to the beautiful cream-coloured house in the middle
distance flanked with palms against a far-off blue mountain
peak.

The new rose-garden promises very well; we were peacefully inspecting it when a roar shook the air.

"I am blasting for a tank," she said undisturbed; "I
have two wells but I am never able to profit on account of
the pressure; I am now putting in a pressure system, something like five thousand feet of four-inch pipe, so we will
have sufficient pressure another year."

The ground is all stones between which bore the taproots
of the much treasured live oaks (quercus agrifolia). She did
not speak of digging a "spit" deep, as we do,—but of
"taking off the soil one stone deep."

She never buys anything but top soil,—and the roses,
it appeared, were exceedingly special, for them the soil was
taken off four stones deep.

It was a pleasant grey day. "There may be rain," she
said hopefully. (Not exactly a word to cheer the English
heart beside her!) Her beautiful grass took my eye at
the word "rain."

"It is Bermuda grass," she said; "it is green all winter
and we take care of it. In December we give it a dressing
of bloodmeal; when it gets cold at nights in January, about

the fifth to the tenth, we give it a dressing of hot fertiliser,
. . . guano; about this time of year, after some rain, we
give it bonemeal. Most people don't understand the
Bermuda grass, they think it takes care of itself; but it
chills in the winter and gets grey. One does not need to
do anything with it in summer; it takes very little water
being a hot-weather grass. Because this is not a hot
country it must be encouraged by being warmed up in
winter."

I could not help feeling glad that grass is easier to grow
at home in England; our green gardens are very restful.

"I feel the oaks are a great responsibility," she sighed;
"I water them, feed them with bonemeal, boring three or
four feet; we water first and then fill up with bonemeal."

Southern Californians adore great spreading green trees
and have very few. I remembered how Pete had looked at
my wide English oaks (quercus robus) with longing.

"We have no trees like these," he said,—and I had
sympathised. For in the days of my sandy Surrey garden
I had often longed for the wise great foreheads of broad-
leaved deciduous oak and beech and chestnut among the
straight dry pines. . . .

We went to the Blaksley Botanic Memorial Garden,
presided over by Dr. and Mrs. Bissell; it was given by
Mrs. Bliss in memory of her father Henry Blaksley, a
lover of nature, the object of it is particularly to show the
best drought-resisting plants to be used in California.

It was a charming place, systematically labelled . . .
grouped artistically without the (often unfortunate) trick
of planting according to family,—it was rather community
grouping . . . the Indian trail, the Island trail, and so on.

The next day I dined at LasTejas, and found Mrs. Stow
Fithian acting hostess as Mrs. Oakleigh Thorne was in bed.
The cold was no longer to be denied.

It was a happy evening for me, but it lacked her laughing
wit. Among the guests of a very nature-loving party were
Mr. George Owen Knapp of Arcady and Mr. and Mrs.
McDuffie of redwood fame. Sequoia sempervirens, the

redwood, is in danger of extinction by real estate and other materialists. Or rather *was*. A league called "Save the Redwoods" was started some years ago,—about 1924 I think, —and it has already conserved for California many thousands of acres of virgin redwood forest; the total remaining standing is just on a million acres, it has meant much public spirit, much generosity of time as well as money to do the valuable and sensible work so far achieved; I was glad to meet Mr. Duncan McDuffie, a member of the council, and find in him the fire of a real enthusiasm.

The trees of Bull Creek Flat are about the finest growth to be found the world over; there they are, the last stand of the giants.

"To go into that grove of redwoods," said Mr. McDuffie, "is to step into a dim cathedral, lofty, pillared, peaceful. The Great Architect has been building it for a score of centuries; and it is nobler than any made by man. Its nave is loftier than that of Amiens and longer than that of St. Peter's. Its wine-red shafts, rising clean and straight over two hundred feet, number more than the pillars of Cordova; its floor is carpeted with a green and brown mosaic more intricate than that of St. Mark's; its aisles are lit with a translucence more beautiful than that which filters through the stained glass of Chartres; its spires pierce higher than those of Cologne; its years are greater than those of the first lowly building devoted to Christian service."

I listened hypnotised. Those great trees! How they exhausted me to see . . . and how would one grow to love them . . . I remembered what Joseph Hergesheimer said of them when he contemplated the axe about those primæval boles. . . .

I realised, hearing the conversation around me, that I had not seen a tenth of the gardens to be found in Santa Barbara,—and that it was one of the liveliest and most beautiful garden-towns upon the Golden Shore. They asked me to stay longer and see more of the place and people.

But I explained very carefully, and quite clearly I regret

to remember, that I "had an assignation with the azaleas at Charleston and they would wait for no one. . . ."

"Assignation," it appears, is a word no one uses in America. It means a love-tryst only, and apparently quite a squalid sort of love-tryst. Lucia flushed delicately, and looked forgiving.

Mr. Oakleigh Thorne is the kind of man to drive women to matrimony; they can't help hoping they may find someone like him; I revolved names in my mind, while I listened to his talk thinking how few men are quite as nice, and what an enchanting couple they make. He is fond of cattle, she of gardening.

"I have about two thousand head of cattle now," he said, "but I really enjoyed them more when I had a hundred and knew each by heart; the sweetness of life is intimacy."

He was right; but not every man knows that.

He has the beautiful manners which make women all over the world love to meet General Sir Charles Crewe; and make them long to slay Winifred Peech that they may capture Jim. I am too fond of her to want to do that myself, but I often watch them moodily wishing he were like a greenfly and could be parthenogenetically re-duplicated in vast numbers to present to lonely women, or those whose husbands are not so polite.

Mrs. Stow Fithian promised to show me her cactus garden, and so she did. A gay little "desert" garden,— full of ideas and very decorative . . . like herself.

Mrs. Oakleigh Thorne sent me kind messages from her room: with a letter to Miss Henderson which would open the gate of her garden to me in Louisiana.

CHAPTER VII

BABYLON AND SERENDIPITY

OFF we went again; the landscape whirling by.
"Hot-dogs" and soft drinks everywhere. What
are hot-dogs?

We spun along through lima bean country and I learned
that in the Ojai Valley (pronounced "O-high") writers and
artists can live more cheaply than at Carmel or in Santa
Barbara.

I looked round longingly: but Ojai was already passed;
Harry is a devil of a driver. The words "live cheaply"
had an attraction. My conscience was troubled by the
dreadful way Pete and Lucia Norfolk were behaving,—
their hospitality was boundless: I did not know what to do
with them. I hoped they would not be living on bread
and cheese for months after these goings-on. I was much
puzzled by the lavish ways of California—as if money had
made itself out of the air.

From Ventura to Camarillo is a wonderful avenue of
palms like giant pineapples; after that a green-roofed
white-pillared highway of eucalyptus.

While I scribbled notes, the shadows of that highway
mottled my page in a dance of little feet . . . I kept thinking about the terraces and water gardens of California.

To a great many people the idea of a garden is closely
associated with terraces; or with the varying levels of rock
and water gardens. I live on the pastoral slopes of the
Weald of Kent, a country of bland pools, fruit orchards,
lawns and flowering shrubs, where rock does not naturally
outcrop and therefore is not harmonious in the garden
scheme, and I am often brought up sharply against this

narrow and definite view in other gardeners; every time
I meet it I savour again the romance of history which it
divulges,—catch a glimpse down the long, long tunnels
of time to the old lost gardens of the East, the terraced
gardens where streams ran singing,—the gardens which,
through the Crusaders, influenced so greatly our European conception of garden design; even to the point
that the Italian school still to-day remains almost purely
Persian; gardens reflecting (faintly we doubt not, but still
reflecting) the mysterious beauties, the majesty and scale
of the famous terraced gardens of India, Byzantium and
the traditions of Babylon.

Gardeners to-day still stand on level plane above level
plane set with flowers and rich with perfume; their eyes
still lapse down a garden in wide and genial degrees to
find the distant view of valley and river-bed; still does a
noble design of terraces satisfy the human craving for
feet set among the solid comforts of beautiful earth, while
the eye plunges free into the attractive dangers of space;
and still to a great many people a garden of terraces is
the only true form of a garden.

It is curious to realise that this world-wide conception
had its beginning in the cry of a homesick girl! Far
away in the mists of tradition shines a starry ever-recurring
tale of the "hanging gardens of Babylon," the seventh
wonder of the world; every garden-lover has heard the
thrilling phrase from time to time, and many have wondered
what it really means.

Imagination stirs at the unusual sound, and wakes to
lively speculation at the mysterious silences which meet
an eager question.

The historical books of Ctesias are lost, we only possess
fragments of them in Plutarch, Athenæus, and Diodorus,
and there are references in other authors, Pliny and so
forth; he was the family physician of Xerxes, and lived
in Babylon all his life in the fifth century B.C. A man of
wide enthusiasm, he spent his spare time writing books
on the history of Assyria and Babylon, treatises on rivers,

Persian revenues, and India, and descriptions of the hanging gardens made long before his time by Sardanapalus.

That monarch, an uxorious and extravagant prince, had to wife a young Princess of Media, as Persia was then called. Transported to the flat alluvial plains of Mesopotamia where the Euphrates was used in a tidy network of regular canals for irrigation, she pined for the flowery hills, the sparkling waterfalls, the broken skylines and romantic valleys of her own land; one can feel, at this long distance of time, something of the way her heart turned in sick loathing from the flat plains of her husband's country after the beautiful landscapes of her own.

Nowhere in all the world can one find the Spring break in such a glory of flowers as in the high table-land of Persia and the rugged country lying East and West of it. It takes time to succumb to the magnetism of flat country. A hill-dweller shivers in great open spaces and longs for the abrupt shadows, the comforting accustomed cloak of the hills . . . just as one may see a farmer from the bald-headed prairie or veld cower in fear when he finds himself among the mountains, complaining that there is not room to breathe there; gasping for his own more spacious skies.

Sardanapalus perceived his young queen drooped, and made the famed amazing "hanging" gardens to cure her. She wanted a mountain in his plains, and the sound of singing waters? . . . She should have them!

The word "hanging" here means "terraced"; Gilbert White speaks frequently, in his *Selborne*, of the long "hanging" wood called "the hanger,"—a wood set back on a hill.

The hanging gardens of Babylon were set back in terraces, and Ctesias would have us believe they were 1,200 feet above the level of the plain. Some of the temples must have been 500 feet high, and were made in the sacred planetary number of seven pyramidal stages.

Sardanapalus would want his queen's "Mountain" to look over the temples and he would avoid the sacred

number of seven in his pleasure building, so one may
venture to assume they rose to seven or eight hundred
feet, even if one cannot credit the 1,200.

Stone was hard to come by on the Babylonian clay,
and the terrace walls would be of burnt brick, backed by
sun-dried brick; or, as they would say in California, lined
with adobe; those used in the water-courses were probably
glazed.

The young queen must have revived as she saw the
stupendous efforts to which her plaint had roused her
royal lord,—or else he fell in love with the work for its
own sake, for it is clear that the great gardens must have
taken a long time to complete.

The king had engines placed to lift the waters of the
Euphrates up to the top, so that the terraces might be
amply irrigated and bright waters go tumbling and leaping down, back to the river below, bringing again to her
the memory of sweet water-voices on her ancestral hills.

To-day at the Villa d'Este and in many a Californian
garden modelled upon it, we hear runnels and streams of
water laughing down stairways of brick and stone; falling
from level to level in bright cascades; only that in these
more favoured climes the water is more of a plaything, a
gesture, than in the gardens of Babylon where the very
spirit of every flower-paradise was in the running water
which alone makes growth possible. Irrigation was the
first essential of the enterprise when Sardanapalus planned
his gardens.

Then to these great platforms and terraces came fruits and
flowers of all the known world; avenues of cypress which,
by the time Ctesias saw them must have been majestic;
roses, weeping willows, cedars, almond, apricot, lilac, jasmine and wide enchanting carpets of tulips, crown-imperials
and the lesser fritillaries,—irises, hyacinths, dazzling blue
scillas and sweet narcissi; hollyhocks, delphiniums, peonies
and pinks.

There would be fountains and bathing pools, arbours
and shady walks by the pleasant waters; and into his

garden-paradise the King of Babylon brought gazelles and nimble squirrels, pheasants imported from India and bright-plumaged birds to companion the song of nightingales among the roses.

Some savants believe that the terrace walls were faced with glazed and decorated tiles; but most of us are more content to picture great mellow retaining walls of plain burnt brick, glowing softly in the sunshine, draped with roses, or rich with trained fruits.

Though the most famous and mystic terraced garden of all time was made by the waters of Babylon, where the captive Jews "sat down and wept, hanging their harps on the weeping willow trees," yet the inspiration for it came from Persia. We talk of the Japanese love of flowers, of the way earth-beauty in Japan is taken into the fabric of daily life, but it has often seemed to me that the Persians had at least as great a national passion.

Again it was the Persian wife of a Mogul Emperor who inspired the building of the famous Kashmir gardens; still, near Shiraz, can we see through all the sadness of neglect and decay, traces of the ineffable beauty of the garden of which Hafiz sang so sweetly,—one of the great terraced gardens of the world, one that carried on the direct tradition of Babylon.

Love of a garden rings so full in the poems of Omar Khayyám of Korassán that it has survived the acid test of translation into every language. The terraced gardens of Italy, piled up in splendour on the hills over Rome or Fiesole, are nowadays taken as the source of inspiration for all garden design in California where commanding views and springs of water are to be found; but why are not the far more lovely gardens of Persia remembered? "Hard to reach and falling to decay," will probably be urged; but those might even seem to be, to some courageous souls, good reasons for visiting those gardens, and catching their beauty before it passes utterly away and is no more seen. There are further wells of pure inspiration to be found for garden-planning in the terraced gardens

H

of the Indian foot-hills, and those by the Dal Lake and the Shalimar of song.

I am never able to rid myself of a sensation of something heavy and worthy about most of the large terraced gardens of England; they do not seem to spring in a gush of fantasy or like pure poetry from the heart of a hillside, flung out in a passion of joy before some supremely beautiful view, as they appear to be in other happier climates; it is probably the lack of clear sunshine, and the soft clinging mists of Britain, which give one that feeling; or is it perhaps that so often, instead of "hanging" in sheer glory on a mountain-side looking over valley and river to distant hills, these lordly terraces lead tamely down to a park and deer?

I was so lost in thought that I was startled when Lucia touched my arm:

"Where have you got to?" she laughed.

"I was thinking," said I, "of the touch of Babylon."

But as she had no idea of the thoughts that went before, the poor darling looked sufficiently puzzled.

Suddenly, after all this travel I was sleeping in an orange grove at Green Valleys ranch.

Pete built the place of redwood to his own design, it is simple and very comfortable; a weeping willow bursting into leaf made a veil over the face of the moon-wraith clouds, boughs of oranges swung, heavy with ripe fruit on every side; the scent of orange blossom and nutmeg geranium lingered in the night air. . . .

Meadow-larks were singing in the morning; and at breakfast I learned something of the fruit habits of the Californians—salads were served with orange blossom on them; we had Australian saucer peaches, which being too soft to travel are unknown to most people; very flat little peaches of an exquisite flavour; green, with rosy cheeks. By every plate at every meal was a tumbler of orange juice freshly pressed from freshly picked oranges.

"Now I am going to take you to the house in the trees," said Pete—"my 'eveless Eden' where you shall be

permitted to write.   I will show you the cantaloupes and
tomatoes they raise here under little hats of wax-paper; it
gets them past the first frost so that they come in a month
earlier than anyone else's.   You shall see the Cadota fig
farm, too, for canning and preserving.   It is a new under-
taking; the Cadota is a delicious white fig with a little
drop of honey in the cup when ripe."

Presently I found myself writing in a walnut tree.   I
know now that, driven by the gadfly of many possessions,
Americans very often create for themselves some such form
of retreat;—a ranch in the hills, a bungalow by the sea,
a place in the desert; a study in a tree-top; or whatever
it may be.

Pete had built himself a studio up in a big walnut tree,
his "eveless Eden"; sacred to himself when he wants to
get away from the hurly-burly and do some contemplating,
read, shed the world.

I was not perfectly convinced of the nature of the compliment paid me when I, alone of all, was made free to
write there; it seems a bit two-edged.   An "eveless" Eden?

An "*insinuendo*,"—as who should say?   The gathering
years bring their smarting privileges. . . .   One must
submit.

Anyway, it was a nice Eden; high up in the branches
of a huge native black walnut tree, then just bursting
into leaf and thickly hung with green catkins; the
fringes of them hung all round the windows and doors,
sometimes shaken lightly by the birds which shared my
eyrie,—or by vagrant winds which blew over the hills
sweet with orange blossom.

It had only one room, but in it were chairs, tables,
divans with excellent springs, a bookcase inset in the
walls, a great open log fire; a shower-bath and toilet;
also a balcony where presently I ate lunch in perfect seclu-
sion, looking over the garden to the ineffable blue of the
snow-capped hills with the bland green rolling foothills
in front.   A waterfall made its music under the boughs
of the walnut tree trickling through a rock-garden of many

delights; it was curious to hear the silver sound of the water under my feet down on the ground below.

There was no telephone—it was a perfect place.

A long way off a muffled hammering told where a super-pavilion was being built between the swimming-pool-to-be and the tennis-court-that-is. The pavilion had a dance floor, a stage, service-room, closets, showers, dressing-rooms, and by and by in front of it there will be that swimming-pool.

All these pleasant things set bang in the middle of an orange orchard, seemed to me to be the last word in week-end luxury; there Lucia and her many guests could ride the green hills and play out of doors.

The eveless Eden was Pete's own particular bolt-hole; away from the farm, the saddle horses, dancing, swimming and all the rest of the fun.

I looked from the eyrie upon the long lines of flight cages, where industrious pigeons bred the succulent squabs for market; an avenue of Jacaranda trees led to the road and the orange grove beyond it, where the house and outbuildings were hung with bougainvillea, bignonia and Dombeya. Under the ferny leaved Jacarandas, bloomed a furnace of stocks and petunias, sweet-peas, marigolds and daffodils. A woodland planting of young silver birch just breaking into shrill green, completed the confusion of seasons to my English eyes, accustomed to the dormant winters of our Northland. There was something disorderly about sweet-peas and daffodils in full bloom together; not to mention hedges of roses out in every colour and of every fragrance all round the boundaries of the property. On every side stretched acres of orange trees, lemons, grape-fruit, tangerines, sweet limes and avocado pears.

There was another citrus fruit also and of a rarity, which made the most excellent cocktails, far better than grape-fruit, and I had been accustomed to believe that was quite the best one could have. It is called a Samson tan-geloe, a cross between grape-fruit and tangerine; it is about the size of a Valencia orange, the thin fine skin is full of juice and has none of the tiresome tangerine pippiness; this fruit had only a pip or two, sometimes none. The flavour was distinctly of both parents, with more of the bitterness of the grape-fruit than the sweetness of the tangerine. The essential oils of the skin had a very distinctive and pleasant fragrance. Pressed into a cocktail they gave it a new enticement, a strangeness.

"The ranch carries itself," said Pete, "it is fifty acres of fun. We have ducks, geese, turkeys, hens, the 'squab' pigeons, fruit, vegetables and the horses: it is all fun."

I sat in the Eden writing . . . but it was not easy to concentrate. The lovely out-of-doors called and called. When I wrenched myself back to pencil and paper the faces of Pete and Lucia came floating between and I had to think of them.

The secret was out. A guest had uttered a word the night before at dinner. . . .

"Have you sunk any more wells, Pete?"

There is only one kind of "well" to-day in California.

"Have I been the guest of oil magnates all this time?" I asked.

These two—simple, great-hearted—had touched hands with that terrible form of romance—sudden wealth.—Oil had been found on the land where first he lived. Never a word had they said to me of their great adventure, the deceiving hussies!

But now Pete suddenly talked.

It was an absorbing evening, while he told of the long strain of it all,—the thousand pitfalls for a man who could not look after himself in the mad fever the word "oil" lights directly it is even whispered about any locality . . . the plots and counterplots . . . the suspense of drilling . . . the reaction after the gush. . . .

"When we first met you we were just getting over that really dreadful experience," laughed Lucia.

I remembered the grubby English inn where we had bickered and I laughed too; a little wryly.

Why are our hotels so bad?   An uncomfortable darling land, mine is!

I kept thinking of them.   Level-headed, young, happy people; all who worked for them loved them—the acid test of character.

I could not help being relieved to know their story . . . the oil would well up for them and bring more money and more easily than all those poor little pigeons I had dreamed of them feverishly killing as soon as I had gone.

But I had hurriedly to adjust a lot of ideas about the wealth of American squab farmers; they would not all find oil.

I was taken to see Mr. Paul Howard's plant-selling place on South la Brea Avenue in Los Angeles; he calls it "Flowerland."

Men in white overalls have "Flowerland" in green letters on their backs; there is a spacious in-and-out driveway to the shop with its gay flower frieze, its wide windows full of flowers, vases, seats, bird-baths, small "chip" boxes of pansies, daisies, godetias, petunias and what-nots, all ready to take away in the car on the way back from one's office and plant out in a trice in little gardens.

In the long lath houses behind, there were myriads of tiny pots with sturdy little plants of different kinds to choose from.   The "lath" house was new to me.   They do not need glass for warmth, but they do need shade and protection from winds and heavy rains in the climate of Southern California; the "greenhouse" of wooden laths is the perfect solution.   In my ignorance I thought I had come across a row of buildings ready lathed, and awaiting the plasterers—when I first saw those houses!

So many seedlings in pots rather give an English eye the impression that California's amateur gardeners must be somewhat idle and extravagant, also that they must miss a good deal of the fun of their gardens.

In England we enjoy growing our flowers from the seeds we sow ourselves; the Californian pot habit was explained when I learnt how the hot climate with its con-

stant need of watering kills so many seedlings that the
people prefer to buy "a proper little plant" in a pot, well
started, and ready to plant out. They know then what
they have, and are saved many disappointments.

There are acres of seedlings and of pots at Flowerland:
there are roses in cans . . . I found "Marion Cran" among
them (looking a bit sick from the quarantine efforts of
the "bug-hounds") . . . but still sprouting her characteristic bronze and copper shoots. There are, of course,
potting sheds and packing sheds, motor parking places
and a range of offices over the shop; there are redwood
trees in tin cans—astonishing sight! They make tremendous growth and shoot up twelve or fifteen feet the second
season; there were Monterey cypresses in five-gallon cans
to plant straight out at any time of year. A hundred of
them five feet high make a good quick hedge for impatient
American gardeners in six months out of those cans.

There are also fruit trees in the nurseries (in cans), tall
well-grown weeping birches, and large conifers in the
ground to ball and burlap, for people who can afford them,
for transplantation in the astonishing manner of the country.
Some very big trees were all ready balled and burlapped
(which means that a big ball of roots is wrapped round
in coarse canvas and sewn with packing thread). They
stood plunged deep into coarse wet wood-shavings, and
I was told that they could be kept two or three months
in that way without suffering a setback.

There were "old" Florentine well-heads cleverly copied
in stone, with wrought-iron buckets and chains; statues;
groups in marble or lead, garden seats and garden "features"
from the simplest to the most elaborate.

In this "rus in urbe" the mocking-birds and blackbirds
were well content; they even nested in the sample hedges.
The blackbirds were intelligent little wretches, very fussy
and courageous. Mr. Howard, who treasures his hair, was
walking down the path when a cock blackbird flew out to
have a look at him, and finally lit on his shoulder and began
pulling his hair out—I suppose he wanted a lining for his

nest! Anyway, Mr. Howard, who views approaching bald-
ness with horror, tried to shoo him off; then the hen blackbird flew down to help her mate, and pulled even harder,
so he was completely frustrated.

They call Pasadena the "crown of the coast" and so it
may be; there is water to be had which is lacking in Santa
Barbara, so growth is richer, and the claim still leaves
plenty of regalia to ennoble the other lovely cities sparkling
down the glorious Pacific seaboard.

I was amused to hear people say as they showed me
round their beautiful gardens, patios and bowers: "This
is only three years old . . ." and "You know, Mrs. Cran,
it's only *two* years old!"

In Virginia later on they said to me with that indiffer-
ence which is the fiercest pride: "This is two hundred
years old," and I had to adjust myself in America accord-
ingly, to enjoy these varied prides, in order to understand
the garden sense which utters them.

We were going to meet the Diggers' Club in Pasadena
and I hoped to see Mrs. Francis King again; I heard she
was there, and wanted to renew a happy memory of our
meeting in London long ago; but we missed by a few
minutes.

Whatever people say about America now I *know* there
is a warm and seeking soul in the houses and gardens of
it. In the Pasadena Diggers' Club each member actually
gardens; works with her own hands in the lovely common
mud of earth, and does not hire a troop of gardeners to
tread that soul-path in her stead.

The Vista del Arroya Hotel has many bungalows each
with a garden, which it lets to visitors who do their own
digging and tending! A significant feature of Hotel life,
new in my experience, and most luminous; it points the
way to the herd life of the future. I found, later on,
that several places have their lively practical Diggers'
Clubs, offshoots of the more socially involved Garden
Clubs.

In Mrs. Gate's garden I had a shrub pointed out as

"oriental" lilac and found it to be syringa Persica, the
first lilac (in our sense) that I had touched and sniffed on
the Pacific Coast. I lingered in that garden of ranun-
culus and alyssum saxatile, baby blue eyes, blue flax and
blue-eyed Mary to touch again the fabric of a real lilac!

Two beautiful and really mature gardens in Pasadena
grow side by side and belong to two sisters, Mrs. J. B.
Cox and Mrs. Severance. There were large oaks on the
lawns, deep ravines filled with azaleas, tree-ferns and running streams,—drifts of forget-me-nots, red-berried cotono-
asters, masses of clivias, the queer bird of Paradise strelitzas
and sparaxis-like bilbergias with their long pink drooping
stems hung with green bells. Under the camellias grew
carpets of cyclamen and violets.

There are violets everywhere in America; most of them
do not smell, though I noticed that the violet which grows
in the shade at Mr. Orpet's nurseries and which he calls
"California" is very fragrant. He says it spreads rapidly,
and I was much interested in it, for in colour and scent
it closely resembles the large amethyst blooms of "Tina
Whittaker" which I grow in my own English garden
from plants Mr. Whittaker sent me from his garden in
Palermo, Sicily. The variety originated there and he
named it for his wife.

In the Huntington garden at San Marino I met William
Hertrich, the superintendent of the grounds; a man who
loves his plants, especially the palms and succulents, though
he has specialised in acacias and eucalyptus species. While
we were studying the great Agathis robusta, the tree
conifer with a tap root and a height of seventy-five feet,
he told me he was born at Basle and has travelled a great
deal among gardens. There was a Montezuma cypress,
grown from seed, which looked like a lovely weeping larch;
and a bottle-brush tree with a queer peeling whitish bark
which felt like soft cork—or well-hung venison,—when
you press a thumb into it! I told him how I had seen
in Arcady at Montecito, a weeping pittosporum, a tree of a
golden grace with creamy yellow flowers and yellow fruits.

That is a very noble garden of Mr. Knapp's between the mountains and the sea, one of the great ones.   In it Italy and England, Greece and California blend in a bewildering series of vistas.   The blue garden alone sent me spinning giddily from Africa to Australia, Peru, Costa Rica, China, Spain and the West Indies, as I looked at agapanthus, eugenia myrtifolia, heliotrope, solanum Wenlandii, ceratostigma plumbaginoides, viola cornuta and Duranta plumieri reminding myself of their easier, dearer names, lily of the Nile, Australian bird-cherry, cherry-pie, potato creeper, leadwort, horned-violet and golden dewdrop!!

I liked Mr. Hertrich and we had a long garden chat together; while Lucia, a miracle of patience, waited for us.

"Now I am going to take you to the Serendipity to lunch," said she.

My heart stood still.

"Serendipity?"

In Shepherd's Market, Mayfair, London, Everard Meynell had a bookshop . . . he called it the "Serendipity" . . . and then he had a cough and went to California.

Everard with his dark eyes and the short, black beard. . . . I can see him still on his mother's arm as I took their picture together before he sailed away, and never came back.

Time ceases at a word.

"Serendipity"! . . . and I am in the Sussex garden where I first met the kind eyes of Alice Meynell. . . .

Walk quietly here for she has passed on and it is a garden of memories now, full of "that silence which is music mute."   Here is the red-tiled farmhouse, the midden it once surrounded made into a smooth green lawn; against the far wall grow tall poplar trees, slender shafts of green. They stand like sentinels, straight and strong before the house they guard—that house where the arts are treasured. They throw long shadows at eventide and make a tracery on the walls in the cold moonlight, soft shadows on Alice Meynell's windows of the trees she loved and wrote about.

. . . Come round to the south front and see where balm
grows and rosemary, too, with pansies and forget-me-nots;
—this tall green tree was struck from a cutting taken from
a tree by Shelley's tomb;—here is Rosa Mundi, the Rose
of the World; and here is lavender. Coventry Patmore
said of Alice: "Her body is so like her, straight as a stalk
of lavender." She is beside us as we walk on her accustomed lawns, immortal—her dark eyes burning. . . .

We lunched at the Serendipity. And it had known
and loved Everard. . . .

CHAPTER VIII

THE CUP OF GOLD

MR. GOULD is one of the very, very few Americans I met who enjoy the dawn! He uses his lake at Pasadena as a mirror for the glamorous hour.

"People here miss the best of this wonderful climate," he said to me, "they do not understand the early morning lights!"

So I sojourned with him in the pearly morning-tide, for I, too, have always loved the uprising of the sun. His is a Tiberian soul with a sylvan leaning. He has built a small *temple d'amour* in a little green valley. Just then it was sweet and fresh as an English Spring, with its drifts of flowering peach and plum and quince and crab-apple; there were magnolias carrying their cups of ivory, pink and deep wine-red; bridal wreath hung over carpets of white iris. We breakfasted over the lake on the terrace of the "temple," which is a spacious room, very Italian in manner. A beautifully furnished room in the woods; in it his friends take tea and hear music looking over his lake and the valley of blossoms. He seems to use his "temple" as a retreat from business and people. An al-fresco idea embedded in the extreme of luxury, Italy; Californicated, so to speak.

Letters began to come from the east bidding me to be careful not to miss the azaleas. Why did people want to keep on bothering me about them like this? I had seen plenty of them at English and European places . . . azaleas!

I was the guest now of Mrs. Chauncey Clark at the Woman's Athletic Club in Los Angeles. Every day Lucia sent one of the cars for me to sojourn among gardens and meet delightful folk, and here and there in the coming and going I would note some delightful flower —passiflora princeps, the loveliest of all passion flowers; buddleia Madagascarensis, a honey-scented yellow, growing almost like a climber; the glorious erica Melanthera; in Pasadena a memorable beauty is vested in the shiny bronze-gold of the young shoots of the camphor trees. . . . Sometimes I had a happier time than usual in some simple garden.

Mrs. Forest Stanton gave me one of those hours in her garden at Flintridge. In an agony of bereavement she had turned to a garden when her little son was killed,—and found healing there. She works in it alone with a Hindoo for her only help. She was charming in her enthusiasm. . . .

"Look! This hedge is three foot thick and six foot high. It is only three years old!" . . . and: "These Italian cypresses—three years ago they were so small, just a yard high and they only cost twenty-five cents (about one shilling) each"; or: "I sowed the lawn,—isn't it lovely?"

Mr. Evans at Santa Monica had another of these intimate well-beloved gardens, but his is that of a scholar and a man of keen discrimination; one in which one could live for ever and learn a new lesson every day. He was one of the most distinguished amateur gardeners I met in America, though I realise his garden is not understood of many Californians . . . it is one for the travelled.

He likes the best of everything, especially everything South African, and nothing easy. Listening to his pleasant voice as we went round, I pricked my ears and learned without surprise that he was at Marlborough though they have been in California forty years. Here were the best hibiscus (Agnes Gault); the best acacia; the best bougainvilleas; the best sophora; eucalyptus pyriformis—it has enormous dark-red yellow-pointed blooms four inches across, and grows to twenty feet or more.

Eugenia Smithii, he told me, is the "lilly-pilly" which I used to see in Australia and only knew by its common name. His great bush of buddleia colvelii roused me to powerful sighs of envy . . . the waxy pink flowers measured individually half an inch across! I told him how I had found buddleias growing wild by a bastion not far from the hills of Basutoland . . . and mention of South Africa once more made us wander off to look at the protea he flowered. It was not really a happy sight—proteas do not seem to like California—and how one wishes they did! I tried to describe their beauty in the Cape, and he listened attentively. "Everyone who knows them speaks like this," he commented, and then went on: "You have seen B. Y. Morrison, I hope?" I was about to say good-bye, having been finally routed by seeing the red orchid that has bloomed continuously for five years. I thought he spoke of some further miraculous flower.

"Which is it?" I asked, looking round.

He laughed, standing under the great wands of grevillea leucopteris with its grey-blue whiskers and spectacular wands of fawn and pink; "cones" which would become white.

"He is a daffodil-lover and grower from Washington, D.C.," he answered.

But I did not see the daffodil man in California.

There were some things in the gardens of Los Angeles and Pasadena which made me very envious, and one was the way that dear little rose Cécile Brunner grows; it makes a hedge as our hawthorn does; they clip it, so neat! I first noticed it with Mr. Raymond Gould, who took me to see his Villa Evarno, a house of austere and lovely taste in the Florentine manner. There was a loggia at each end and a suite each end with guest rooms in the middle—a perfect house for a brother and sister. I often think that the best and sweetest companionship on earth is that one—husband and wife have much to endure as well as to give each other, from their alien blood-streams; the relationship of children and parents is perilously poised in separate generations; but brothers and sisters are of the same united blood-streams—have shared childhood with its terrors and exaltations, nothing surprises them in each other when they are grown-up, remembering the night-mares, the shared rebellions. . . .

Mr. Paul Howard took me to see a garden he had laid out round the town house of Dr. and Mrs. Isaac Jones. It was built in the English manner with a roof of redwood shingles mellowed brown, the levels were cleverly treated to give perspective and the illusion of space, in a double city lot—there were an arbour under a mulberry to watch the tennis, a paved tea-place, crêpe myrtles and flowering plums and cherries, with bulbs below a weeping willow by a running stream; a charming place.

I met in Los Angeles Mrs. Dan Murphy whose cinerarias at Pebble Beach had so wrought upon my eyes. Here, in her Italian garden, I found proof that this delicate little lady loves colour. She had delphiniums before most people had them in California. The garden was being re-cast, to a more exciting design; there was an open-air theatre in cypress, and a studio for her sculptor daughter, Bernadine.

Californians it seemed to me do not read. I talked to them in a foreign tongue when I spoke of my familiars—R. L. Stevenson; W. H. Hudson; Alice Meynell; Francis Thompson; Lewis Hind; Wells; Galsworthy; John Masefield; Axel Munthe; Gilbert White—names that meant nothing to them. But Bernadine is a book-collector; it was a great pleasure to talk to her, the lovely, serene young thing, slender and tall in her yellow silk dress with her straight dark brows under red-brown hair, smiling at us out of luminous beautiful eyes. Mrs. Murphy told me how, in their garden operations, they sank for water and found oil—a most inconvenient material when it is not wanted —apparently she was sick of oil.

"We shut it up quickly with cement," she said, "and drilled to another plane, where we got lots of water."

I couldn't help feeling I would be glad to find a spot of oil myself. . . .

On Beverley Hills Mrs. Robinson had lunch for us on a loggia under trails of a great vine bearing enormous bowls of yellow waxen flowers; it was the famous, the thrice-desired Cup of Gold, Copa d'Oro!

"It blooms from Christmas on," said my pretty hostess,

I burn still and grow hot all over to remember the entertainment and accommodation we offer travellers in England;—and what we charge for it, too.

Frank Miller is a dreamer who built a "tavern" out of his dreams; it is a remarkable tavern. Irving Bacheller wrote of it:

"In that Inn, we have found a wider vision of the man into whose keeping people deliver their lives for a season. It gives a man rest and strength and cheer for his further journey. It is a half-way house between antiquity and dreamland. I should say, moreover, it is well out on the long road into the future."

The truth is that Mr. Miller felt the history of California as Lummis did, but instead of writing about it he collected Spanish treasures and put them in his inn which thus became a museum of the country's heritage and history.

In the "Garden of the Bells" he has over seven hundred bells collected from all over the world; he has a Spanish art gallery and gold altar; a court of the birds, and Spanish patio (which make open-air dining a romance)—one walks down a corridor which might be the cloister of an old monastery in Segovia,—finds a fountain that once spouted in the Plaza of Cordova. His "Tavern" is his castle in Spain.

I enjoyed the hour we spent talking with the visionary whose energies are always definitely directed. He is first of all a poet. He imagined travellers thronging the city among the orange groves at the feet of the mountains. He foresaw a growing interest in California's history; and this business of keeping an inn in a country town, developed him and led him far, into important service for city and State.

For he had vision.

He has some pet mottoes: "You cannot buy happiness; you must get it out of work"—"Without vision the people perish"—"Sentiment pays."

Grand Duke Alexander of Russia lunched at the table next ours; tall, thin, bearded, with long sensitive hands

and an abstracted air—he had come to talk in America
on the need of international closer relationship to Christ
if this civilisation is to exist.

But need it?

We are so far from Christ; we have put up the Golden
Calf of Church in His place.   What priest dare live to-day,
or dares to preach, the Sermon on the Mount?

Riverside is on the Santa Ana River in Orange County.
On the historic Rancho Santa Ana, which runs for several
miles along the river, Mrs. Susanna Bixby Bryant, the
owner, is making a botanic garden of native California
plants only.   It is situated upon the hills overlooking the
wonderful orchards of the Santa Ana Canyon and (on the
river's farther bank) the State highway between Riverside
and Santa Ana.

She told me she is making the garden in memory of
John W. Bixby, her father, who some fifty years ago bought
several old Spanish grants which now constitute Rancho
Santa Ana.

Since 1809, when the first grant of "Santiago de Santa
Ana" was secured by Bernardo Yorba, that part which
is now known as "Rancho Santa Ana" has belonged to
only two families—the Yorbas from 1809 to 1875 and
to John W. Bixby and his heirs since the latter date.   To
the original grant Bernardo Yorba added the adjoining
"Canada de Santa Ana" and re-named his holdings "Rancho
Cajon de Santa Ana."   Mr. Bixby added more acreage
and named the whole "Rancho Santa Ana."

This is an interesting bit of Californian land history,
for very few of the old or original ranches, in the "new"
and rapidly-changing West, have remained intact in the
hands of two pioneer families over so long a period as
one hundred and twenty years.

The picture I saw of "John Bixby, Pioneer" showed
an exceedingly handsome man with a very noble head.
I believe the word "pioneer" would be enough to make
me admire a grotesque! Passionately I reverence the
daring blood, the generous, self-spendthrift blood of

pioneers. But in this man's picture was beauty as well as fire . . . I admired him very much.

Of the long, happy hours I spent at Mrs. Bryant's ranch there stand out now as usual, the small things, Mrs. Oscar Lawler and I quarrelled at lunch, I remember, about national flags . . . in a great austere, beautiful room . . . where every idea grew big in my mind. We played and laughed together, making fun in our fighting, for she is a dear woman, and Mrs. Prince told of her school of Store Service Education. I heard afterwards that her system had revolutionised commercialising in the United States.

We saw the herbarium and drove across the rolling foothills where great blue shadows lay,—I thought they were cloud shadows, but they were blue lupins—acres and acres of wild blue lupins! There are about seventy species indigenous to the United States and most of them are found wild only on the Pacific Slope.

We saw the pretty "tidy-tips" (Layia platyglossa) Brodiœas and mariposa lilies,—showy, exquisite, mottled butterfly flowers trembling over the wild grasses. We found buttercups of the same golden sheen and same foliage as that which gleams in our English May meadows, but the flowers have more petals and grow taller than ours. We saw the great orange lands, and drank tumblers of the pure juice, fresh-pressed, ice-cold, and my last memory is of the beautiful snapdragon from Santa Rosa Island, antirrhinum speciosum. It is an island species not found on the mainland. It has long, slender blooms of pure sealing-wax red on a spike; the habit of the foliage is pendulous; a memorable snapdragon. I shall hope to meet it again some day somewhere else in the world. It comes from seed, and where it has water it blooms continuously; it lives longer, however, when it has had to lie dormant through a dry period.

We passed Signal Hill at Long Beach with its tale of history big with romance, for it was there that oil of the deep sand was first found.

In Mrs. Fred Bixby's garden among lovely old pepper trees, I saw that rare thing in America nowadays, a pioneer's adobe house. The feeling of coolness, solidity, and height in the rooms was reminiscent to me of the glorious old Cape Dutch farmhouses. No modern comforts really make up to the sensitive for the personality and the character in old houses, where can still be felt the giving hands which strove there against many difficult conditions and made—and won—a home.

Mrs. Bixby's "friendship" garden was in harmony with the beautiful mellow house. It was a small enclosed place smiling under the sun. There is an oleander walk and a patio between two wings of the house wherein peace, spacious comfort and memories are treasured.

CHAPTER IX

SNIFF GARDENS

MARY PICKFORD'S garden is like her ringlets were—very pretty and well kept. There is tilth in that rich valley bottom soil of hers because her Dresden gardener is fond of his job. He came from German West Africa, and we had a long talk among the chrysanthemums, dahlias and gladioli—he gave me a bunch of sweet peas. They were of nice form and bright colour.

He put them carefully into my hands:

"It is good they keep their simple name," he said. I agreed, heartily.

While so many of our ordinary garden flowers are known by their botanical names—antirrhinum, cheiranthus, artemisia, and so on—the sweet pea has preserved its old-fashioned title with becoming obstinacy. Hardly anyone refers to these butterfly flowers of the summer-time as lathyrus odoratus, though the perennial or "everlasting" pea is quite frequently called lathyrus latifolius. Some day it may happen that psychologists will take note of these curious streaks of custom in the use of flower-names and give us a treatise on their possible explanation. There must be a reason for them, and it would be interesting to know it.

I do not grow sweet peas enough at home; I have an obstinate longing for lathyrus splendens—the one I saw at Everton Grange by Mrs. Kemmis's bendy walls. But sweet peas do very well on my heavy soil, and as a race they are grown very extensively in England, chiefly from seed ripened in America, I am told!

Delicacy of form, an enchanting range of colour-tones,

134

and a strong delicious perfume ensure to the sweet pea the crown of its genus—no other pea competes in the flower garden with this popular hardy annual. There is the interesting blue "Mummy" pea, to be sure, but it is scentless and not nearly showy enough for table decoration. We have within the tribe of lathyrus odoratus enough diversity of form and colour, enough beauty and enough usefulness to keep us well occupied, and well content.

The original species came from Europe and India. Sicily and Sardinia provided us, as long ago as 1650, with the purple and the white sweet peas; from Ceylon came the fragrant pink-and-white one known as "Painted Lady." Rather more than half a century ago a Shropshire man, Henry Eckford, began to work on the six or seven common sorts known to gardeners, and about twenty years later people began to take notice of the size and colour of his fine new varieties. Laxton, whose name is now almost wholly associated with fruit, also did a great deal to introduce and establish the merits of new sweet peas.

Nowadays the lovely flowers are grown in hosts of colours and forms—bi-coloured, picotee-edged, striped, flaked and self: blush, carmine, blue, cerise, cream, crimson, fancy, flushed, lavender, maroon, mauve, orange, pink, purple, rose, salmon, scarlet and white—an iridescent bubble of colours to float up from the dark earth for us, in the warm, still weeks of summer.

Mary Pickford's Dresden gardener and I, browsing among the tall pink peas and gossiping, had a lot to say about the Kalahari desert which he loves. I was hoping to see something of the Californian desert and he was interested to hear I might be going . . . sand and cacti were beginning to sizzle in my blood. I was weary of sappy, rich-fed things.

I went into Charles Chaplin's garden with a sinking heart; the curly drive was hideously suburban; cement played a loud part in the stone edging, there was the everlasting carpet of blue periwinkle; there were the awful gazania and geranium mixture; there was the familiar blend of plumbago and bridal wreath which custom could never stale to my eye, see them never so often,—and also that ugly stark affair, a hard tennis court, glaringly dreadful under the afternoon sun, set round with wire protection and powerful lights; for play at night, I suppose.   No one could call it an attractive garden feature.

I wandered down the hill, much discouraged . . . all this gravel and cement! . . . this devastating ugliness! . . . How could that man project such sensitive beauty in his legend upon the screen, . . . and live in this?

And then, suddenly, I found the man of the screen expressed.   Charley had had the hillside planted with a pink ice-plant,—I do not know which mesembryanthemum it was, and the dark pines swayed over acres of clear pink,—a glowing carpet under the harsh dark trees on the dry, rocky soil.   Everyone in California uses that plant, but they niggle with it, a bit here and a bit there.   It needed Charley's mind to see it grown in the brave simplicity of one grand planting.   A garden is always the mirror of the human who lives in it.   I might have known I would find some such stroke of genius there.

Charley will not have anything hurt, so the place is alive with gophers, snails and squirrels from the field near by, and he loves his pink hill; he comes down specially to look at it.   The father of Mr. Chaplin's young gardener was a great orchid man; his mother came from St. George's Hill, Weybridge, in England—where rhododendrons grow tall as trees and flower in towering masses.

"Like music the colour of them must be," said the young gardener.   "Mr. Chaplin is a musician.   He can feel the music, too, in the colour of his hill.   Only those who work with him know how clever he is."

He looked up toward the marching pines.

"It took a long time to plant all that creeper," he said.   So it must have taken a long time; but it was worth it.

It was just after seeing Charley's hill that I saw Mr. Ben Myer's garden at Beverley Hills.   It was designed by

CACTI ARE STRANGE CREATURES: THEY FLOURISH ON ADVERSITY AND LOVE THE DEADLY, ARID, WATERLESS PLAINS

Mr. Paul Theyne.   A charming place; green velvet lawns
with no hard and fast edges to the flower borders,—beautiful
groupings of iris, tulips, columbines, tritomas, watsonias,
gladioli and cinerarias very well placed for form and colour—
a green pool on the green lawn with green box-balls reflected
in the green water; a green wrinkle in the water where the
spring flowed in; a wistaria-hung pergola; a nice manurey
rose-garden newly spread with luscious fare; nice manure it
was. . . I wished I were spreading it on my own roses
at home. . . .

That was a big banker's house and garden set on a high
hill,—very admirably laid out by a man who could afford
to buy good taste and had the taste to find it.   But I knew
that Charley's dreadful garden, with its one flash of pure
untutored vision, was far more spiritual—to me far more
acceptable.

More than anything in the world a garden displays
personality; the seeing eye walks softly in each new garden
it enters, for it is about to discover the owner's very soul.
The bias of his mind is there, the range of his ideals, his
courage or his slackness under difficulties, his sense of
order or disorder, his education, his breed, his tastes, his
nature are written in that tract of earth.

Harold Lloyd's garden is full of features—beside flowers;
a private golf course, two hard tennis courts and a miniature
English village for the young daughter.   It is a medley of
styles, Spanish barbecue, Italian ballroom, Japanese lily-
pond, English village, Indian canoes, Arizona cactus garden
—one thing after another.   Most exciting!   Terraces,
orangery—as one ecstatic female says: "the Harold Lloyd
estate in California is comparable only with the gardens of
the Caliphs."   Oh, poor Harold!

The azaleas began to bother again.   There was nothing
to do but to leave these dear people and chase off to the
South, apparently, and see the wretched things and get
them over.

"You need not start for several days," said Lucia, "it
is a late spring, they won't be out yet.   Come to the

desert with me.　Mrs. Chauncey Clarke wants us to go to
her date-gardens at Point Happy."

I would have cast all the beastly azaleas into the Pit
before I would miss living such lovely words . . . words
have always done terrible things to me.

"Come to the date-gardens at Point Happy." . . .

I had never seen dates grow.　I only knew them in flat,
pretty boxes on our Christmas dinner tables.

*　　　*　　　*　　　*　　　*

Harry at the wheel again:—and on through Riverside
to the great green plains beyond, ringed with mountains:—
out into the wild and lovely places:—to the singing sand.

Jack Rabbit Range is a series of hills covered with sage
brush, round grey bosses of sage brush . . . silvery-grey
goose sage! . . . It is so named because this growth
always makes cover for a lot of Jack rabbits.

The mesas of Beaumont were full of cherries in bloom.
A "mesa" (pronounced "May-sir") is a piece of land between
mountains, a flat high valley.　The tender spring green of
almonds against the bare stone hills was a haunting thing.

We began to come upon desert flowers: an amethyst mist
covered the ground.　I stared at it unbelieving, while
Harry whirled us relentlessly along.　On one side the
peaks of the mountains were clear rosy red: on the other,
indigo blue; behind us they were soft grey and in front
were low hills of a hard brown.　In this coloured bowl
we sped across sheets of lilac-pink flowers.

"Sand verbena," said Lucia, peacefully:—she was used
to it!

I found out afterwards that the fragrant flowers are
salver-shaped, with a long tube in many-flowered, long-
peduncled heads, terminal or auxiliary, on trailing succulent
stems; its name is misleading, for it is not really verbena,
but abronia; the variety I saw at Indio was either A. villosa
or A. aurita, or both.

"Our desert wild flowers are rigorously protected," said
Lucia.

That was a comforting thing to know.

They call it Point Happy because of an old settler who loved the rough freedom and the beauty of the desert . . . "Happy" was the only name he ever knew.

And now Point Happy is a place of poets and dreamers; there is a spell upon it . . .

I have a friend who remains to me for ever the type of woman I should want to live with if I were a man—gay and wise, full of energy and of sympathy, witty and accomplished, a traveller and a poet. Kate Hayter Reed has travelled out of sight now, but she is waiting round a bend in the road, laughing to herself because we think we have lost her . . . people like Kate do not "die."

Here and there I find her kin, her sisters,—women of the same sweetness and strength, and they are my friends; whether they know it or not.

Mrs. Chauncey Clarke is of that elect line. A most alive and brilliant woman—living poetry in every hour.

We were taken to the guest house to bathe and change after the long hot ride. A mocking bird sang, sweet as a nightingale, on a Chinese umbrella-tree outside my window; tumblers of grape-fruit juice waited in our rooms. That may sound dull, but let anyone travel for hours in that dry air, and then come upon such nectar pressed fresh from Marsh seedless grape-fruit grown in Coachella Valley!

Oranges grow too sickly sweet in the desert heat, but those grape-fruit were a revelation. Great pale, thin-skinned globes bursting with sweet crisp, ice-cold juice, . . . with a nutty taste under the sweet. And I cannot take out one adjective. . . .

Mrs. Clarke had collected a "diggers" party for our welcome; Mr. and Mrs. Carr had been in the Oasis for fifteen years; he pioneered there, and now has a profitable date-garden.

"One can figure on seven hundred dollars net profit per acre on dates once in full bearing," he said; "the Deglet Noor will only ripen in this valley in America and it is a marvellous date; there is a great difference in varieties, you know."

I did not know.   Also "Deglet Noor" was Greek to me.
But a squabble on the other side of the table took up my
attention. . . .   "My place will be lovely in five years,"
our hostess was saying, "for my dates are growing, too!"

"You wait till our baby grows up," said Mrs. Soper
haughtily, and then they all laughed, for it seems that
Mrs. Soper has bought a square mile to make a desert city
on—an architect's dream.

Meanwhile, they were living every second in rapture.

"We have grey walls of tamarisk round our place, thirty
feet high now, to make a shelter from the tearing wind.
When we first came we realised quickly that to make life
bearable we must have wind-breaks, so we planted tamarisk
even before we had any tools or any hired help.   When
the fearful wind tore the little tamarisks out of the ground I
would stand before them and save what I could,—I wore
the silver tablespoons thin scooping sand back on their
bared roots—my nails and my fingers wore out too, and
the cutting sand went screaming past my face and legs so
sharply that it drew blood.   It is like sand-paper.   I could
not bear to see the poor trees torn up.   And now they
are tall and strong.   They protect us.   They knew us.
Inside their shelter we have flowers and fruit, and we can
grow *such* asparagus!"

She babbled on and I listened in a dream.   Beside each
plate lay a "posy," a bunch of desert flowers set primly head
to head; tightly bunched in a formal design of varied
colours; the posies reminded me of the ones people took
to weddings and to Court in Victorian days.   My childish
eyes had seen them, with reverence . . . sometimes the
village children would bring one made of wild flowers to
our door hoping for a glass of milk, or a piece of bread and
jam.   Mrs. Soper it was who had made these pretty offerings for Mrs. Chauncey Clarke's guests.

"Mrs. Clarke is our 'Mother' and our lure.   It was
because of her we came to the desert—to be near her,"
said the architect.

I could understand that.

It was born in on me as dinner progressed that everything was of a very exquisite flavour as well as perfectly cooked. I am well accustomed to that clever cookery which disguises poor material and makes it seen rich and seductive; the French excel at it, but sometimes one finds the inspired house where all the material is of the freshest and best—vegetables full of the sweet earth-tastes, fruits warm with sugar of the sun, meats fed on special fodder—and all these things cooked with imagination and served with poetry . . . Some expression must have crept into my face for I found Mr. Carr smiling at me.

"The turkey here is good, isn't it? It is date-fed, you know; dried onions and dates; stones and all; date-fed pork is good, too."

So that was why this fine white meat had the rich delicacy of Devonshire cream!

"Date brandy is pretty good, it has a 'kick,' " he went on, "and don't the coyotes love 'em? They steal the dates near the ground."

Poor Jock! Barking away in Kent at every tramp who passed the lonely house while his mistress was gadding in what, to him, would be pure paradise; Jock adores fruit!*

I listened to the rattle of the palm leaves overhead through the dark, soft night of the desert. The nights are vital there, full of life; all creatures come out in the cool air, and humans awake to enjoy life and each other.

There were hammocks under a pergola, real lie-down hammocks over the grass, where one could sleep; there were roses around, stocks, rosy larkspur, nasturtiums, hollyhocks, petunias; sweet alyssum . . . too sweet in this warm air! . . . sweet peas bloom there for months on end; the desert garden had a drive set with alternate orange and oleander bushes which grow to dazzling perfection through all this country.

The pageant of dawn began—a winged splendour, transporting the soul—all round the property was a secure

* See *Wind-harps*.

boundary with locked gates; I wondered why they were so
carefully locked against what would appear to be emptiness;
I set out for my morning walk full of eagerness, but was
somewhat frustrated to find a brown man of violent aspect
attach himself.   Up in the rosy sky a buzzard hovered, I
was not encouraged by the omen.   Every book and every
film I ever saw had described Mexicans as treacherous,
murderous, dangerous folk who—apparently—would always
see you sooner dead than alive.   It quite spoilt the accustomed ritual of the early morning walk for me to have this
man padding beside.   He seemed very pleasant, too.

After a scramble over granite rocks, we came to a breath-
catching view of a snow-capped mountain—below us lay
Mrs. Clarke's swimming-pool, and broad date-gardens,
bounded by glossy, dark grape-fruit trees hung with the
pale round globes.   A flock of quail flew up from the rocks
at our feet and settled down again a few yards away; their
sober little bodies (lost to sight at once among the browny-
grey boulders) merged with the background.

At breakfast over polenta and eggs and fruit and coffee,
I expounded the tale of the bandit who had walked with me.
and learned he was a devoted servant of the estate wishing
to protect and guide the visitor!

"These Mexicans are the dearest, gentlest people," said
my hostess, "it is too bad that people think ill of them—
they are splendid gardeners, and very tender in the way
they handle young things.   You wait till you go round
the dates with José!"

I had to change all my ideas of Mexico at once.   It is
a pity, when there is so much to learn in this short life, that
a great deal of good time has to be wasted unlearning the
things one has learned wrong.   I was glad I could now like
Mexicans.

"Mr. Morgan is going to drive us to Hidden Springs
to-day," went on Mrs. Clarke.   "You must see our desert.
This, of course, is an oasis; we all have artesian wells and
irrigate our crops.   Wherever there is water we can grow
wonderful crops of choice early vegetables and fruits for

Eastern and Western towns. You should see sixty acres
of asparagus—and oh!—our pomegranates!"

I asked about grapes, but could only hear of the "Thompson Seedless" which are made into "rubyettes" and "emerald-
ettes" for cocktails! The grapes must be like sultanas,
I fancy.

Off we set for the drive through the desert toward
Death Valley. We were going to look at Hidden Springs,
and every puff of hot air that went by the face was sweet
with the scent of aromatic herbs, and grape-fruit blossom.
I sniffed rapturously. Some people seem quite indifferent
to scent; for over-civilisation has relieved us of any real
need for that keen sense of smell which was a vital matter
with our remotest ancestors. What was once a warning
has become a not very fashionable pastime.

Generally speaking, we are indifferent to scent—and
do not trouble to analyse perfumes. We accept them in a
glorious jumble when we notice them at all, the wonder is
that man retains in such a keen degree his much-neglected
power of smell, for it is still there, quite sensitive and acute,
not atrophied as some would have us believe. It has a remarkable vitality, a little practice and observation will bring
it back very quickly.

The nose and palate between them make up a very delicate
machinery, fine enough to detect the smallest possible trace
of scent, so exquisitely sensitive that it can be fatigued
by too much of some kinds—violet is a tiring scent, and
musk is another—there must be something in the molecules
of these perfumes which temporarily paralyses the olfactory
cells. After tiring the nose with violets we find we cannot
smell them (or any other perfume of the same quality)
until we have rested from smelling for a while.

Naturalists have always noticed the perfumes of the
country-side, one sees it over and over again in their works.
It is Tickner Edwardes in his country calendar who speaks
of the smell of hawthorn-nectar brewing in tens of thousands
of tiny vats in the beehives, to make the finest honey in
the world. He speaks of the "incense of it steaming hot

and fragrant through the squad of fanning bees at every portal."

It is W. H. Hudson, the great naturalist, who speaks of the moving power of scents in his last book of all, those wonderful books he wrote—"Intellectually, we know," he says, "smell does not rank so highly as the other two senses, but it is on the other hand more emotional and stirs the mind more deeply than seeing or hearing."

And F. A. Hampton, who has studied the subject very closely, says in his delightful work, "This is a characteristic quality of scent, that the feeling it evokes is strong, even poignant, while the sensory impression is vague and difficult to describe or recall . . . the emotion comes back first and is followed as a rule by the memory picture."

I noticed the sweet airs of the desert with appreciation and it was with lively interest that I suddenly saw the car was passing a nursery called "Sniff Gardens."

How wonderful these Americans are, I thought, here is someone who knows the commercial value of a sense man had almost laid aside, and yet it is but in harmony with their passion for cleanliness and healing; it is consistent that they should be sensitive to the physical effect of perfume; as well as to the dear enchantment it gives to a garden. I was glad of this Nurseryman, though I deplored the name he chose for his gardens!

There is a great deal more charm in scented flowers than in unscented ones; it is as though the ones with fragrance have a soul in their frail and lovely bodies,— they give out of themselves more than the others;—something definite of which we do not know the name, but which we humans accept into our brains and bodies when we draw in the scent. That is not a fantastic statement. If we breathe in the scented air and then breathe it out again, the scent has gone. It is left with us, "caught in the small area in the upper part of the nose where the brain is prolonged into direct communication with the olfactory cells,"— some scented molecules have been left with us there, to be transmuted in the chemistry of our bodies.

No one has found any flower which has the light and yet rich, full fragrance of the damask rose, and all those roses—Dame Edith Helen, Zephyrine, Ophelia, and so on —which smell like it. It is the scent we call the "Old Cabbage Rose" smell. Roses stand in a group alone, sub-divided among themselves into definite classes; there are also the tea-rose, faint and sweetly delicate; the fruity class as in Lord Lambourne and Golden Emblem—rather like pineapple; and the spicy smell of the hybrid-musk roses, Cornelia and its cousins.

As we go sniffing about our gardens we discover the lemony trace in some of the fragrant water-lilies, in magnolias and the smaller evening primroses; the turpentine in conifers, the camphor in sage, tansy and thyme (camphor which in rosemary is somehow mixed with a nutmeggy smell),—the sulphur in onions, garlic and shallots; and then our researches begin to open up other avenues of interest, for we find perfume in all sorts of unexpected places. We learn the sweet, rich smell of that lovely single "anomala" peony; and on a hot spring day when berberis stenophylla is out in long sprays of yellow bloom the garden becomes full of a gorgeous spicy perfume which we never expected, for there is no nurseryman's catalogue that remarks the scent as one of its attractions. We begin to appreciate, too, the combinations which make an especial sweetness in the garden—the mingled scents in the cool of the evening, . . . of border pinks, newly cut lawns and the Ceanothus Papillosus, . . . for instance.

"Scents are surer than sounds or sights to make our heart-strings crack," says Rudyard Kipling.

And which of us is there who does not know the memories which some whiff of unexpected scent will bring—a lost hour—place—or friend;—youth, perhaps, or love . . . materialised again for an unsubstantial darling moment by that ethereal sweetness, beguiling us back to the old raptures, the lost illusions.

"Sniff Gardens?" I said to Mr. Morgan, who was industriously driving the car along, "it's a funny name,

K

but a topping idea. I never heard of a 'smell' nursery before. What do they grow especially!"

Mr. Morgan laughed in a hollow way as at a bad joke. "Oh, everything."

"Everything that smells nice?" I said.

"Not especially," he answered.

"Why call them 'Sniff Gardens' then?"

"It's the man's name."

I had at once to undo a lot of admiration for American vision and enterprise, falsely conceived because a man's name had put me on to a wrong belief.

But why not really have 'Sniff Gardens'?

By and by we come to Mecca, of the "large soft dates"; where every date-garden bears an inviting sign to lure you in to eat some. A cry from Mrs. Clarke and Lucia at the back of the car:—

"Oh, wait! Oh, wait, here are the desert lilies!"

They are the loveliest things. We kneeled by them on the burning sand enraptured. Long snaky undulated leaves lay on the ground. "Crinkly" Lucia called them;—a foot or more long and half an inch or so wide, and from them rose the noble white trumpets streaked with grey on the back. The perfume was a clear, fresh, fruity one, most unexpected in that burning arid land. The bulbs, I was told, are very deep-seated. It was an experience to remember—those proud, white trumpets standing up tall and silvery on the glistening sand.

"They only grow in Coachella Valley of all the world," said one.

But I have heard (elsewhere) that the desert lily (hesperocallis undulatus) grows from the Salton Sea eastward into Arizona and southward to Mexico, so that this piece of information may have been a burst of local pride.

We came to the Salton Sea—that is to say, we came to near outlooks of it—a strange mystery, a dead sea 200 feet below sea level. Mr. Morgan told me it had only been there since 1905, when the Colorado River "broke," the break only stopped in 1906 and since then the "sea" is fed by waste water from Imperial Valley. There is good mullet in it put there by the Government; and all round its shores, for those who want such a thing, are opportunities to build here a Western Nice.

Its blue looked ineffably lovely under the changing lights which are the magic of the desert—smoke trees made their own peculiar beauty on the hills—and sheets of rosy sand verbena gave an exotic touch to the colour scheme.

I was exceedingly happy . . . The company was after my own heart; our wise, witty hostess; Lucia so pretty; and Mr. Morgan slowly unfolding a sensitive quality under his rather business-like manner. Mrs. Clarke had not only told me to wear what I liked, but did not seem to mind when she saw how awful what I liked was . . . a shady hat, sneakers and a short-sleeveless garment of simplest form. One of the reasons I hate towns is because one has to dress up, and here I was let loose in old clothes with nice people, under the sun, to enjoy a thousand flowers never seen before!

"Have you noticed the warm aromatic smell of most of these twigs and woods and leaves?" Mrs. Clarke asked. "I want to make a desert incense some day. It should be quite distinctive."

(Now I wonder if she has since done it?)

Incense, of course, is a gum-resin from the Mohr trees of Somaliland or Arabia (genus Boswellia). That is to say true incense; frankincense or olibanum; but I do not see why "desert incense" should not become a known variant even if it is made of fragrant leaves and twigs instead of gum, so long as they contain enough inflammable essential oil to give off a sweet odour in burning. It seemed a pleasant idea. The flowers on every hand were bewildering. I was entirely out of my depth—the only things I recognised were the "sand verbenas" in carpets of amethyst and an etherealised Californian poppy, tiny, pale, exquisite.

There was a plant like our self-heal; bushes of mauve lupin, much of the strongly aromatic greasewood or creosote plant (adenostoma fasciculatum) with its evergreen needle-like leaves and showy panicles of creamy flowers; it carries tiny, white, what-o'clock seed-vessels at the same time as the flowers. In the mass it looked like heather.

On the hill-tops were hundreds of the Candelabra de Dios, the candles of the Lord. They have a flower like a flame; the stems are ashy-grey and thorny, the leaves fleshy, thorny, cactus-like. If it is, as I imagine, Ocotillo (a relation of the tamarisks) the stems are fragrant; they are waxy and resinous and inflammable.—An ingredient for the desert incense? These candelabra make their own remarkable shrine in the desert. It is not easy to forget the long, flowery tips on the hills,—lit up with flaming bloom.

There was a lovely salvia they called "white sage," a silvery-grey thing with pale lavender or white flowers. "It makes wonderful honey," said Mrs. Clarke, thoughtfully, "a clear, pale, exquisite-tasting honey."

Anything she said about flavours I would trust. She is one of those rare women, of a type all sensible men should seek with tears, and for long years undaunted till they find one . . . a woman with a fine palate.

There was a bush they called cat's-paw acacia which was just like a small edition of the South African wait-a-bit thorn, and a fine, silver-grey "desert holly" (reminding me of certain olearias) which they told me keeps, when cut, for months.

They were all kind, eager to help, but I needed a botanist with me to catch gleams of the oddly beautiful forms around. Again and again I deplored my ignorance . . . it was exasperating to be split on the rock of it like this!

"If we only had Miss Eastwood here," lamented they— and once again I wished she had not gone to Europe just when I wanted her to tell me about "old Abraham" and these lovely so-surprising flowers of rock and sand and sun.

Jim Peech in his garden at Beaulieu has a broom of which he is very proud, and with reason. Sir William Lawrence grows it, too, very successfully at Burford—genista Oethnensis, a fragrant Sicilian broom—here on the desert I was frequently reminded of Jim's pet broom by the feathery grace of palo verde, the much loved green desert-tree

LA QUINTA, INDIO

The Inn built like a Mexican City in the Date Gardens of an Oasis

(Parkinsonia Torreyana). In the Canyon of Hidden Springs we found it growing against pastel shades where the rocks are coloured as if an artist had painted them in vast harmonies of rich and delicate tones.

It was in the canyon that Mr. Morgan's "trial by mistletoe" started. I had admired along the burning, bumpy difficult trail (for by now we were well off the metalled high-road) an appearance in certain trees as of beads strung in close bunches. At first I thought they were bird's nests, but by and by I found they were beautiful beads, translucent, ruddy, and amber. Mr. Morgan noticed my frequent glances turned in admiration on these clusters of jewels, pressed thick and close on many a tree; presently he arrived with a branch.

"Our desert mistletoe," he said gallantly.

"In the New Year the berries are as red as blood," said Mrs. Clarke.

I was much touched by this offering, especially as the beautiful round beads were even lovelier on close inspection than at a distance,—and I carried the bough about the canyon for a while, till the heat made even that light gift a burden, and I laid the mistletoe and a handkerchief in the car on my seat.

At last, much wearied with clambering about, and the strain of seeing new wonders, meeting new enchantments— I flopped into the seat, the car bumped off, and in due course I needed my handkerchief; I fished it out hurriedly and it stuck to my face. The more I tried to get it off the more I stuck everywhere; my fingers stuck to each other, then to the handkerchief firmly welded on to my face; then wherever I put them. I tried to turn with signals of distress to Mr. Morgan, and found I was stuck to my seat!

When Lucia and Mrs. Clarke could speak for laughing they made the car stop. The gallant pulled me apart from the seat and took me on to the sand where I immediately stuck to him. The desert mistletoe is surely "viscum" something or other. They make bird-lime out of the sticky, glutinous berries of our English mistletoe (viscum album) but this stuff was sheer glue. Face, dress, hands, arms, and the car seat, were liberally rubbed with dry sand and to his glory be it recorded that Mr. Morgan drove the strange object beside him without turning a hair, and would not even *admit* his car seat was spoilt. If a man wants to get a woman to stick to him he had better try wooing with desert mistletoe.

We dined at La Quinta at Indio that night; an inn built like a city—like an old Mexican city; a series of low houses among tamarisk, pepper and palm trees.

There was a spacious, unhurried deliberation about the bungalow suites spread round the central dining-hall, in that oasis on the burning desert sands. White-washed walls, unadorned but for the moving beauty of sharp shadows, deep roofs of heavy hand-made tiles with every chimney a different pattern; floors of square polished brick, sun-bath tents, plenty of running water, very little furniture; dates, figs, almonds, grape-fruit, pomegranates, grapes, asparagus and the choicest vegetables—grown there and served fresh to the table—date-fed pork and turkeys served with a naïve poetry; bright flowers around the dishes, orange blossoms on the salad; their ivory buds cool on the chrysoprase green of crisp lettuce leaves (so that perfume was added to the cool pleasure of them), lumps of fresh golden pineapple and pale creamy avocado pear.

There is a quality in the luxury of La Quinta which has come out of the very essence of the man who conceived and built this strangely beautiful remote hostelry. It is very well "done," planted out in the wild solitudes; sought by the elect, by those who love nature and the silences; by the thinkers, poets, writers, philosophers.

Mr. Morgan, the hero of the mistletoe bough, whose dream that inn was, "is a native son of the Golden West." The son of a pioneer. He was born in California, a land peopled from far and near, which has few "native sons" of middle age. He has expressed at La Quinta, his love of the wild, his love of comfort; and has made an amazing,

unique inn.   It is unspoiled by the vulgarity of crowds—
God forbid they ever find it!

After the wonderful day, the wonderful night . . .
under the desert stars. . . .

Gusts of delicious perfume came across from grape-fruit
trees in blossom; gleaming ivory plumes of date-palms were
bursting the rough brown leather of their sheaths;—a
mocking bird sang on the tree beside the window a rich
full-hearted song, sweet and long-drawn as a nightingale's.
Bluebirds were clamouring around the red berries of sticky
desert mistletoe, and it seemed to me they were better
fitted to cope with it than frail humans.   Robins, meadow-
larks, humming birds woke the singing morn; all around
on the hot, dry sand, scrambling in sheets of rosy amethyst,
were the carpets of sand verbena; there were handsome
bunches of fringy bloom on the castor bean bushes, and
the great pink double oleanders were out.

Beyond the oasis, away on the stretch to Death Valley
or to Hidden Springs past the mysterious Salton Sea, I
knew now that there were stranger things, odd twisted cacti,
puncture weeds, Judas trees, pale great Yuccas, mountain
snakes, lizards, chuckwallas and such fry, companionate
with the deadly, arid, waterless plains.

bottle for ten years and secured a perfect setting of fruit with it. It must be kept absolutely dry; mildew destroys it very quickly. And, of course, it is always best, if one can, to use it fresh."

José cut some twigs from the great cluster of white flowers, went back to the date garden, and climbed into a female tree; there he opened the protecting sheath of brown velvet and disclosed the white virgin within.

The female looked like a sheaf of pale ivory buttons on the ivory stem; the male when it had come out of its trance and burst out into its proper manly form, looked like a graceful plume. José cut off six inches from the top of the poor damsel (this love business always seems to make women suffer), he then parted the truncated sheaf and put three fronds of the male flower into the middle;—they were put at the top of the fruit cluster with the open flowers turned downwards, and tied in place with a strip from the palm with a clever slip-knot that would stretch as the fertilised shaft grew big with seed.

Left to themselves date-palms bear irregularly and sparely. With cultivation they become a highly profitable affair.

A good deal of restraint has to be observed, however, in this hand pollination for, if a palm is allowed to produce large crops of fruit at an early age, it will develop few off-shoot buds. Increase of plantations is done by these off-shoots so the value of every young palm of a desirable variety is not measured solely by the quantity of fruit it produces but in a large degree by its ability to produce offshoots to increase plantings. Under favourable conditions this increase should amount to tenfold every six years.

The development of this fascinating new industry, only seventeen years old, on the Pacific Coast is amazing. Coachella Valley seems to be peculiarly suited to the growing of the Deglet Noor, a grand date which is very sensitive to moisture, either rain or dew, when the ripening process begins; but there are other varieties not quite so fussy about dew-point conditions which promise well; and the United

José, with a Male Date Flower in the right hand and a Sheathed Bloom in the left

States Department of Agriculture has not been lacking in enterprise, scrutinising the commercial value of various dates,—Tafilet, Saidy, Fard, Halawi, etc.,—and studying with closest attention the history, past and present, of the Egyptian oases where the men of the palm orchards have cultivated dates.

They thrive in a wide range of soils from a heavy adobe to a light, sandy loam; but a rich, well-drained sandy loam is the ideal. Irrigation is a necessity. These trees can only grow where they can get abundant burning sun and abundant supplies of water.

The Saidy is a date of the Libyan oasis and is now being grown at Tempe in Arizona and at "Mecca" in California, "Mecca of the large, soft dates." It is rich in sugar; when freshly ripened it does not have the peculiar indefinable aroma and flavour characteristic of the Deglet Noor, but it has something the Deglet Noor has not—an improvement in flavour upon storage due to a slow granulation of the sugar content; a quality unique with this variety.

The sleuthing out of the varieties of any new fruit best suited to the requirements and climate conditions of a country to which its cultivation is as yet experimental is a long, slow business vested in certain valuable but seldom showy and noisy people. They do not run with banners and trumpets about the Life-road, telling everyone what a lot they are doing, they burrow silently through the tunnels of the years, travelling; observing, recording, experimenting, rendering a rich service to their generation and seldom rewarded by as much as a "thank you."

Later on in my travels I visited the Department of Agriculture at Washington, D.C., and listened to the hasty way each grave man after another would pile all the credit upon his neighbour, shaking praise off, as if it were an awkward load—as a dog shakes a wet coat—whenever anything they had done cropped up that seemed admirable, or had a hint or taint of success about it. One could not but contrast them with some of the people who subscribe to horticultural societies and get gold medals and things.

I had an illuminating hour with Mr. W. T. Swingle and Mr. T. H. Kearney. Between them they managed so to confuse me with their passionate modesty that I finally left with a belief that to say anything in compliment to their work would be to besmirch the purity of their escutcheons, unspotted of publicity or the vile praise of froward man.

I found it a trifle disappointing (although I greatly admire such delicacy in public servants) because I very much wanted to say how their work had impressed me, and (much more important) what Mr. Rankin and Mr. David Fairchild said about that which Mr. Kearney did in Tunis in 1904–5 and Mr. Swingle in 1909 (as well as before and since) for the lively bantling date industry; but evidently the thing they will most appreciate is that I leave them to blush unseen, and cast their "sweetness on the desert air." To the great advantage of the desert.

Mr. Swingle, a tall lean sardonic attractive dry good-looking man, who chased the fig and found the date, also explores for rubber; he told me that more than twenty million pounds of dates a year can be produced from the date-palms already planted in Coachella Valley and that he has got one or two very remarkable seedling Tafilets from Cheapside Jews!

There is romance in all the date story as in most of the fruits city-herded humans take so lightly . . . there is a long tale of the wasp he tracked for the Smyrna figs! . . .

Mr. Kearney is really the cotton "god," and he told me of the long-staple Pima cotton, bred in Arizona, of which the seed is taken back to Egypt, being more productive! Yet 200,000 bales of cotton are still imported by the States from Egypt. "Maarad" is the Pima seed from Arizona!

He told me that Australia is made to raise dates, and South Africa too; or at any rate Rhodesia . . . anywhere where they can get artesian water. I had an interesting time with those two, and left them in their tidy Government Office each still trying to fit a halo on the other's head.

I first heard of the date experts of Washington, D.C., from Mrs. Chauncey Clarke in her date gardens in Coachella Valley, that "little Arabia" of California, after we had watched José pollinising; she was interested in all research work, and was allowing glass plates to be let in the earth round some of her valuable palms in order that their root system might be studied by Government experts.

I hated leaving the desert. We went to see the architect's "square mile," and found him marvellously hedged with the tamarisks they had planted in the high winds, when the sand cut their faces and wore the spoons thin! Everything seemed to grow for those two and I tremble to think what their place will be like soon for they will not kill anything; there was already Lilium, and Beserita daughter of Lilium, the cows, not to mention El Torito growing more ambitious daily;—dogs, male and female, in abundance, starting with Mr. Grey the wall-eyed sheep-dog crossed with collie.

Their grape-fruit trees were just coming into bearing; with ceremonial ritual I was given the first. Their very first grape-fruit after all these years of waiting for the tree to bear.

"We love our date gardens here, you know," said the pretty brown-eyed woman, "when the sun slants under the palms at dawn or at evening time, the bunches of ripe dates look like jewels of transparent amber and cornelian. The Deglet Noor especially is pink . . . luminous . . . and turns to a golden amber. You would never imagine such colour was in them—our date gardens are green caves hung with jewels."

Harry at the wheel again! We were away to Palm Springs and the Desert Inn; we walked the palm-set Canyon and saw a lot of young things in riding kit being filmed there—a "Hollywood outfit," very much out of key with the beauty of the oasis. The Desert Inn started twenty or more years ago as a tiny hostelry for a few intermittent visitors, to-day it has a thirty-five acre site, with a large open swimming-bath fed by mountain water and there are golf and riding to be had, so that it is now a fashionable winter resort. It lies under the beneficent shade of Mount San Jacinto, from which two streams of purest water gush to make that garden of the sun.

The great country whirled by, hour after hour. We were in rolling green hills now, like the Sussex Downs, passing miles of orange and lemon groves.

"Let us go and look at 'our lease,'" said Lucia.

So we went to the oil derricks where life had sprung up out of the earth in a new form for Pete and Lucia. . . .

The monstrous machinery towered like gallows—what had been a green land was a blackened wilderness of scaffolding—but from this ugliness their own lives had blossomed like a garden and grown wide and fair. . . .

"Before you go South we must have a picnic and grill our steaks in the open," said Lucia.

We did. I saw in use that odd feature of California gardens—a grid of iron bars on bricks;—I had noticed them in many a garden and been told how the people like to roast their meats in the open over a wood fire.

We feasted under the wide tree—the two pretty daughters were there, and the Japanese man and woman of the ranch. She was busy and competent waiting on us with smiles and quick little gentle movements, but he was lost in contemplation—standing in the rich glare of the fire under the heavy shadows of the tree, dressed all in white, leaning on a stick.

"I believe he is a philosopher, I don't believe he is a servant at all," said Lucia, helplessly, regarding her minion; "it is his wife who does all the work."

"He is always thinking," chirruped the little daughter.

He had once asked if he might read one of my books— to my embarrassment, for I did not suppose he could read English and was sure he would not want to read mine, anyway. But he asked again very prettily through his so-nice wife. I only had the *Gardens of Good Hope* and so he went off browsing on this treatise upon South African gardens, embroidered as usual with the what-nots which

creep into my garden books.   When he brought it back
to me he said:

"It is all poetry."

Sleep is sweet in an orange grove.   I lay and listened
to the frogs, to the sudden, sharp sound of the redwood
timber which cracked with a loud noise now and again, to
the sleepy cooing of the fat pigeons dreaming; all round
the house swung the golden oranges with fine essential
oils sealed tighty in their silken skins; some had dropped
down to the tilled earth and lay there on the rich valley
silt of the perfect citrus soil; passion flowers and roses
hung round the house; Prince barked in the still night,
—and the green hills rolled in billowing curves around
the beautiful valley.

The azaleas were imperiously marching into my plans.
I hated the things by this time . . . there they were in
some place called Charleston bursting into fat buds, bother
them! . . . and the Mississippi lay between—and the
Grand Canyon. . . .

*　　　*　　　*　　　*　　　*

Lucia stood by the train with a large basket of oranges
from the ranch; covered with orange blossom.   Pete had
a couple of books for me to read. . . .

"Got your ticket?" he said, in a grumpy voice.

I felt suddenly very, very lonely. . . .   That tone of
voice was of the long-ago, sheltered, forgotten years;—the
voice of a man seeing a woman off on a journey;—snappy,
cross, anxious, protective.

"Got your ticket?"

I had my ticket—yards of it, flapping about. . . .

CHAPTER XI

THE LOST GARDENS OF THE SOUTH

MICHAEL RIMMERLEY'S red roses were as good as they sounded and well worth seeing, but I did not think much of his Grand Canyon. It is over-sold.

You don't see much when you look down it, because you don't really look down it at all; you look across. The Colorado may be a wide rushing river . . . it only looks like a turbulent, muddy trickle when you get a glimpse of it a mile below, among the rocks, through field glasses. I stayed at El Tovar and saw the sun rise over the Canyon;—but I have seen it the same colour in Africa . . . with the same swift changes. . . . I was disappointed. There was something cynical about the Indians, too; they were obviously accustomed to show off; like the Dutch in certain parts of Holland much infested by tourists.

Now this is only my personal reaction to one of the most famous scenic wonders of the world; I have set it down honestly, because this book is after all but a series of snapshots of a much-travelled Continent,—taken here and there through the lens of an alone-woman's eye. That I did not see the Grand Canyon from a more impressive angle is my loss; I am full sure that it could catch my heart in wonder. But I happened to find only the tawdry commercialised side. . . . I know that it is a "remark-able example of earth sculpture produced by erosion and of immense scientific interest because it discloses a great perspective of the geologic past." . . . I know that.

I saw of course that its general red colour glows in the sun and that it is a phantasmagoria of changing tones,

THE LOST GARDENS OF THE SOUTH

pale buff and grey, delicate green and pink—and in the
shadows chocolate brown, slate grey, and olive green.   In
the distance it takes on that miracle of African mountain
colourings—a transparent blue-purple haze, indescribable
against the green pine trees on its rim and the intense cobalt
of the sky.   Ultramarine birds flew among the green trees
and made their own perfect note in the colour scheme;
birds of a dazzling blue.

If I had seen the canyon from the river at Fern Glen,
or from Marble Gorge looking up walls a sheer 2,000
feet high; if I had stood beside Sheer Wall Rapid and
ridden down the thrilling mule trails with Michael Rim-
merly or some such fiery-tongue I would have been enriched
by the famous beauty-spot.

But I can only remember the wide flatness . . . the
tourist business. . . .

My road lay through Arizona and Texas to Louisiana
. . . Sam Houston's Texas—The Lone Star State . . . I
was motored through the desert,—the "Painted Desert"
of Arizona and learned during that arid wonderful ride,
on a bumpy trail in an open car, why eagles can be called
"golden."   (I wonder why we cannot learn everything in
life in that adventurous sudden way . . . at first hand?   It
makes each new scrap of knowledge a possession.)

We had passed through a "village" of prairie dogs,
queer engaging little creatures . . . and were bumping
along over the rough dry scrubby grass between interminable sage-brush hummocks in a shimmering world of pastel
colours when I happened to look up,—and there poised
in the sky above us were two transparencies.   The eagles
hovered very, very high in the burning azure,—their mighty
golden wings outspread; luminous.   I knew of course,
that golden eagles breed all the way from Labrador to
New Mexico, but I was not thinking of them then,—
nor had the name ever conveyed anything to me; suddenly
there they were, hovering overhead; like amber with the
light shining through it.

The Painted Desert is well named; it is sheer colour,

exquisite, unreal. We skirted deep chasms, met Indians and flocks of goats in most untoward places where passing was difficult; and moved in a burning furnace of heat, and unbelievable colour.

An orange made me a flashing moment. . . . I had one of Lucia's large juicy ones in my hand when we were caught up in a patriarchal tangle of flocks and herds; the dark eyes of a Hopi Indian glanced at the fruit lying idly in my lap; a glance like lightning,—swift as a dragonfly . . . it was there and was instantly gone; an oblique glance; observant, expressionless. It did not interest me. But a few minutes later I was aware of the dark eyes of a tiny Hopi fixed on the orange with passion.

I held it out—the little one stretched eager hands to take the gift . . . and a pleasant smile came to me from a taller, older Indian near by; a radiant and sweet smile.

As we moved away I understood . . . oranges would be nectar of the high gods, and of a rarity, in that unwatered desert of burning sand . . . the first glance I had caught had been one of intense longing, but the manners of a courteous race had made the young Hopi purge every bit of expression out of his eyes. . . .

When we children were very young the first thing that was put in our Christmas stockings was always an orange; it was in the toe . . . the precious *"bonne-bouche"*; they were expensive in England those days; we looked forward to the toe of our stockings very much year after year. It makes one muse upon the luxuries we accept without a thought in this era of grace; so much accustomed to them that we hardly remember the lean ways of long ago . . . oranges were a very rare and heavenly fruit in my childhood; passionately adored!

The herd of goats was at last negotiated and the big cream car moved on toward the "Petrified Forest"; I looked back and saw a small dark face glistening with the sticky juices of Lucia's orange!

Cold mountain snows look down on Flagstaff; Mrs.

Perry gave me a box of "cactus candy," a pleasing sweet-meat much like angelica, and I boarded the train for New Orleans.

The impression I had of Texas was of a land of rolling prairie plains,—with a flora that appeared to be principally nutritious grasses though I knew that in some of the plateau-canyons grow peccan, sycamore, walnut, live oak, and cypress.

It is stock-raising and dairy country but very rich in petroleum, natural gas and oil which provide cheap and unlimited fuel,—and keep the living costs low . . . I wonder if Sam Houston had any real idea of the great value of the land he acquired for America when he fought in 1846 in command of 743 raw troops and routed 1,600 Mexican veterans? That triumph lured him back to peace and power; but the parts of his life I like best to learn about, and which coloured for me the whole rich smiling Texan lands as I travelled through them, were the shadowed places; once when he fled from the post as clerk in a trader's store which his elder brothers had found for him, and lived with the Cherokee Indians for nearly three years in East Tennessee;—a thing as surprising as if my own brother had upped and gone to live with the gipsies, with the Romany folk,—when mother and father with frugal foresight removed him in early youth from Oxford, and placed him, much subdued, as clerk in a bank! There was the dark valley Sam trod when Eliza Allen, the young wife whom he worshipped, left him after three months of marriage. He was Governor of Tennessee then; the ball was at his feet; he was a tall, popular, handsome figure of romance . . . no one ever knew why she left him; he never told; but at that blow to his heart he abandoned the world and cast the bitter dust of the "civilised" from his feet.

He went back and lived with the Cherokee Indians again. Six years later he was Commander-in-Chief of the Texan army.

A chivalrous dreamer, this Sam; of fearless candour;

a man who knew the price of nothing and the value of everything.

It was Michael Rimmerley who painted the romantic outline of that wild American upon the canvas of my fancy . . . he turned a pair of English eyes from an old, old house in the Weald to look with more than a little of hero-worship upon a dead Virginian soldier. They say of Michael that he is stupid and irresponsible; I find him the last to an exasperating degree but never the first! Certainly not stupid, except where he wishes; and there is cleverness in that. . . .

He led me a long, long trek with his words; they were whips that drove me forth;—spurs that stung me into travel. . . .

On Passion Sunday I was on his Mississippi—"Father Mississippi." . . . I possessed it all . . . the enormous, muddy, swirling water, the levées, the plantations, Baton Rouge, the green, green land and even Mark Twain's rear-paddle boats! Under the sunset light the brown clay went out of the colour of the river and it shone like a fire opal;—the cruel Mississippi that keeps what it takes; those who are drowned in it are not found again. . . . It is a colossal affair, over 15,000 miles of waterway are capable of being used for commercial purposes,—the river and its tributaries between them drain over one-third of the area of the United States.

"The peccan tree is never fooled," said Miss Sarah Henderson; "it knows when to come out."

We were driving down Esplanade Avenue in New Orleans where the green walk and the wide avenues of trees resemble New Amsterdam in Holland. I like peccan nuts; so this piece of information was carefully stored.

"This is a lily country," she went on. "Every kind of lily grows here, except madonnas,—and our official city flower is the oleander. But I wish you could see the crêpe myrtles in July!"

So did I wish it. This charming gentlewoman spoke of things I loved to hear; I could feel the famous "Southern

charm" in all her ways; and was drugged by the soft
Southern languor in the beautiful old city; I could see
the scars and the stars of History; could read a richer
legend in the streets of New Orleans than the brisk boulevards of Los Angeles and Hollywood have yet had time
to spell.

With the tiresome azaleas swelling their buds fuller
every day and beckoning me to South Carolina, my time
in the old plantation gardens and Spanish patio-type gardens of Louisiana had need to be no more than a scamper.
I had lingered full long with Pete and Lucia. . . .

Over the pompano at lunch, Mrs. Labrot became lyrical
about miles of blue irises just coming into flower; so off
we set under graceful quick-growing hackberry trees to
find them in the swamps "by the bayou."

It seems one is guided by bayous in that place! They
are the marshy offshoots of the river; they are, on a vast
scale, what we in England call "backwaters"; but these
backwaters of the Mississippi,—these bayous,—are each
one like the River Thames itself; and the boat life upon
them and on the river-banks is exactly the same as we see
at Maidenhead and Marlow. The Southerners love them;
they are full of splendid fish and wonderful things to eat;
they live on them; and by them. There is always life
on the bayou . . . always a boat.

We drove along the dusty white roads of crushed shell
between tall green trees with the swampy lands stretching
either side, green and cool; New Orleans is famous for
its shell-fish, the best oysters in the world, lobsters, crabs,
prawns of a succulence beyond belief,—but one needs to
see those long white roads of crushed shell to realise the
limitless resources of her waters. Everyone fishes in
Louisiana!

Among the green grasses of the swamps stood up gleaming umbels of white spider lilies (hymenocallis rotata), the
pure cup of each flower be-whiskered with its long white
spidery spikes,—like stiff white baby-ribbon. The blue
irises, with the perversity of things that are meant to be

shown off, were there in acres and acres of green rush
and bud, but only a few flowers had yet come out! They
were very beautiful, blue in many shades, with a yellow
streak,—iris hexagona, I suspect; the native one is the
brown iris fulva and the blue swamp irises that grow from
North Carolina to Washington and Newfoundland are
I. cristata and I. verna.

We looked down on the coastal marshes of Louisiana
by bayou Barartaria where the herons come, and where
the coloured sunsets shine on miles of goldy grass; it was
once the scene of lively exploits by the famous pirates Jean
and Pierre Lafitte who made it their rendezvous because
it gives access to the Gulf without stemming the current
of the Mississippi. Everything is "Gulf" down there . . .
Gulf gasolene . . . Gulf food, etc.

The beauty of the bayous was extraordinary to me after
the desert travel through which I had just come; the dark
sparkling water, clear, green-shadowed, was "paradise
enow"; there is another unexpected beauty in these streams
in the way they suddenly broaden out into "ox-bows,"—
to basin-lakes,—now and again.

Here I saw for the first time the famous aerial plant
"Spanish moss" hanging from the great oak trees; its
floating rags and shreds of grey gave a dreamy softness
to the reflections in the bright water. There were gardens on the way where Easter lilies, hollyhocks, sweet
peas, camellias and bamboos made each their picture.

The old plantation gardens have splendid lawns; and
beds of flowers grow against a glorious background of
shrubs . . . azalea, crêpe myrtle, oleander, jasmine, purple
clerodendrons and justia.

Water hyacinth grows in miles of pale mauve upon the
water, so luxuriantly that it is a menace to navigation;
it was Dr. William Allen Richardson (whose name to most
people stands for a lovely old-fashioned orange-yellow rose)
who first brought the water hyacinth to New Orleans and
threw a few bits in the water. He was Miss Sarah Henderson's neighbour,—and I shall always regret not having

questioned her more closely on his reactions to the beautiful
blue flower after he had learned its greedy appreciation of
the new home he had found for it!

They have gardens of sentiment, of history, and of age
in Louisiana.   We walked in Mrs. Stauffer's green place
of lawns and trees, with small lead figures in the formal
rose garden and stepping-stones in the grass.   There were
borders of flowers of the west wind (Zephyranthes)
round the rose beds and pink Cherokee roses on the
arches.   There were pillars of solid cedar in front of the
lovely old colonial house, where cardinal birds, orioles and
mocking birds sang rich and clear.

"This is the proper approach to all New Orleans gardens," said Miss Henderson staying by a path bordered
with Louis Philippe roses and fleur de lys; "some of the
people still speak no English, you know, only French!"

The Louis Philippe rose is a Bourbon; both Bourbon
and Bengal roses do well in New Orleans; and the best
doer of all the hybrid teas is Radiance, red and pink.
The pale salmon pink H.T. Mrs. Charles Bell is another
reliable rose; but the Pernetianas do not thrive well.
Emily Gray, Paul's Scarlet Climber, Mermaid, Dr. Van
Fleet, Dame Edith Helen, Killarney, Mrs. Benjamin
Cant, and Mme. Abel Chatenay are good.   Apparently
fish scrap is a good manure, easy to obtain there, with the
advantage of being free from weed seeds and insects.

New Orleans is on the old Spanish Trail which runs
from San Diego in California to St. Augustine in Florida
. . . a long, long trail . . . and the streets of the Vieux
Carré are narrow,—but in the newer parts there are wide
avenues and boulevards.   The French influence is strong;
picturesque, beautiful; it made one's heart ache to see the
heavy paw of Northern "efficiency" in skyscraper buildings in New Orleans . . . commercial minds full of that
vulgar grab and run idea, which is the assassin of peace
and of happiness, have not spared the historic city.   The
graceful characteristic balconies and lovely old courts have
been pulled down to put up the inappropriate skyscrapers

beloved of the ant-heap city of New York.   An incredible piece of vandalism.   While I mourned aloud at this Mrs. Labrot assured me that the Louisiana Historical Society is very keen; which cheered me up a lot;—it is an active agony to see beauty despoiled.   New Orleans has character; one finds the dull simple-seeming houses on the streets have the most lovely backs; patios and courts, beautifully made doors, and balconies . . . that which looked parochial even frowsty on the street proved, when seen from the hidden, intimate side, to be of a delicacy and an invitation inimitable.

The lost gardens of the South!   One finds them overgrown and all the pattern softened with neglect, for want of money.   Louisiana has had a troubled, dramatic history; and lives ever under the menace of its dæmon, its god, the terrible, glorious river; but it has compensations; the soft voices of the people woo one's heart away.

"We have a great deal of happiness, for our relations with each other are sweet," she went on.   "We love our servants, too, they do not presume; our workpeople have a niceness; our houses and lands are destroyed by flood, our sugar frozen, the Industrial Canal handicaps us with its heavy dues . . . trees and sky are all that are left and the happiness of each other." . . .

It seemed to me that they were richer than most, "having each other." . . .   It is true that they suffer from one thing after another. . . .   In 1926 their sugar-cane plantations were nearly extinguished by mosaic disease; but in 1929 they were planted with P.O.J. canes and are now recovering from what threatened to be crushing disaster.

A sense of insecurity invaded me now and again as I realised the city in which I was enjoying much enchantment was below high-water mark.   The lower parts of the city are below Gulf level; a fact that the cemeteries, of all cheerful places, brought home to me as much as anything.   They were like towns of stone and marble for the people are buried above ground; with fine vaults to guard their bones.

I am not enamoured of cemeteries. I would never choose to go to one unless it might be to sit beside a lost friend and renew there some precious memories; however, I admired the handsome edifices of the departed;—and turned to livelier prospects, the beauty of the water oaks with their shiny handsome leaves and the many varieties of that stalwart quercus race of which my own old house in Kent is built (there is in it at least one that must have been a sapling in 1066 when Norman William conquered Saxon Harold; it was built in 1320 and my oak stands still as hard as iron after 600 years of buffeting by time and weather!). They have white oaks and red oaks and live oaks as well as water oaks and many more in New Orleans.

"Why doesn't everyone come here to live?" I asked, wondering, at last.

"The mosquitoes save us!" they said; "we have a terrible lot of them; and we are used to them. In summer there are smudge-pots put out all along the streets to keep them away!"

Besides the famous shell-fish, the strawberries of Louisiana are the best flavoured and the most valuable in the United States; the country is rich, too, in fur . . . mink, otter, musk-rat as one might guess in so watery a land!

One has to learn the graces of unpunctuality in the South; I have cultivated the astringent virtue of working strictly on time in my life . . . it has advantages, in several ways—I arrive punctually to fulfil obligations and I expect other people to do the same by me. This smug edifice speedily tumbled about my ears down South. I found myself, sticky with apprehension and perspiring freely from apology, delivered from one appointment to another never anywhere near the hour arranged, only to find my frantic excuses quite unnecessary. Nobody cared!

After the glare of the desert and the joyous friendly blare of California I found myself in this phantom place; wandering round peaceful overgrown gardens with the gentle-voiced exquisite lady of breeding,—who loved the stars.

Money means nothing to these people; they have lost too much; they are content, they do not grab; they know how to go without. Proud, self-sufficing, sensitive people . . . and *how* they love their State!

There were many things that were new to me,—the milk-and-wine lily was one (crinium augusta) in umbels of creamy milk stroked with wine-stained hands; and that small yellowish magnolia they called "fuscata" with powerful fragrance like pear-drops, or nitrate of amyl. Magnolias grew everywhere enormously.

I was due to be with Mrs. Olsen the first Vice-President of the New Orleans Garden Club Society at four o'clock. I arrived at 6.45 suffused with shame; and was welcomed with airy good-will; never was a less rancorous land! The people do not argue; they just accept. Mr. Olsen is a very hospitable Dane; and we had a merry dinner preceding a lecture at Community Place, where my hostess was showing slides. She was very earnest in her love for her city and its gardens. . . .

"The creation of beautiful home gardens, public squares, playgrounds and parks has passed beyond the realm of personal gratification or local interest," she said, "to the broader field of civic pride and good citizenship; we want our city and state to be known for the natural beauty with which nature has endowed it. The passing tourist learns little more of a city or State than the beauty of its landscape; but that speaks for itself and is a very valuable asset well worth conserving."

A lady was to drive us to Community Place for Mrs. Olsen to give her lecture; which was advertised to start at eight.

I found myself getting hot and cold as eight arrived and passed . . . it had grown to be part of the flesh and fibre of my life never to keep an audience waiting. . . .

At last a lady with a soft drawl arrived and took us off in her car; at 8.40 she asked the time. I told her, rather snappily;—my voice edged with sympathy for the Lecturer.

"Well now; think of that!" she said in her sweet slurred voice. "Won't they be pleased to see us?"

She trundled along, driving perilously over the boulevards, shooting the stop signals and charging into the oncoming traffic. We arrived at last to an uproarious welcome, and I had an evening of intensive education in the gardens of the Vieux Carré which are part of the history of New Orleans.

"Every pretty garden is a personal contribution to the beauty of our city," pleaded Mrs. Olsen. "Whatever we create of natural beauty around our homes, city, State or country will be the tradition of future generations and the heritage by which we shall be judged."

She went on to show beautiful lantern slides of the old courts and patio gardens.

In many cities of the United States there exist old buildings and houses of the early settlers that have been sensibly preserved. New Orleans is especially fortunate in this respect for the houses of the Vieux Carré are an historical evidence of the necessity of closely set buildings due to the limited area of the original city; and the courtyards are the outcome of limited space left for outdoor beautification. It was obvious to me, as she talked, that the tradition and preservation of these old courts will soon be regarded in the light of a personal obligation by every citizen of New Orleans.

The New Orleans Garden Society is an active body with lively avowed objects in view; such as to get in touch with all garden lovers; to help growers of plants to identify and correctly name their plants, to profit by the experience of other growers in determining the best plants to grow; to encourage an interest in plants in schools; to encourage and promote the beautification of the City Parks under the direction of the Park Commission; and to distribute flowers to hospitals and asylums.

There are separate committees formed to deal with each

one of these aims, and a glance at the year's programme of "events" showed how closely they were followed.

The fair unpunctual driver was waiting to transport us home again—which she did eventually;—but first she declared we must have a "spumoni" and so we went round and round again at her erratic will. I had never heard of the thing and did not know if it was a fish, a flesh or a fowl . . . but the name sounded uncomfortable . . . "spumoni." . . . After sundry adventures we found a stall where a boy produced a degenerate-looking ice-cream. We surveyed his offering dubiously.

"It's all right when you get a fresh one," he said; "why not have a Good Humour?"

Americans give their ices peculiar names . . . spumoni?

Though plenty of people will say I am wrong I have always stoutly maintained that the little creatures, birds and dogs and toads and fish and cats and babies and such small fry are part of a garden, and so I was considerably disappointed at missing "Willow Pond," Mr. McIlhenny's bird sanctuary at Avery Island for the preservation of the Louisiana heron, American egret, blue heron and green heron; in about two acres between the hills he has some 22,000 nests by actual count. He places little bamboo bird-houses among the dells and experimental stretches of his gardens, where swallows, flickers, owls, and three kinds of woodpeckers make their nests.

I missed the herons and many more things I wanted to see; I was informed by wire that the "azaleas" would wait no longer . . . so I uprose sorrowfully; left Louisiana and its soft musical voices; left lovely old New Orleans where one can live for ever on the most marvellous oysters in the whole world . . . those plump, firm, exquisite-flavoured oysters of Bay St. Louis.

CHAPTER XII

AZALEAS

I WONDERED what they did in that house?—It was a wooden shack in the sand—the train had stopped, puffing heavily its black and repulsive coal smoke. I had grown used by now to the clean oil-driven trains of the West, and resented this old-fashioned, out-of-date dusty coal. A grey and white pussy came out of the little wooden house and wagged its upright tail gently, like any other puss in any other home. There was a blue enamel jug thrown by a rotten tree-stump; the pale dry sand of the "garden" in this wayside Florida place was littered with rusty tins. The Easter green of a young almond tree in leaf was the only beauty there, except that living streak of grace—the cat!

This was not at all the Florida of which I had dreamed. Florida of 35,000 clear lakes, and sand and woodland streams; of tumbling surf and sparkling spray; of colour sea-changing; of fire-flies and flashing fish; Florida of pines and palms and moss-hung forest deeps, of orange groves and tangled mangrove swamps, and tropical foliage in scented breezes; of green grasses in the everglades and white clouds in a blue bowl sped by faithful Trade Winds. Florida of golden sunsets in fiery seas, of moonlight and silver mystery mottled in shadow . . . "Florida"—the name had a melody.

The kind conductor opened the door for me, and I leaned out to speak to the puss-cat. It lifted its white and grey face, opened a pink mouth wide, and mewed confidentially.

What do they do for a living in that house?

Perhaps they collected cups from the trees that bled
turpentine! There were stands of slim young trees each
with a gash, and a "V" under it; below the point of the
"V" was a tin to catch the shiny gum, the blood of the
tree. From that they make turpentine and ship cartloads
of barrels from Pensacola. There appeared to be two
varieties of pine tree tapped—one looked like the swamp
pine (Pinus Australis) and the other the loblolly (P. Tæda),
but I had no means of knowing which gave the best turpentine.

The journey in the coal-dusty train was a bore. To
find the insistent azaleas it appeared that I must go to
a place called Charleston in South Carolina: "A very
lovely old place, Mrs. Cran, you will enjoy it." Everybody said it was beautiful and very old in history. Meanwhile the long, slow hours dragged on, and I watched
the country . . . and then suddenly I saw dogwood. . . .

There was no need to ask what it was. I knew it in
a moment. I knew directly I saw those planes of white
among the wild woods:—dogwood sparkles, it is so
white.

On the leafless boughs the wide flat shining flowers
look like spots, or gouts of whiteness, afloat in the darkness of the forest. Suspended; hovering;—purity's self.
I wished I could stop the train and go and pore over those
bright flowers. But at last I had seen from afar the very
flesh of the famed dogwoods; I had come to the fringe of
their blooming.

After I had got this azalea business over I was hoping
to see the woods of Virginia in spring. I had had a letter
to the Tiddlywinks—a poet gave it to me in London before
I sailed to the States, and when he gave it he spoke in a
way that made me look forward very much indeed to
meeting them. But though he talked of them kindling
he did not say a word about their fleshly manifestation,
so I had the pleasure of complete uncertainty and all the
freedom of my dreams. As the long, dusty travel unrolled
I visualised Tiddly—with a long, white beard, ancient,

patriarchal, deep-rooted in the soil.   He and his meek,
sweet old wife would receive me with ancient courtesy,
and we would roam together in an old Virginian garden
of roses and box.   I could shake the dust of travel and
be at peace; talk of our poet and refresh my soul.

Or again, I would see the Tiddlywinks as a pair of young,
slim, eager creatures, receiving me with laughter and making
a merry break in the journey;—chasing dogwood with me,
perhaps;—I made up my mind I would ask them to show
me the way to some quiet cottage deep in Virginian woods
where I could write and walk, alone and free; live close
to the blessed earth for two or three weeks; find the
woodland creatures and singing birds; learn the simple
ways of simple people in an American home far from
noise and far from cities. . . . I felt sure I could ask my
poet's friends to guide me to some such home, they would
understand . . . a place where I could see spring unfold
in Virginia.

Meanwhile, here was Charleston.

We were shot out of the train at some distant point
and taken to the town in a bus.   As we drew near it
nauseating smells greeted us from an oil refinery; we went
along a squalid roadway under dead, withered palms, and
I gathered from the conversation of fellow-travellers that
I had strayed into a land of commercialised gardens.

A disgust seized me.   I wanted to go back to the cool,
green bayous . . . to Pete and Lucia.

"Every place was full up," I was informed, the azaleas had
filled the town and no one had a bed to spare.

How I hated those damned flowers.   I was glad I had
ordered a room weeks ago at the hotel Mrs. Oakleigh
Thorne recommended.   We got there at last; very wearily
I went to my room.

A message came presently to say Mr. Schuyler Parsons
had called; and we sat on the verandah while he told me
that Mr. Norwood Hastie wanted me to see his garden
at sunset time.

I fidgeted uncomfortably, and then came out with the

truth . . . it is a form of self-indulgence . . . though it has a value at times, this speaking the truth business:

"I have seen so many gardens, Mr. Parsons, I am dreadfully afraid of being disappointed in these azaleas you all talk about."

He looked thoughtful.

"That is interesting! Let me know just what you think of it. Some people like Middleton best; but I advise you to see Magnolia first."

"Magnolia?"

"Yes,—it is called Magnolia garden, but it is famous for its azaleas."

Magnolia! Then they were talking of these same azaleas after all when they wrote me in California to be sure and see "Magnolia Gardens."

I girded up my loins and went.

I could hardly have approached one of the great emotional experiences of my life in a more ungracious mood.

There is nothing like Magnolia in the world.

All that there is of rebel in me—all that tugs against the everlasting *laid-out* gardens, against the coerced corseted beauty of formal terraces, walks, and ornamental waters, found kinship here. The man who planted the garden was not enslaved by any "science" of landscape gardening; that which is obvious, banal, conventional, yea and vulgar in the best "laid-out" affair was utterly missing. I stood at last in a garden of form purely informal,—in that which I had longed for always and never found perfectly expressed. Here was no preconceived notion of European methods; but imagination of a delicacy and of a strength, in perfect sympathy with the spirit of its surroundings.

Here is shown to all the world what love can do without the aid of masters.

John Grimké Drayton was entirely uneducated in the "arts" of the landscape gardener. He loved nature; he loved growing things; and he expressed the lover and the poet in his garden.

A wild tranquillity, a passionate peace prevail. It was made by a poet out of the stuff of dreams: it is the Mecca of all my garden wanderings; it is the place to which unknowing but obstinate I have striven all my days; among the great green oaks and seven veils of floating Spanish moss shines the Holy Grail. The heart of a man burns steadily there, on a furnace of colour in a garden shade.

The man "whose vision beyond the veil is translated in the garden of his making" inherited the estate on the Ashley River on the sudden death of an elder brother. For 250 years it has been continuously owned by the Drayton family and its descendants. Mr. Norwood Hastie, the present owner, is the grandson of the John G. Drayton who designed and planted the garden. The family is of English stock, bearing a coat of arms, a cross gules engrailed on a field argent with crest, a helmet with a starling statent—and the motto "Hic iter ad Astra." It is the old Drayton coat borne about 1190 by the Crusader Walter de Drayton, a great-grandson of Alberic de Vere, Earl of Oxford.

Warned by his doctors that if he was to live he must work in the open air, John Grimké Drayton turned his attention to the land he had inherited, and conceived the idea of making a garden. From a red rose and a white at the foot of his ivy-covered steps his supple genius developed this garden lovely beyond any in the whole world.

The azaleas are rose, and red, and white; which was a great surprise to me. I was not expecting furnaces of red, twenty feet high. I had thought of azaleas in the soft tones of cream and buff, peach and yellow as they grow in the English gardens. I should, of course, have known better but for some reason heaven blunted all my senses in this approach to my great hour. I was blind, deaf, dumb and stupid with the reiterated word "azaleas" . . . I was utterly unprepared. . . . Like a person shot out of this mortal life in a second, I was suddenly without warning pushed into Paradise.

One approaches the garden through an English park

M

of wide, green spaces set with huge live oaks. There is nothing in that to warn the visitor of the breath-taking vision about to break. . . . Mr. Norwood Hastie took me round personally, for which I am grateful. He knew when to turn away and leave me alone. Indeed, in that garden one flings "the soul and body down for God to plough them under."

I turned to him exhausted. "Take me indoors and tell me things," I begged. "Do other people feel like this?"

And then he told me that other garden-lovers have felt the same emotion and some of them hardened garden-travellers, too!

Owen Wister appeared to have approached Magnolia in much the same spirit of contumacy that marked my own!

"I was not prepared for much," he said, "my experience of life had already included quite a number of azaleas. I have seen gardens, many gardens in England, in France, in Italy; I have seen what can be done in great hothouses, and on great terraces, what can be done under a roof, what can be done in the open air with the aid of architecture and sculpture, and orna-mental land and water, but no horticulture that I have seen devised by mortal man approaches the unearthly enchantment of the azaleas at Live Oaks (Magnolia Gardens). It is not like seeing flowers at all, it was as if there, in the heart of the wild and mystic wood, in the grey gloom of those trees veiled and muffled in their long webs and skeins of hanging moss, a great magic flame of rose and red and white burned steadily. You looked to see it vanish. You could not imagine that such a thing would stay. All idea of individual petals or species was swept away in this glowing maze of splen-dour, this transparent labyrinth of rose, red and white through which you looked beyond, into the grey gloom of the hanging moss and the depths of the wild forest trees. I turned back as often as I could, and to the last caught glimpses of it burning, glowing, and shining like some miracle, some rainbow exorcism, with its flooding fumes of orange, rose, red and white merging magically."

"Why do you call it Magnolia?" I asked.

"The estate took its name from the many fine specimens of Magnolia Grandiflora," Mr. Hastie answered; "in early May these blooms will be exceedingly lovely, but the azaleas have outgrown every other feature. My grand-

father had a stroke of fortune, of course, in planting his
garden over phosphate rock; it is that which makes everything grow so tall and strong that it seems to want to
climb!"

I begged for an adequate photograph to put in my book,
to show my English readers something of that which I
can never convey in words.

Mrs. Hastie looked at me helplessly.

"No one can paint it; no lens can take it!"

I realised that was true.

"One of your English novelists tried, but he could not.
See, this is what he says:

"A painter of flowers and trees, I specialise in gardens, and freely assert
that none in the world is so beautiful as this.   Even before the azaleas
come out, it consigns the Boboli at Florence, the Cinnamon Gardens at
Colombo, Conception at Malaga, Versailles, Hampton Court, the Generalife
at Granada, and the La Mortola to the category of 'also ran.'

"Nothing so free and gracious, so lovely and wistful, nothing so richly
coloured yet so ghost-like exists, planted by the sons of men.   It is a kind
of paradise which has wandered down, a miraculously enchanted wilderness.   Brilliant with azaleas, or magnolias, it centres around a pool of dreamy
water, overhung by tall trunks wanly festooned with the grey Florida moss.
Beyond anything I have ever seen, it is other-worldly.   And I went there
day after day, drawn as one is drawn in youth by visions of the Ionian Sea,
or the East, or the Pacific Isles.   I used to sit paralysed by the absurdity
of putting brush to canvas in front of that dream pool.   I wanted to paint
of it a picture like that of the fountain by Hellen which hangs in the Luxem-
bourg.   But I knew I never should."

The writer was John Galsworthy!

It was interesting to learn that I had shared my soul-
seizure with these two men; particularly that John Galsworthy had felt the unearthly beauty which the grey moss
and black waters give. I had never seen clear brilliant black
lakes before. The powerful acid in the roots of the cypress
trees, which grow straight out of the pool, like huge pillars, turns the water inky black. "Like a Lorraine glass,"
said Mr. Hastie. One has to imagine green lawns and
winding paths, banks of camellia Japonica thirty feet high,
towering trees hung with long trails of the green moss

with golden Banksian roses, mauve and white wistarias, yellow jasmine and Cherokee roses sprawling and scrambling among the great limbs overhead, and hanging down in canopies of fragrant bloom.   Blood red camellias, snow-drifts of dogwood, tender foliage of tulip trees, slender crêpe myrtle and garlands of bridal-wreath spiræa, are there out-dazzled by the blazing banks of azaleas,—and all reflected back from the clear, black water of the cypress ponds.

The Spanish moss, swaying like shreds of ethereal grey chiffon in the breeze, makes a merciful veil to temper the fiery brilliance of the azaleas.

Although the alien from the Orient, Azalea Indica, first planted there about 1843, is now the chief feature of the garden, there are many other features to enjoy; they creep slowly into one's consciousness as it recovers from the stunning of the first impact; a Californian redwood, Torreya taxifolia, cedrus deodora, cryptomaria, holly pines, Japanese crabs and cherries, etc. The collection of camellia Japonica numbers over three hundred different varieties; and botanists will be interested in what Dr. E. H. Wilson of Chinese fame, said in the *Journal of the Arnold Arboretum* in 1921:

"The collection is of great interest as it represents very completely the 'Indian Azaleas' known to the garden of the forties and the fifties of the last century. From most modern gardens these varieties have been lost. Many of the original plants are still growing in Magnolia Gardens, and by successful layering, quantities have been obtained and the collection largely increased. The older plants are now much crowded and the largest measure from sixteen to eighteen feet in height and from fourteen to sixteen feet through. The largest plants are R. phoeniceum G. Don and its forms which are richly represented. Apart from the typical species there is the form semi-duplex Wils. with double flowers; also one with white flowers, which I have not seen before. Other forms are f. splendens Wils. (R. pulchrum Sweet), which were raised in England and introduced into America in 1835 and 1836, and var. calcycinum Wils. (A. indica calcycin Lindl.) with very large, rich magenta-coloured flowers which was introduced from China into England by R. Fortune about 1850. Of the true R. indicum Sweet (Azalea indica L.) several colour forms are growing at Magnolia, including the famous f. variegatum D.C., which was introduced into England from China in 1833 to Knight's Nursery and into Boston, Mass., in 1838. For many years this was not only a favourite exhibition plant, but was also the parent of many 'Indian Azaleas' like 'Iveryana' and 'Gladstonesii', Van Houtte's Azalea indica punctulata and A. indica punctulata variegata, which are figured in Flore des Serres XVI. tt. (1618–1621 (1865) and are possible hybrids between R. indicum Sweet and R. Simsii Planchon, are still in the Magnolia Gardens. So, too, is 'Azalea Decora' which is probably of the same parentage and has rich red-coloured flowers. The well-known Azalea indica alba or A. ledifolia (R. mucronatum G. Don) and its coloured form (var. ripense Wils.) are of course represented at Magnolia by many fine bushes."

Thus Dr. Wilson. I saw Magnolia in its perfect hour; at sunset of a day in early April; the light dripping through cedars, cypresses and live oaks silvered the swaying banners of Spanish moss and touched the flowers beneath to an unearthly radiance.

This old plantation garden is set by the broad shining river Ashley,—and from its lawns one looks across to 150 acres of golden coastal marsh where once grew the famous Carolina rice, swept and invigorated by Atlantic breezes.

The original house, a Colonial brick mansion, was destroyed first (God help me, how hard this is to write!) by the British in the War of Revolution and the second building burned later during the war between the North and the South. The old steps of that second residence now lead up to the present cottage,—the spring residence of Mr. and Mrs. Norwood Hastie.

Middleton Place Garden, also on the Ashley River and not far away, claims to be the oldest landscape gardens in America. I visited it also; it appears to be a matter of debate in America as to which one should prefer— Middleton or Magnolia; that must remain a matter of individual taste—and perhaps, too, of experience. As I have said, I saw Magnolia in its perfect hour; the other might be better to live in constantly . . . but it has not the ecstasy of Magnolia.

Middleton *is* a "landscape garden." A very beautiful one, but I have seen better. I have never in all the lands or in all my days seen anything like Magnolia.

About 1740 Henry Middleton sent to England for an experienced landscape gardener under whose guidance a hundred slaves are said to have worked for ten years. One can believe it.   Henry Middleton, Governor of South Carolina, invited André Michaux, the French botanist, to his place, and from him obtained the first camellia Japonica ever brought to America.   He set out four plants of which three are living yet, and blooming, after a century and a half!

It was in 1846 that Middleton Place was planted with Azalea Indica.   The range of plant life in this favoured part of the States is unlimited,—the deciduous forests of the North blend here with the eternal summer of the far South; and besides the camellia Japonica, Michaux introduced to Middleton the Japanese varnish tree, Chinese candleberry, the maidenhair tree, tea-plant and mimosa.

It is a garden of open squares and courts framed in azaleas, of brick walks, curving terrace lines that sweep down to two planned "butterfly" lakes.   Beyond the Long Terrace are the sunken gardens once the bowling green, the rose garden and several camellia, azalea and spice walks; there are five lakes at different levels; an ancient rice mill; the size of the venerable live oaks hung with immense curtains was truly astounding.

I remembered Mrs. Oakleigh Thorne at Santa Barbara drilling holes to water her live oaks and feed them with bonemeal,—they were not planted over rich phosphate beds—poor lady!

These two lovely old gardens are not to be called the "lost" ones any longer, because the great upwelling of interest in gardens throughout America has brought thousands of visitors to see them; at a fixed charge; so they earn enough to restore them to their former splendour, and keep them up.   It is a heavy tax on the pocket to keep such places perfect.   Mr. Hastie told me it cost him $1,000 (£200) a year to clear one weed alone from its water!   I had been told in New York that the gardens

The Swamp Garden at Dean Hall, South Carolina

of Savannah were "older and less spoiled," but I did not see them.

I saw a very remarkable swamp garden thirty miles out of Charleston, however, the only one of its kind in the world, I was told by Mrs. Dawson, who drove me. It was at Dean Hall, where Mr. Kittredge has cleared the swamp and made a strange garden of tall cypress pillars rising sheer from the black mysterious waters; there are islands, bridges and little boats, and on the rising ground, between these sombre stretches of clear, dark water, he has planted daffodils in myriads to make a golden glory in spring. Mrs. Kittredge took me round as her husband was not there; and my heart sank as she unfolded his dream; for I could not imagine the northland daffodils thriving and increasing in that place.

"It is the first year of the daffodils," she said, "the paper whites were in a year earlier, but they did not bloom the second year; we hope they will next!"

Daffodils love my buttery loamy clay in cold England and grow there well . . . this did not look like cool clay to me . . . of course, they were likely to bloom the first year with their bulbs stored full of food. . . .

There were five miles of paths in the swamp garden. It must have taken a very great deal of time and labour, and a fine system of pumping to drain and plant it, but its beauty was unique; a strange water garden, unlike any other; a garden of reflection. It made my head reel to see the splendid trunks of the cypresses rise like pillars sheer out of the black water in an endless vista—"it is planted for winter blossom as well as spring," she told me as she pointed out the queer, knobbly, grey, elephant "knees" of the cypress roots standing up out of the water; "they breathe through them!"

Drayton Hall is the only pre-Revolution house left there, still standing. It has remained in the same family; and the sixth generation from the original English stock is living there now.

Down the long, red road that passed it, grey tatters of

Spanish moss flew in the wind, from the overhanging trees; it was a strange canopy under which to pass. The colour of the road was like the red roads in Worcestershire, England; or Johannesburg, South Africa; beside it stood little old St. Andrew's Church built in 1706.

A sense of history was beginning to creep upon me. I tried to shake it off, it was not possible to talk much history in America without getting back to that unhappy place, the War of Revolution. I did not care for it. I wish the parting between England and America had been done cordially and kindly; it was an inevitable parting but I wish we had said good-bye as a father says "God-speed" to a handsome, capable son well able to look after himself . . . with affectionate admiration . . . with tenderness and pride, instead of fighting our eldest-born.

Charleston unfolded itself in time to me. I was able to meet for a second its tight-shut difficult heart. The dead palms, the horrible smells, the long, dreary ride from the train, the cynical exploitation of visitors to the gardens by the taxi-drivers and all who had anything to sell had no longer power to make me hate the place as I started by doing. After all, commercialising its history and romance as it does, Charleston is the gateway to Magnolia, some seventeen miles away; and its people are sensitive, charming, hospitable as soon as one escapes from the rôle of a visiting stranger, and gets to know them.

I was fortunate in the hotel; Mrs. Dawson's pleasant Villa Marguerita, where in March and April the tables round the big goldfish pool in the centre court are crowded with visitors from all over the world; visitors who have come to see the gardens of azaleas; it remains in my mind as a place of rest and recovery from the lively emotions that wait on one in Charleston!

Mrs. Beverley Mikels took care that I saw some of the beautiful little gardens in the town itself—as distinct from the plantation gardens I had been visiting. She was a real plant-lover, and it was fun going round with her lively guidance, for she quickly realised that the places

where people "do it all themselves" had a meaning for
this traveller.   I have always loved more than size and
splendour the evidences of character in gardens.   That
is the wonder of Magnolia—it expresses in epic terms a
wonderful personality; long observation has taught me to
look for it mostly in little gardens; I am accustomed to
search diligently in humble places for signs of the authentic
poetry of the heart.

It was there in Mrs. John Simond's garden, fresh, cool
and watered, with its wall fountain and pestle bird-bath,
a golden arbour of Banksian rose, tulips, bearded irises,
snapdragons and stocks; in Mrs. Mikels's own garden
where she echoes the purple wistaria in purple iris and
stock, and fills her window-boxes now with pansies, and
later with clear Rosy Morn petunias to catch the note of
a large pink mimosa which blooms in May.   It is a small
garden in Church Street, but one of sweet character—
stone was used nicely in stepping-stones in the green lawn
and a paved court by the guest-room where tall hollyhocks
stood on guard.

We saw Mrs. W. B. Ravenel's green lawn and oleanders,
Clara Butt tulips, larkspur and madonna lilies in their
simple and attractive planting; and Mrs. Geer's overhang
of yellow Banksian roses, her gingko, weeping almond and
wonderful weigelia rosea.   There was a very fine fig tree
which took my eye; and Mrs. Mikels laughed.

"There is one in every Charleston garden!" she said.
"It is a small green sugar fig, the 'celestial' variety."

It was a pleasant walled garden with a wall fountain,
a rose circle, and cool blue plantings of purple stock,
blue irises and Rev. Ewbank tulips.

Dr. W. J. Pettus loves birds!   Everybody seems to in
Charleston; I saw a great number of bird baths and drink-
ing bowls; there was a cardinal bird nesting in a pittosporum bush in his garden and he was entertaining on
the subject of his mocking bird, a very pugnacious fellow.

"He attacks everything and gets fearfully lit up with
rage," said the doctor; "he even attacks the wax-wings"

(the cedar birds) "in the air as they fly over on their migration flight!"

The mocking bird is one of the Mimidae—and he has a marvellously sweet song; he is, in fact, the American equivalent to our nightingale. I grew to love the little creatures with their soft grey and white colouring and wagtail flick of the tail; they flutter their wings when walking and have a hard life driving off snakes which eat both eggs and young if they get a chance.

Dr. Pettus's house was built in 1775 and was on the point of a bathing beach, but now the old sea-wall is buried under lawn, and he has two hundred feet by about a hundred and eighty. The old slave quarters have been made into a garage. It is a walled garden with a fountain and box-edged beds; there is a beautiful lace-work iron gate dated 1735 and he told me that Swedish iron does not rust because there is practically no carbon in it.

One of the things one noticed particularly about Charleston was the extreme beauty of the wrought-iron work everywhere.

Mrs. Caspar Chisholm of Sword Gate in Legare Street (which is pronounced "legree") showed the old formal daisy design garden she is slowly uncovering,—and then whisked me back to Kent and the homeland by finding a book full of pictures of Sir Edwin Lutyens' "houses and gardens." We sat in a wistaria arbour and turned up Benenden House now tacked on to Great Dexter,— and the picture of the things he did to what was once a nice old house at Great Maytham! It was most upheaving; I lost touch with America, and was transported to a garden of green lawns and golden daffodils where poor little Jock watched month after month unavailingly for his adored morning walk. No one else takes him out before breakfast.

The grey draperies of Spanish moss festooned the roadways under the young spring green of the leaves; the ferny, fairy grey moss. Mrs. Mikels showed me the brown husk of its flower,—the little green bloom it bears

in spring . . . I was once more confused with wonder.
It was too much, this Charleston,—with its violence and
its exquisite gentle sweetnesses . . . the dainty, fairy filament, then, had a bloom. Had a husk. Had seeds!
When it comes in this fragile perfection life is so wonderful that it overwhelms.

The botanists give it an ungainly name: Tillandsia
usneoides.

It was left to America to show me what can be done
with a country town in which every householder grows
flowers for the general picture; if the Santa Maria Inn
is the flowery inn of all my travels, Summerville in South
Carolina is the flowery town.

Hidden away in a forest of "long leaf" pines, it is the
place that began life as a summer resort and refuge from
malaria for the rice planters before the Civil War. It
was they who built many of the charming old-fashioned
houses with their wide verandahs and lovely gardens where
camellias and violets bloom all the winter and in spring;
wistaria climbs to the tops of the tallest pines, dogwood,
azaleas and roses glow on every border and the woods
are full of fragrant yellow jasmine, lilies and wild honeysuckle of the most maddening perfume in sheets of cream.
It is a happy town, for there one can shoot and fish, play
golf or tennis amid a very paradise of bloom. The roads
intrigued me;—they meander through the pine trunks
under canopies of wistaria, jasmine and Cherokee roses—
and on every side pretty houses are set back irregularly
in gardens of miraculous colour. Summerville grows tea.
I believe it is the only tea-garden in the States; but there
it is, and while on the subject I may say quite frankly, that
most Americans do *not* know how to make tea. Such
stuff as they give you there! They make marvellous coffee,
which we in England make very badly:—most of us.

The night before I left I dined with Mr. Schuyler
Parsons and spent an evening I can never forget.

He is a man of taste with a very charming house in
Charleston and by the time I arrived there I was so battered

by the beauty of everything, by the sense of history and
the rich, forceful personality of this land of America of
which I had been deplorably ignorant all my life, that
nothing surprised me any more.

So when I found among the guests a handsome man in
a frilled shirt, black stock and fob and all the rest of an
ancient garb, I took him for granted as part of an astonishing town in which Time had vanished, and one moved
in another age.

It appeared, however, that he was going on to a con-
cert where his was the dress worn by the male voices; and
later on I heard him sing with the rest of the Charleston
Society for the Preservation of Spirituals.

In England we know (and love) the negro "spirituals"
because Paul Robeson sings them to us in that glorious
voice of his, but here was something we, in my little Island,
never know.

It was a collection of Southern gentlepeople whose
families had loved their "slaves" (and freed most of them),
and they, when young, had been brought up under the
sound of the melodious negro voices, swayed to sleep
by the rhythms of their strange folk-songs. These
"spirituals" were none that we know by record; they were
handed down by ear alone. Songs saved by the white
people whose childish limbs had been swayed to sleep, and
eyes soothed from tears by the sound of them.

It was a fascinating performance; the singers were a
very handsome gathering. Here were the finely-drawn
faces of plantation owners whose old homes had suffered
material loss; had been burned out and ruined by the
disastrous Civil War in 1865; whose people had lost all
but their pride and the traditions of their blood.

They sang the haunting half-savage melodies, swaying
as they sang, and clapping their hands in perfect rhythm
as the black mammies do; I did not know most of the
people but noticed the young wife of the architect, who
drove me to Dean Hall, and the beautiful shoulders of
Miss Rutledge rhythmically swaying, abandoned to her art.

Mr. Norwood Hastie had asked me to see the sun rise at Magnolia the next morning. I was up before the mocking bird, but transport broke down, I could not walk the seventeen miles. In an agony I saw the sun come up while I paced the streets looking for a car unavailingly. The negro drivers of taxis were all lapped in sleep waiting to pounce on their tourist prey at a more seemly hour.

I had touched the garden of all dreams; Magnolia faded like a mirage . . . I had not possessed it in all its moods. I lost the moonlight on the waving banners of Spanish moss; I lost the sunrise over the black still water.

I left the loveliest garden in all the world with much of its beauty undiscovered, and the desire for it will stay with me till I die. Once received into the blood there is no recovery from the longing to return, and to return.

CHAPTER XIII

B——Y PESTS

I USED to know an untidy, rather dirty, artist's studio in Chelsea where the chief spark of attraction to everybody was a niece. She was Irish, with twinkling legs, a dimple, white teeth and uneven blue eyes; she used to sing "O Shenandoah, my Shenandoah" in a sweet voice, rousing in me a variety of emotions. I liked the tune but I did not know what the words were about:—Who was "Shenandoah" and why did he babble about some rushing river?

I liked to watch the dimple push in and out as she sang (it was one of those conscious voluntary dimples), but I wanted to go away and hide, for she would call it Shenandore, religiously rolling the imported and hideous "r"! I always ended up by listening to the end because the song had a sadness in its sweetness; I did not know why. That song was so wound up with old Jim and his niece that I could not get them out of my head when I suddenly found myself in the Shenandoah Valley where the "rushing river" runs; I had to send them a box of apple candy with pictures of the miles of apple blossom on the lid, so that in future they would have some idea of what Shenandoah was, and looked like.

The valley runs from the Potomac River to Roanoke;—it lies between the Blue Ridge Mountains and Alleghanies; and in the Shenandoah national park there is the largest stand of Virginian hardwood timber in the world. The valley grows apples; and every spring the town of Winchester, Virginia, organises an "apple blossom festival," to which I was taken by Mrs. F. S. Shelton, the sun-and-shade April lady of a long ago meeting in England!

Of the festival itself the least said the better; it would have been charming had not a spell of bitter cold come down, blasting miles of the pink blossom brown, and making the children shiver in their pretty flimsy dresses. It was borne in on me, there, that the climate of England is not the only uncertain one in the world.

The town was crowded and Mrs. Shelton had taken rooms in a house; it proved to be a delightful, simple Virginian house, with plenty of daughters and an old mother whose word was law. We had a great time running to and fro with each other's suit-cases, all of us being noble and giving each other the "best" room, when all were so clean and neat. I was left at last, all unworthy, with the material comforts but none of the glow of unselfishness. I asked one of the girls if there was much noise of traffic; and she answered proudly:

"Well, it's right smart just now!"

The house was known to Stonewall Jackson,—the soldier of fierce fights and stubborn magnificent soldier-craft in the Civil War; he helped to protect the father of the house, then only six years old! At supper, over home-cured ham smoked in apple-wood, pickled peaches, pickled water melon, grape jam, (weak) tea, omelette and wonderful cake, we learned that they have four acres of apples and wish they had more. Apples pay in the Shenandoah Valley.

Mrs. Shelton asked where my American articles would appear, and I said:

"*Harper's Bazaar* (London edition), though I do not know why they publish these innocent matters among all their witty, risqué, fashionable stuff."

A Virginian girl of the house piped up:

"Maybe you ain't so bad as you think you are. I never heard a writer brag yet."

I wished I could stay there a month and a day; with the slim old mother in command; the many patchwork quilts; the outspoken girls. It was a real home.

The hills of West Virginia are covered with Judas trees (cercis siliquastrum), dogwood, and carpets of wild violet, flowers, was not greatly enamoured of the plant; and it sprawled untidily, as if it knew! But it is treasured up in Maine, where Sally grows it at Blue Hill and cherishes the legend that it bears: "If thou hast it with thee, thou shalt be prosperous and ever acceptable." A very sensible, not to say, probable legend, if one considers its name.

I found it also, equally beloved, in Mrs. Shelton's garden at Castine. In England it is the plant which passes from hand to hand, always given, never bought; for the people say that you may share but cannot buy the "joy of the ground." A pretty custom which may obtain, for all I know, in America, though Mrs. Wheelwright did not seem to know it, and was interested to learn the legend that goes with the plant.

The beautiful mertensia Virginica was just passing over; —they call it the Virginian cowslip, though heaven knows why! In no way do the blue flowers or the habit of the plant resemble our own cowslip,—primula florindæ is far, far more like cowslips . . . It was exciting to find the carpets of beautiful blue phlox devaricata wild in Virginian woods.

There was something exquisitely sympathetic about Mrs. Wheelwright. She divined my horror of cities and the herd . . . she made me one of her home and healed me of streets. I was among the blessed scents of the earth and growing grass again, serenaded by the mocking bird; and a whip-poor-will, whose voice I had never heard before. I liked it. I liked everything in that kind place, from the gentle old ladies, the witty husband and peach-bloom daughter, to the cows and chickens.

We walked over to Miss Frances Cole's sandy garden of very choice plants, a gardener's garden at Chester,—and then she took me to Drewry's Bluff—where at Meadow-brook Mr. and Mrs. Thomas Jeffress took me round their garden personally. It is a spacious garden set in formal beauty, but it is stamped in every direction with the hall-mark of affection and good taste. . . . Here were daffodils, carpets of lily of the valley, rosa Hugonis, sheets of nierem-

In a Virginian Garden: Drewry's Bluff at Meadowbrook

bergia rivularis, ivy, "confederate" violets, box terraces, Virginian cypress (a beautiful pointed tree), crocuses, sweet williams, irises, hollyhocks, hepaticas, with a myriad more and Sirene tulips spread out wide and rosy with their twisted petals; there were lusty peonies under a privet hedge; native sand lilies; a swimming-pool set round with wistaria; a "James grape" arbour; and borders and edges of blue violets.

Mrs. Jeffress showed me her "real English holly." . . .

"I had only female plants," she complained, "for I did not know they were diœcious, and chose only the berried ones! Now I have got a male flowering one; do you think it will be enough?"

Now how was I to know how many men those holly women want? Her eye sought mine, and then the trees, anxiously; it looked a small bush to cope with all those large wives.

"Anyway, you pay him a compliment," I reassured her. "For all we know Solomon was a little fellow."

There was a hedge of honeysuckle down the drive,— and we found the master and mistress of the beautiful place very busy scattering magnolia seeds in the shrubbery among the Judas trees and glorious dazzling dogwood.

Meadowbrook is on Falling Creek where, in 1619, one hundred and fifty expert workmen from Warwickshire and Staffordshire, in England, came over to start the first iron works in America. They made very fine iron from bog ore found in the neighbourhood. The story was interesting to me, being a Dudley of Staffordshire stock, with a whole long history of iron making and iron research in our ancestry. All went well until 1622, when Indians broke up the works (which had cost the equivalent of 100,000 dollars to put up) and killed the manager, Mr. Berkeley, with all his employees, except a boy and girl who managed to hide in the bushes.

Mrs. Wheelwright drove me back to Buckhead Springs in the soft spring sunshine.

"You must see Gunston Hall and Oatlands, near Lees-

burg, as well as Mount Vernon," she said, and went on:
"The shad-bush is in blow; so the shad are coming up the
Potomac!"

What lovely sounds words make. . . .   "The shad are
coming up the Potomac!" . . .   And shad-bush? . . .   At
last I had found a word out of Mrs. Hutchison's book,
Wychwood,—Shad-bush! . . .   I looked eagerly where she
pointed,—and saw small woody shrubs growing by the
wayside covered with delicate feathery white flowers; I
had noticed them before and wondered what they were,
but grown weary of asking.   All the beauty of American
roads and woods had drowned me in wonder and delight;
—for Virginia has a belt of wild flowers famous among
students of botany.

"It is an amelanchier," she said.

That told me it was a relation of the snowy mespilus
which Geoffrey Hurd-Wood grows for the bees in his
sandy Surrey garden; it veils the distant blue of his views
in a soft whiteness.

"When the shad-bush blows we know the best fish in
the world are coming up the river.   Wait till you have
some shad-roe!"

I had it next day; and I looked upon the pretty white
flowers of the shad-bush thereafter with a new interest.
Shad is a very delicious fish indeed . . . it is of the herring
family with the upper jaw notched in front; and though
we have the allis shad in our European waters it is the
American one that is of princely excellence. . . .   There
is a fresh-water variety in Killarney and some of the Italian
lakes; but to everyone who has once tasted it there is for
evermore but one kind of shad!

I kept wondering what the golden knobs were, on a very
frequent tree; and learned it was sassafras;—when one
gets close the knobs are clustered heads of exquisite little
flowers.   The tree has a furrowed bark, bright green twigs
and queer, variously-shaped leaves, some of them like
mittens.   Good house-wives call it ague tree and use
sassafras in their home medicines; the oil is used by per-

fumers. I liked the aromatic bark and foliage; like so
many virtue-yielding trees it belongs to the laurel family.
Mrs. Edward Harden (*née* Vanderlip) built her lovely
woodsey Japanese garden all because of a sassafras tree!

"What is Joe-pye weed like?" I asked her. I wanted
to see more of the Wychwood flowers.

"It is a handsome thing," she said. "I can't show it
to you now; the big compound cluster-heads are anything
from flesh-pink to deep rose-purple. It grows tall and
strong, rather rank indeed. It is eupatorium purpureum."

"The country names are so much more descriptive and
poetical," I said faintly.

"All this Latinity is trying," she laughed, the wise,
quick woman, "but it has its use, as we both well know. I
think it is a pity to use botanical names for every plant;
with some people it is a passion—almost an offence."

"The country names have legends and traditions folded
away in their sweetness," I complained. "Call Bouncing
Bet 'saponaria officinalis' and what does that tell one of
the vigorous, lovely, irrepressible thing? The trilliums
are 'wake-robins,' the wild godetia 'farewell to spring,'
the pretty layia of the Southern coastal mesas 'tidy-tips.'
There are myriads of these affectionate pet names for
flowers throughout America; names that only spring from
the heart of a people. They are not the botanist's cumber-
some, if well-meaning, crack-jaw labels. The vernacular
names are precious for the emotions they give us."

Her charming face was thoughtful.

"Yes, there is that elusive power of association; do you
ever feel that an element of vulgarity, even of snobbery,
creeps into gardens?"

"It is that I flee from as I flee the wrath of God," I
answered quickly. "One finds it in every land; but it
has been the great surprise of all my years to find in this
rich, bustling, passionately self-satisfied America the secret
hidden sweetness of a genuine flower-love. There are
people I suppose who belong to your Garden Clubs because
of the social *entrée* it gives them,—rich people who order

a garden to be made and kept up because it is the fashion,
—but the spirit of your people knows how to love the airy
grace of flowers; poetry is here. . . . I have been so
much surprised!"

She glanced at me, amused.

"What will you tell your English gardeners?"

"I don't know how to tell them anything," I said, in a
moment of desperate truth. "I can only spin words and
words—and trust that here and there some imagination
will quicken, to the real America . . . there is such a
hideous travesty of your country painted for us by the
Press and on the screen. . . . Why don't they give us
some of the sweetness and the vital humanity of your
homes? The *stuff* they give us! Tell me something
about the Garden Club Movement in America to tell
them in England," I begged.

"It was started by a small group of Philadelphia women,"
she said. "They decided that it would be a wise and
pleasant thing to meet regularly at a fixed date and hour to
discuss their plants and exchange personal experience and
knowledge of garden lore, forming thus the first Garden
Club and the nucleus of the Garden Club of America.
They probably had no idea that it would grow and spread
until now almost every community has an active group of
women who are working not only for the beautification of
their own gardens but also for the cultivation of garden
taste and the preservation of natural beauties in the
community.

"Plant hybridisers, collectors, horticulturists, nurserymen, are all leading busy lives endeavouring to meet the
demand for new plant material; American landscapers and
garden owners are becoming more discriminating in their
field of art, and American sculptors are beginning to produce some really exquisite garden statuary and other plastic
art forms. Recognition of them is being made in the
annual exhibit of garden sculpture now held under the
auspices of the Garden Club of America in New York
each year for the encouragement of original work.

"A reflection of all this stir and movement among the garden and beauty lovers of the country is the more or less concerted effort toward community-beautification which is being made in most States, the preservation of trees and other natural beauties, and the improvement of roadsides. Trees may no longer be nonchalantly chopped down to make way for the spread of concrete and other masculine ideas of progress; woods and wild flowers are being protected, campaigns against billboard advertising are being conducted, and even the Chambers of Commerce have come to recognise the potential value of conserving the natural scenic beauty of a locality. This is a long step forward, and the possibilities of all these activities are infinite—and infinitely fascinating."

"With all your resources of natural beauty and the deep poetic sense among your people, you will soon evolve gardens of American type," I mused. "You have copied Italy, Babylon, England, France . . . and all the time you have the perfect garden in your own land, built of the heart in splendour—the type the whole world might journey to see and be the richer for its lesson." . . .

I saw "Agecroft"; they told me it was built in England in 1320 (the same date as my own old house in the Weald!), and was transported to Virginia from Birmingham. There is an oriel window; the barge boards are not carved.

I also saw "Virginia House," which was once Warwick Priory in England.

As she bade me I went to Oatlands and to Mount Vernon and also to Gunston Hall. Mount Vernon, of course, was the home of George Washington, the man with a big mind in a big body (he stood six feet three inches), and a very nice idea of home the man had. The garden was planted with much very old box; a queer effect came out of the air as one heard the sounds of great leathery leaves of magnolia clattering in the wind over a broad wall of box. Lavender, white tulips, allspice (calycanthus) in full fragrant bloom . . . there was the broad Potomac shining in silver far below . . . many trees in graphs are kept in the Library of Congress; she is one of the women one does not forget; joyous and vigorous; difficult and gentle. Her garden pictures are the best I have seen in my life. Another distinguished woman I met and enjoyed was Miss Violet Oakley, "our first mural decorator," as Dr. Putman described her when we met in the Congressional Library at Washington.

It was in Washington that I found the "daffodil man" of whom I had heard in California. He is B. Y. Morrison, and the name conjured up to the mind of iris lovers that distinctive bearded iris named for him. He is a tall young man, and broad; of many gifts; they unfolded gradually as I got to know him better; at first, when Mrs. H. H. Rousseau and I found him in his office where he edits the *National Horticultural Magazine*, he was faintly official; that thin and insincere frost melted at once when he took us round his gardens, both public and private, next day; there a charming personality unfolded itself in which, though warm and eager, one felt the cold, clear sense of the scientist, searching ever relentlessly for truth. I suspect that America has in that man a valuable servant; iron in the cause he serves; but to us, wandering with him among his seedling daffodils, mulch-paper experiments and one thing and another, a "laughing fellow-rover." We went back to Mrs. Rousseau's house to lunch, and there he sang to us, in a soft bass of great feeling, playing his own accompaniments; it transpired also that he made the beautiful woodcuts in the *National Horticultural Magazine*. A gifted fellow!

Together we looked at Mrs. Rousseau's charming rock garden in Georgetown, where she grows iris tectorum among her blue and mauve phloxes, tradescantia (which we call spider-wort), mertensia, aubrietia and a score of other beautiful flowers. The pale yellow reflexed petals of Ellen Willmott tulip swayed against the blue and the mauve in a lovely rhythm of colour and movement.

Many moons later we all three wandered together again in my own garden in England, and I discovered, by close observation, the place he holds in our world of flowers;—

B. Y. Morrison in my Garden finding boils and blains, plagues
and what-nots

Mrs. Arthur Curtis James's Mirror Pool in the "Blue Garden"

or that it seems to me he holds . . . that of liaison officer
or interpreter between the scientist and the public; between
the botanist and the ignorant, ardent amateur. He makes
the language of the one understood by the other! A
peculiar position, requiring rare gifts: wide knowledge and
utter integrity, with vision and perfect sympathy.

I must say that "B. Y.", as he had become to English
gardeners by now, was much appreciated in my own
country. I kept hearing about him all over the place;
now it was Dr. Hilton from Vancouver Island, sitting by
my garden pool, who said he had seen him at Vincent
Square,—then Mr. Hew Dalrymple in his famous primula
gardens in the New Forest,—and then Mr. Richardson of
daffodil fame . . . then he was away to the Rothschild
gardens . . . and presently he was having a peaceful week-
end with me, recovering from the impact of many people,
the exhaustion of much to see. A state of affairs I could
very thoroughly well understand!

"B. Y." and his pests! He got my garden fuller of
plagues, boils, blains, blisters, blights, beetles and what-
nots of despair than any of my most morbid imaginings
had ever dreamed. There was not a leaf whole or sound
by the time he had done with me;—nor a disease known
to the living world of plants he did not manage to fasten
somewhere or another. Yet the seasons come and go in
beauty . . . as I write these words the garden is full of
roses and peonies, and the house, too; and three boxes
go by the night mail full of them to cheer town-prisoned
friends.

It has sometimes occurred to me that it is possible to
lower disease resistance of both mind and body, in both
man and plants by being too busy with preventive nostrums
and prohibitive laws. . . . But there it is! Another age
may say me wrong and these poisonous sprays and washes
right. Certainly I am no anti-vaccinationist!

But too much of this coddling makes gardening a bore,
—which is not the way to enjoy the earth. Sooner than
spend my time fumigating and spraying, washing and

slaying, I will live in the garden of the wild, and watch nature adjusting the balances in her own way.

I shall always remember that tall and pleasant youth bending over the tulips.

"A trifle of 'fire,' do you think, Mrs. Cran?" And then, among the roses: "You have black spot?"

Of course we have! I wish we hadn't; and I do not know what to say about it, except that a bed which came badly infected from a nursery some years ago is now very healthy and nearly cured; all I ever did was to hand-pick (and burn) the discoloured leaves, and cut out relentlessly all infected wood. I never sprayed. I hurried him past the hollyhocks which had, I knew, some rust,—and turned his eye upon the holly gleaming in a hedge; but he found something or other there, too, and that finished me.

It was amusing to learn that he had found as many diseases at Kew. I forebore to name bore weevil—woolly aphis (which we call American blight), Japanese beetle, mosaic disease and a few more to him because he was a guest . . . a very delightful and appreciated guest.

But "B. Y.'s" b——y pests became a joke in the English fashion of jesting in the face of disaster! There is one thing about all this "protection" . . . and "prohibition" of this and that in America—they give people a lot of fun in evading them.

I met Dr. Marlatt in Washington,—the perfect bureaucrat, who lobby-wangles the balance of nature. The test of sincerity is time; his jest will be forgotten.

The young American work-people I searched out were most interesting and dear to me. The man was temporarily a "pieman,"—he drove a car full of cakes, I gathered,—and she was an embroideress at Julius Garfinckel's store. I met Mr. Garfinckel—a sunburned prince of commerce with white hair, piercing eyes, strongly marked brows, good-looking, dynamic; a fierce worker and loyal to his employees. I was glad to meet one of the type I had so often read about.

The young woman and her husband worked hard and

were very happy; they had a car, an "apartment," or as we should say, a flat, with labour-saving devices, very prettily furnished and beautifully kept. He was of an old Southern family, which came to America from England in 1736 and settled in Virginia and Kentucky. His great-grandfather was a colonel in the Confederate army (the Southern army) during the Civil War, and he organised and led a company of soldiers. The young "pieman" spent nineteen months in the Great War in France, and was a very fine fellow.

His wife had a romantic story. She was English, and also well-born. Her mother had been married in extreme youth to a man who was neither provident nor faithful. When she was at last freed from him she made over her marriage settlement to the girl, believing she was safe-guarding her daughter's future. As a matter of fact, the reverse was the case, for the father kept the young girl rigidly beside him, waiting upon his (third) wife, until the unfortunate girl was twenty-one. The day she came legally of age he induced her to sign away to him her rights to the settlement money as the price of freedom; and packed her off to America, with five pounds in her pocket, through the submarine-infested seas of the War! He never allowed her to get in touch with her own mother, who made several vain efforts to find her daughter and make sure of her welfare.

Tossed out into that terrific cauldron of New York, (this was in the days before the "quota") the English girl had a long, hard struggle. Her mother found out the story of greed and cruelty at last, and tried to help. But the iron of life had bitten deep. The girl was difficult, proud and stubborn . . . and it was by her own efforts alone that she finally "made good." With the peace of a happy married life she softened and became gentle towards the mother who had suffered herself a harsh and difficult wringing because of the quality of the man to whom she had been married in early, ignorant youth.

The pieman and the embroideress and I spent Easter

together; among the golden forsythias, lilacs, fruit-blossom and anemones of the Pennsylvanian Mountains; they told me their dream of a farm in the mountains . . . "an up-to-date farm!" Some day I hope they get it. They deserve it.

They were delightful in their enjoyment of the brilliant spring sunshine. And by way of helping my American education they took me to Gettysburg and re-fought the battles of 1863. I had to see the place where young Jenny Wade was working her dough to bake bread when she was killed . . . and I felt the war-grief closing down on my heart—heavy and black. The useless waste of war! I was still too near the anguish of 1914–18—and, anyway, I have never had a passion for cemeteries . . . so we left the battlefield and cheered up elsewhere.

I told the story to a friend when we got back to Washington, and she said:

"Oh, Gettysburg,—how dreadful! I'll take you to Arlington."

Having no idea of what "Arlington" was, I went; and behold, it was the national cemetery!

I surveyed with horror endless rows of tiny white oblongs of uniform size, which stuck up out of the grass. Nothing will ever reconcile me to those dreadful white tablets. In a city like Washington, full of surpassing beauty, it was bitter to find these mechanical effects in memory of the dead . . . those daring, gallant hearts under the standardised tablets were not any two alike—except in courage, and that was never of such puny, machine-cut shape! I shall always marvel that Washington, with all its tradition of artistic beauty, its poetry in stone and marble, its inspiration of tree-planting, has not found some way of recording her glorious dead other than this appalling display of rows of stark white tombstones.

My friend, when she saw my dismay, turned my attention to a handsome solid block of marble—the tomb of the Unknown Soldier, with an armed guard constantly pacing to and fro. . . . But I could not be consoled.

That marble was heavy and cold enough to keep any young hot heart for ever dead beneath its icy weight. . . . I remembered the passionate beauty of the living flame which burns day and night upon the Unknown Soldier's grave in Paris under the Arc de Triomphe, which speaks in pulsing terms of a deathless spirit, and makes the living strong to face life still.

I can't say I care much better for the way we have buried our own Unknown Soldier in Westminster, either. . . .

I muttered uncomfortable words about my experience at Arlington to Miss Frances Benjamin Johnston; we were dining together at her nice Arts Club and having a heart-to-heart talk about amber, which we both love and wear. . . . She was all lively sympathy at once: "Arlington? Oh, I understand! . . . I'll take you to Rock Creek."

Now, I had heard of Rock Creek Park—and fell once more into the trap. For the dear soul took me to Rock Creek Cemetery to see "Grief"!

I had studied Augustus Saint-Gauden's work a good deal in 1920, because Lewis Hind saw to it that I did; he was very wonderful in the way he drew all his friends to share the beauty of the world with him wherever he was; and as I have already set forth in this book, he took me about and taught me much of American art, especially in sculpture and architecture. "Grief" is, I should think, one of Saint-Gauden's greatest works,—though it looked more like "Peace" than grief to me; but I was by now satiated with cemeteries, and did not tell anyone else of my series of consolations lest they found me another one.

I stayed, while in Washington, with Major and Mrs. Kyle, sister to the ever-blest Mrs. Wheelwright of Buckhead Springs; and with them I learned the essential alikeness of all artists. Mrs. Kyle had been a singer and a great beauty—a Martin-Talbot (or were those sisters Talbot-Martins?), her gay heart laughed in all difficulty and nothing, it seemed, could possibly repress her wonderful Southern hospitality. I came away with two of the Major's Southern recipes which I have not had ice in the

The supply is limited (though I must confess I saw enough of it to grow weary of the herb), and therefore the possession of it has become the heraldry of blood and money.

Either your ancestors planted it; or you are rich enough to buy it from the blue-blooded who need money more than box.

I found myself a good deal wrung by the stuff. There is love and reverence clinging round it; stout hearts planted it centuries ago in memory of the old gardens in England that they had left behind. Stout hearts to-day make sacrifices rather than part with the ancestral shrubs.

It has a billowy tumbled loveliness in the old Virginian gardens where it is not clipped, as in England, but grows in rounded hummocks of adorable green, and smells very sweetly under the hot sun; but all the same it is a bit monotonous seen in bulk, and there is a distinct aroma of posession in the airs that blow about it. One can buy box. It has lost caste.

I met a man who is building a house in Washington, D.C. Greatly as I fear and hate cities, that is one city I could bear to live in if I no longer possessed "the keye of the fieldes" (which God forbid!). The wide streets are set with trees; it is a beautifully planned garden city. Land values there are high, and likely to go higher with time. He said to me, quite casually:

"I rather thought of buying the next lot to mine; it would make a spacious garden, being a corner lot; but I have heard of some box for sale, and I can't afford both!"

I saw many other Virginian gardens; and found them very much the same . . . beautiful houses—green gardens rather negligible as to flowers and colour, but very splendid in box.

The epic tale of buxus suffructicosa gathers, I fancy, round the national cathedral at Washington, that House set on a hill to which the innate poetry of this sensitive, imaginative people flows in a stream of offerings. There is the "Bishop's Garden"; and there are the Pilgrim Steps; —the Little Garden; the perennial border; much Memorial

Gladys Rousseau has been marked from her earliest days by a passion for flowers in Her Garden in Washington, D.C.

boxwood, and other features upon the Cathedral hillside. Four hundred feet above the city of Washington there is this landscape development of over sixty acres of wooded hillside, a national garden, made by offerings of individuals and from the Garden Clubs all over America.

The aim is to make there the type of garden which they associate with mediæval England in oak, yew, holly, box and ivy.

We in England have to realise that the presentation of a well-grown ancient plant of buxus suffructicosa means in America an enormous sum of money; box is valued for its size. Anyone can grow it; but it takes from one to three hundred years to grow a fine large shrub of this slow stubborn "English" variety.

So box it is which ascends to the cathedral like the smoke of incense to the glory of the Lord. They feel so much about it that one is obliged to view the box-manifestations with reverence and with sympathy; if the plant of their love were a dandelion, one would feel the same;—it ceases to be our dear old every-day slug-haunted box;—it is a symbol; a legend;—the peg they hang a dream upon. . . .

To the transplantation of the large specimens is devoted an immense amount of engineering skill. With beams and screw-jacks, with under-root operations like those of coalminers, with wooden casing for the huge root-balls, with trollies and armies of skilled men, they take the venerable specimen plants great distances and plant them under careful supervision, leaving the anxious after-care squad in possession, to render account of their precious trust to the community in fresh green leaf and bursting growth next spring. A question of staying and staking the plants and months of watering I suspect that this after-care must mean. One of the treasures of the cathedral is a pair of immense box bushes, a couple of centuries old, found in an ancient quiet garden, by Harper's Ferry, where Mrs. Shelton and I had lunch over the meet of two rivers and talked of John Brown and Stonewall Jackson.

Each planting has its story to tell; the cathedral garden is

a book of human romances written in green leaf.   One is
now called the Bishop Harding Memorial boxwood; it
is buxus suffructicosa, a remarkable specimen, of unusual
size.   It was rescued from an unappreciative farmer on a
ruined estate in Maryland, who wanted it removed in order
to build a new pig-sty in its place.   Already he had allowed
a bonfire to destroy a similar specimen.

On another occasion tree-lovers all over the country
united in an offering to save the life of a great pine tree
which, due to building construction, was about to be cut
down.   Seventy feet high, seventy tons in weight,—including its twenty-feet ball of earth,—it was moved successfully
1,000 feet.

The Garden Club of Cleveland is represented by an
ancient yew (taxus baccata fastigiata) about a couple of
centuries old.   In the Little Garden is a stone font from
the abbey of St. Julie in the Aisne—it was found by that
famous sculptor who loves birds of Paradise, Mr. George
Barnard; it is a piece of simple carving more than a thousand
years old, surrounded by box from a house George Washington built in 1761.   The Little Garden was given to the
hillside by a garden-lover as a memorial to her husband;
it is designed on the lines of a monastic garden with the
flowers and sweet-scented herbs of the cloistered days.

The adventure of moving an entire garden of old
English box seventy-five miles was considerable!   It was
discovered at "Ellerslie," a ruined estate in the foothills
of the Blue Ridge, in the Rappahannock Valley.   In their
unusual quality and habit of growth, these wonderful hedges
are considered by experts to be among the finest known.

The Americans do not as a rule clip box as we do; and
I never shall again now I have seen the billowy habit of the
natural growth.   One loves its density and wholesomeness
and the scent of it under the hot sun; an intensely individual
plant, this English box, when left to its own development,
modelled in a grand simplicity with "shadowed under-
cuttings, peaks, pinnacles and irregular knobs and bosses
massed upon and against each other in compact green."

Lake Forest Garden Club is represented by a stone pool, and the Wilmington Garden Club gave four rare young incense cedars from the Pacific Coast . . . but a list of gifts would be endless;—and I have said enough to show the feeling of the place. The most imposing memorial of all the gifts of memory which surround Washington Cathedral is the majestic soaring line of pilgrim steps climbing the hill from the broad pilgrims' road mapped out below.

The pilgrim steps are of noble proportions, a great welcoming stairway, a very Jacob's Ladder, broad and easy; the design was by Mrs. G. C. F. Bratenahl, and the whole splendid scheme was presented by Mr. and Mrs. Roland L. Taylor of Philadelphia in memory of their son. One of the most enduring memories I carried away from beautiful Washington was that picture with its noble planting on either side of box-wood, holly, yew, and magnolia grandiflora.

I met Mr. and Mrs. Roland Taylor later in Bar Harbour and found much pleasure in their company, for they have in a very great measure the real gift of attracting and winning the love of animals; and they have vision; it is like taking a walk over the high hills, or across windy downs to have a good talk with them,—tonic and bracing.

We played together in England later on; and they saw Jock, who promptly lost his heart. He is an obstinate little dog, a highly-bred silvery-grey Dandy Dinmont with all the crabbed good qualities of his race,—not at all given to sudden passion. I was much amused to find him languishing great dark luminous glances at Mr. Taylor's rugged countenance, and mincing beside Mrs. Taylor as if he belonged to her; then they utterly won my heart by loving Siamese cats!

We lunched together one day at the Basque Restaurant in Dover Street, Mayfair, where you get a remarkable collection of rare wines; and we tried the Couteau Layon of Anjou. We thought it was corked, and sent for the "patron" who put us severely and swiftly in our places by saying that which we felt on the palate was the earthy taste of the heavy clay on which this special grape grows!

"When you are educated to it you will prefer it to all other for certain luncheon menus," said the expert.

We looked at each other. (Mrs. Taylor had not adventured with us into these experimental regions.)

"An expert," said Mr. Taylor, "is one who is far from home. He is a Latin."

I have never really cared for the European habit of clipping evergreens into shapes—I like it less than ever since I have been in America, a further blot on my garden escutcheon and proof of a wild heart, which greatly shocked Mrs. Lewis Hind. Now "Hetty" * is a very old friend, —a lady of Georgia who married Lewis Hind the essayist and art critic.

Her beautiful home in Queen Anne's Gate, London, is known to many Americans—and also the Elizabethan yeoman's house in Kent, not far from mine, where we foregather and share flower joys. Hetty was telling Mrs. Braun of Philadelphia that she must clip her box close and neat "as they do in England and in Holland, and as is proper."

"You wait," she went on; "you wait till my garden friend Marion Cran comes here."

We met in that house of many treasures soon after and Hetty was completely frustrated when I said how I felt about box. She lived in Holland for many years with George Hitchcock (her first husband) and had grown to love formal lines in decoration. Anything chastened, austere and ordered pleases her dear mind.

But I myself was thankful to find very, very few topiary gardens in America!

Over in Europe fashions obtain in horticulture, as in furniture and in dress; there was a time, for instance, during the tulip rage when prices soared to so absurd a height, that about 1637 there came a mighty crash, and the tulip passed into a long twilight of disregard. It was not till somewhere round 1889 indeed, that the beautiful flowers came back to favour on the flood tide of the Darwin tulips, recently

* See *The Joy of the Ground.*

introduced and immediately popular. There was a great craze at another time for hollyhocks, which only fell from grace through difficulties of cultivation;—irises, peonies, roses, gladioli, all have their following to-day, and their assiduous biographers to tell the world the story of their conquests and their glory. But of all the fashions in horticulture, surely that of topiary was the most persistent, and is the least recorded.

The strange notion of clipping and carving trees into fantastic shapes seems to have originated somewhere about the time of Julius Cæsar, been widely practised in the gardens of wealthy Romans, and filtered through their conquering hands to the lands they subdued, occupied, and civilised; doubtless many a Roman villa in England was "adorned with the representation of divers animals in box" during the three hundred years of the Roman civilisation, which has left its strong and wholesome mark to this day in the law and language of my country.

There is no record of the exact date when topiary took hold of the garden imagination again, but it was in full fashion in Elizabethan and Jacobean days till, somewhere about 1712, its inevitable fate overtook one of the most distinct and persistent branches of horticulture that gardens have ever known.

The spectacle of living trees diverted by constant correction to an artificial form, far removed from its natural habit, palled at last; a simpler and more natural form of landscape came into vogue; it was no longer the hall-mark of taste to clip and shear box, yew, hornbeam, privet, lavender, and every shrubby herb into animals and fantastics, into globes and cubes, peacocks and pyramids and letters of the alphabet.

But the art had a remarkable day; there is no getting away from that fact; until the hour of disfavour arrived, it was as though one moved through a world of green sculpture; every sweet whimsy of natural growth was coerced and chidden by the implacable shears into weird caricatures of birds and beasts; a strange obsession indeed.

When the turn of taste came, the pendulum swung back
a trifle too far, as is generally the way with sudden reforms;
not only were ancient monuments of yew and box destroyed,
but also many a noble sheltering hedge of architected shape,
which was a pity.

Some gardens courageously preserved their discredited
topiary specimens, and those to-day are famous for their
examples of a lost passion.   Travellers who have seen the
wide yew walks at Melbourne Hall in Derbyshire, the clipped
yew round Mrs. Boscowen's wonderful old Elizabethan
house of the 1560 Trevors in Cheshire, Lady Dudley's
home, Witley Court, Stourport, the famous topiary gardens
at Levens Hall in Westmoreland, laid out by the gardener
to James the Second, or other of the astonishing famous
examples, will be glad that some are left, if only as archæo-
logical delights.

Mazes or labyrinths were a natural development of
clipped hedges and twisted fancies;—they are a fascinating
study about which a whole book could be written,—some
were wrought in mixed plantings, some in solid venerable
yew or box, some (quaintly enough) in turf!   And some,
as one would expect, in stone.   It is possible to this day
to come occasionally across a mirror maze in an old-fashioned
Fair upon an English village green.   They are queer con-
ceits,—all very amusing and difficult to tread.

There is a compact and not very complex labyrinth at
Hampton Court, made of a patchwork planting of privet,
yew, holly and hornbeam; there is a fine one at Hatfield,
the seat of the Marquess of Salisbury, very solidly grown
in thick yew.   There are hedge mazes in Lord Brownlow's
garden near Grantham; and at Arley Hall, Cheshire; as
well as turf ones in Rutland, Hampshire and Essex.
Unfortunately no trace now remains of Fair Rosa-Mund's
Bower, the most romantic labyrinth of all.

To-day in England there is a reasonable revival of
interest in topiary work in garden design.   Used with dis-
cretion and restraint, a specimen or two has undoubted
effect upon the lay-out of a garden, and none will question

the architectural value of well-trimmed hedges in all garden design, or their usefulness as wind-breaks.

Some wealthy people spend even in tax-ridden Europe to-day a very large sum of money to obtain a well-cut old figure in box or yew (the two best materials) for some significant point of their garden picture; but a good number of people, less wealthy and more optimistic, embark on the tedious process of shaping figures out of home-grown plants.

It is generally claimed that topiarists do not "train" their works of art in the sense of tying them to a frame-work; and it may be true of the skilled nurserymen and the clever Dutch growers, but one finds that amateurs invariably use a light wire frame, which greatly helps the shaping process. The first time I encountered this phenomenon myself, a fox was being fashioned in a sporting man's garden, to run (in yew) along the top of a well-clipped and lusty yew hedge.

I was new to topiarists and all their works in those days, being more concerned with the miracle and mystery of the lovely wild flowers of plain and meadow. It was therefore a great astonishment to see that a cage or frame of wire was fixed on the top of the hedge in the place which was to become this creature. Lively sparklets of tender young yew-growth showed oddly through the wire; here and there shoots had already grown through the frame, and then these were caught and bent, tied and twisted to take the form of the prisoning wires.

I have never seen a yew or box topiary figure since then without being seized with a great desire to look within and discover if, hidden somewhere in its inner darkness, may be the same sort of corset. I have never actually discovered any, and am left wondering whether at a certain stage the wire entanglement is cut out, or whether it becomes so imbedded in the vitals of the tormented plant that it is forever lost to human eye.

Regard topiary as one may, with however intelligent an interest and sprightly a wonder, it remains to some of us too

rigid an art to practise. There are those who prefer the
billowy natural growth of box, the wide dark branches of
great old shaggy yew trees, to any of these marvels; and
hold hands in this preference with Bacon, Addison, Pope,
and the sensible people of America.

CHAPTER XV

WATER WITCHERY

AMERICAN gardeners use water decoratively far
more than we do in England. They take it
with a lively gesture, and turn the depressing
stuff into a merry mess-mate, into a jolly comrade of the
open. They use it in a score of ways; they tease and train
it with rough good-humour; they make it show off and do
its tricks. Bright water! Shouting and laughing for them
under the sun.

But nowadays, wherever I am in the round world and
whenever I think of garden pools, I remember a banker.
He has to live within reasonable daily reach of London,
and, therefore, has a more or less standardised garden plot
of the usual size in a (standardised) road of pleasant (standardised) detached, labour-saving houses. He found himself, after a few years, somewhat jaded by his rose-garden,
sundial and mixed border, and so he asked me what to
do to renew his faded interest, and I suggested a lily-pool
where the sundial had hitherto queened it in a large circle
of stone paving. The idea alarmed him until I mentioned
goldfish, and that set him thinking.

"I don't know how to look after them," he said dubiously;
but I explained that the nurseryman who sold them would
give him all instructions.

Thereupon he decided to have a water garden, and within
an hour we had got the plan roughed out, and he was all
agog to get home and start digging operations.

I must confess I had no idea of the peculiar exactness
of his City-trained mind, nor of the myriad questions I
should have to answer before he had a sooth little lily-

pool, with a couple of small water-lily varieties—sunk in their baskets, according to directions—and blue Siberian irises growing by the rim of the pond.

I gave him the name and address of a very good nurseryman, one of whose flourishing sidelines is the supplying of various fancy fish for garden ponds and pools. He was grateful to me and wrote off for "a hundred goldfish." The address probably gave the honest dealer pause, for he slyly wrote back to ask the size of the "lake, in case one hundred were not enough."

Highly excited at this alarming word, my protégé wrote back to say he had no "lake," only a small, artificial tank, or pond, but recently finished. He then learned that "so much cubic space" of water must be allowed per fish. Thereafter letters flew fast and furious, and he finally emerged triumphant with a permit for twelve fish!

"And why not make it eleven goldfish and one thunderfish?" said the good nurseryman; "it is an interesting creature, which lives at the bottom of the water and is never seen except when it comes to the surface and darts about to warn you of thunder."

So the thunderfish was ordered.

And then when the consignment arrived and was duly "planted" in his pond, my poor friend had further alarms and excursions.

"The food! the food!" he said. "How much must I give my fish?"

The unwearied fish expert replied: "As much as will cover a sixpence, once a week."—(Or was it a threepenny bit? Anyway, some such coin.)

"Thanks, but you mean once a day," wrote back the anxious fish owner.

"No! once a week, and do not give more," was the patient reply.

So once a week (or is it once a month?) the tiny ration is carefully measured and cast upon the waters to the great gladness of the bright fish, who thrive upon this meagre business, and grow apace.

"'They know me," said my Londoner, gazing round-eyed through his spectacles, his grey hair sleek upon an utterly truthful brow. "They know my step, or voice, or something, and follow me round the pond, opening their mouths."

I did not doubt it, for I, too, have fish that come to the banks for food; only mine are carp and tench in natural ponds. I knew he spoke truly.

But the thunderfish sulks.

"Little beggar!" said his owner in a note of exasperation; "the times I have hurried home when a thunderstorm was brewing, to see him come to the top. . . . And I've never managed to catch him. He's too quick for me."

I was intrigued at the picture of this grave man, with his many responsibilities, all of a hurry to catch the train at Cannon Street, hoping to be home in time to see a little fish grow lively! But there is no end to the things that water can do to a gardener.

One day he saw an ugly, indeed an obscene looking insect crawl up a rush. He was about to push it back into the pool when his wife called him, and after he had obeyed her wishes, whatever they were, he remembered the beast and told her about it. They went down the sunny garden together to have a look, and when they got there the back of the insect-case had split open, and something was wriggling out. Together they watched the miracle of a dragonfly's birth, and saw what had been a hideous and clumsy grub turn under the hot sun-rays into a flashing jewel of green and gold, freed from the underworld of mud—freed to the blue sky and the light of day.

Lily-pools abound all over America. Everybody has a lily-pool or goldfish pool, large or small, nearly always a formal stone or cement tank. I did not find many natural lily-pools on mud bottoms with natural banks, where waterside plants could grow at will. The treatment is nearly always in the corseted manner; well de-natured. The mischievous element is beckoned to their gardens in divers playful moods, often very attractive; but bitted. That is not to say that wild hearts do not exist among

gardeners there; thank God they do, and I take leave to
foretell that they will increase as the love of nature grows
in a country that is above all responsive to sincerity and
quick to learn.

For instance, I found a natural pond in Mrs. Spencer
Mulford's garden on a green lawn, among gingkos and
rhododendrons. Huge maples towered nearby; and, when
I saw it, the wide white wings of dogwood were spread for
the lovely Eastern spring. I looked down at a sobbing
gurgle in the heart of her pool where the water bursts up
from its source in the ground; thankful to see green verges
and meet a gardener whose hands know when to refrain
from meddling.

"I like some left wild," she said, eyeing me a trifle
anxiously.

At Hartwell Valley farm I found Mr. Mason wandering
down by his spring in the valley, dreaming his dreams.
"I don't want any landscaping or manicuring," he was
saying. "I want primulas and irises to grow along these
banks and spread just as they please." Heaven bless the
man.

And I think that the prettiest thing I ever met was the
rose freight on the stream at Zeerust, Rhode Island, by
the Atlantic. When Mrs. Voss cuts the full-blown roses
every day she takes them in baskets to the little silver river
which flows past her garden and throws them adrift there,
red and yellow and pink and pink and cream. They move
up and down on the tidal stream, and at last are borne down
to the sea.

Swimming-pools in America are expressed in a score of
styles. I expected, of course, to find them in California
and the South, under the burning sun, but they abound
everywhere in the States. Indeed, it was not until I came
east, to Pennsylvania, that I saw two swimming-pools in
the same garden—one always ready for use while the other
was being cleaned out! They made a frolicsome spot in
the garden life.

We are not so blest in England. One of my English

garden friends has a beautiful garden in Surrey, placed round
an old black and white Elizabethan house; he knows a
lot about narcissi, and bamboos; is honorary secretary of
the Roads Beautifying Association; is a much-admired,
distinguished member of the world of garden-lovers, and
likes water.   So there is an open-air swimming-pool in his
garden.   I remember standing beside it with him one day
when it was reflecting a dim grey sky: a cold, not to say
dreary spectacle.

"There are not many days in this climate when we can
have swimming-parties," he said sorrowfully.   "Come and
look at the bog garden; that is heaps more amusing."

And so it was, with its primulas and ferns, globe flowers
and irises, and all the fun of the marsh.   He was a good
deal discouraged about his bathing-pool; it certainly does
seem a bit foolish to make any to-do about an element
which not only surrounds our Isle, but also descends upon
it with melancholy persistence most of the year, in one form
or another!   Best to let it fall into the ground, where it
wreaks mightily and comes back in the happy shape of
flowers.

In the garden of Longwood, Delaware, many a moon
afterwards, I sat on a golden June day in a green garden
edged with box, listening to the loud sound of waters, and
I thought of his love for the babble of streams.   Beyond
the green walls was another green room; and still, beyond
those living walls, rang that loud, melodious laughter—
gay and hoarse.   It is a garden of many waters—not thin
threads and sprays flung up reedily here and there, as is
more usual in ordinary gardens, but great gushing founts
that come up with a gladness and strike the air with force;
hoofs of stallions ridden by Titans resounded to my fancy
in those "courts for ever green."

With all the splendour of the design there is something
simple in the place.   Simple and strong.

It is a very surprising garden; even the open-air theatre
is arranged with a difference.   There is no silken drop-
scene to hide the stage from the audience, but a sheet

of water rises up; it makes a shimmering fabric upon which hidden lamps embroider a moving pattern of coloured lights between the acts.

A wild woodland set with trees leads to the Longwood garden of fountains; under the shade copper fritillaries, white wake-robins, yellow ladies' slippers, lilies of the valley, may-apples and other sweet things grow in sheets of beauty beneath huge rhododendrons and massed azaleas. Wide white planes of dogwood are reflected in the lake. It is an immense place.

From the "plangent tenor" of its many fountains I went to the great glass-houses with Mr. and Mrs. Pierre du Pont to hear about her Ghent azaleas and his new hybrid amaryllidæ, passing on the way the charming old house of poignant simplicity. It was built in 1730 by Josiah Peirce from a grant of William Penn,—a large allspice (calycanthus) was in full bloom of its sweet brown blossom by the drawing-room windows; and the flowers matched Mrs. du Pont's eyes, I noticed, warmly brown. Her husband loves sweet-smelling things, and so when we came to the tropical houses with their vanilla, coffee, bananas and passion fruit I looked round for frangipanni; and there was not one! But I expect there is by now. Their glass-houses are so built as to be forgotten for the flowers, and I discovered Mrs. du Pont's great pride was in the huge plants of Ghent azaleas, and her Rocheas.

The majesty of that garden did not confuse me; I was not bludgeoned by its wealth, as so often happens when one gets first stupefied and then disgusted by overpowering display in a place that should be,—of all the works of men's hands,—the place of the heart.

That was because Mr. and Mrs. Pierre du Pont are unfeignedly keen, they play with information as children with a new toy, and give back their own with an enchanting and eager generosity. Some of my readers will understand how great a thing this is when we find it. . . . The human soul seldom keeps its freshness and its bloom when it has known the rough touch of riches . . . it more often grows

IN MR. AND MRS PIERRE DU PONT'S GARDEN AT LONGWOOD SOUNDS THE LOUD,
MELODIOUS LAUGHTER OF MANY WATERS

a fungus from which the sensitive prefer to escape. . . . It was a happy day; I was with Gladys, then the wife and now the widow of Admiral H. H. Rousseau, the Chief Co-ordinator at Washington, a very gallant and distinguished officer of the American Navy.

She is one of those vivid, beautiful women, with a gift for friendships, whose vital fascination is apparently based upon a wide knowledge of life; but which proves at the test to be drawn from a deep well-spring of natural sweetness and spiritual strength. Her father was a diplomatist; she knows her world; and she has been marked from earliest days by a passion for flowers. She hunted for orchids in Panama, and has three species named after her; wherever she went in her father's wandering career she found her way to the earth,—and by no means could I have found a dearer or more entertaining companion with whom to see gardens.

We had a lot of fun because all down the Kennet Pike I kept talking of the "du Pont garden," which we were on our way to see.

America is full of misleading names;—"Magnolia" is azaleas,—and now I found that "the" du Pont garden was scores of gardens in Delaware; Mrs. W. K. du Pont grows orchids; at Eleutherean Mills, on the Brandywine River, a du Pont, Mrs. F. B. Crowninshield, has made a rock and water garden out of the ruins of the old powder mills. Another du Pont garden belonging to Mrs. R. R. M. Carpenter has one of the nicest swimming-pools I saw in America, beautifully placed among green lawns and trees; the whole garden is of good taste, planned with a large gesture, free and simple.

Delaware is a small State; they say of it that it has three counties at low tide,—and only one at high! The scenery is beautiful;—it is like a very spacious and en-chanted England, with its wide-spread carpets of may-apples, tall, fragrant paulownia trees, green hills and woods and running creeks, cool, clear air, hedges and pretty stone houses.

P

One day in Kent, Hetty had got her homesick face on.
Every now and then she remembers through the muffling
years that she is an American by birth; some small sweet
thing brings back the thought of Georgia, Virginia and Maryland. This time I found her all "gone Georgian," because
a fellow-countryman had leaned over her gate in Kent and
promised to send her some "may-apples." I was very
sympathetic, because I know how flowers and plants make
their spells and bewitch our lives. . . . I imagined may-
apple was a variety of hawthorn,—our mayblossom,—and
pictured large woody shrubs, laden with pink or white
bloom, smelling very sweet. When, therefore, Mrs.
Rousseau now leaned from the car and said, "Oh, look at
the may-apples!" I gazed upward, full of thoughts of Hetty,
wondering if the American had ever sent her the promised
plants to Kent. But it appeared they were quite a different
shape; wide umbrellas of green leaf were spread out flat
in green sheets, a foot or so from the ground. I was loud
in my astonishment. So the car was stopped and I had
to look under the umbrella leaf to find the beautiful creamy
cup of the may-apple flower which is podophyllum peltatum
and ranges south from Florida to Texas and north to
Quebec, Ontario and Minnesota. No relation whatever
to cratageus!

Mrs. Irving Warner took us round the Wilmington
gardens, and I soon learned how absurd my remarks about
seeing "the du Pont garden" had been.

That family seems to own all Delaware county. I may
be wrong in thinking so for my sense of size and distance
went adrift in America; I was lost in bigness. I did gather
the feeling, the old familiar feeling, of a feudal state, under
the cherishing of powerful benignant lords of the manor.
I was brought up in an England of the feudal age and
habit; I know its comfortable content, for those who live
under its *régime* and the strong sense of responsibility which
rests on the shoulders of good overlords. However right
or wrong I may be in that fleeting impression of Delaware,
I am free to declare that I saw a great many beautiful du

Pont gardens there and to utter a belief that no one family in America has done more for horticulture.

Mrs. Harry M. du Pont has a very large and park-like pleasaunce which reminded me a good deal of Mr. Hearst's castle, San Simeon, in California; only she had some splendid cattle instead of wild beasts. Mrs. Felix du Pont, a Miss Chichester of Leesburg—Virginia stock,—had something of the unruly heart that loves the vagrants of a garden more than the garden itself; the song of frogs, the twilight and the early morning. . . . My chief memory of her place was of a pool and pergola and the large, fragrant, well-grown waxen lilies of the valley.

A most delightful young du Pont was Mrs. Simpson Dean, who, as a girl of sixteen, had longed to own "Nemours" one day; and it was there we saw her in the house her French great-great-grandfather built in 1821, now her home, a lovely old house, simple and spacious, with characteristic French carving; it looks out to the Brandywine River. She loves white flowers (unlike Daphne Milne, who abhors them) and masses them against the dark and satisfying woodland background which frames her house and marches grandly up from the Brandywine. A splendid tree peony filled me with envy; and we were sufficiently impressed by the tree-box grown from seed now some forty or fifty feet high. While we talked, a ruby throated humming bird poised over a pink chestnut,—and the beautiful young face beside me took on an absorbed intentness. . . . She loves birds. . . . Presently a thrush called, and we forgot the garden to enjoy the little creatures. A red cardinal yelled for joy of his big worm;—and then she found me a tree toad,—an exquisite grey thing marbled with black.

"Mauchline" is a town garden of great feeling; one in which a personality lingers sweetly yet, though the maker is dead. It was made by the mother of Mrs. Irving Warner, our "little Joshua." She became our Joshua when Gladys Rousseau and I were running to catch the train we nearly missed (to my despair, for friends were waiting dinner for us in Philadelphia!). To keep a train waiting seemed to

CHAPTER XVI

GARDEN PERSONALITIES

WHEN I got to Pennsylvania I knew I was a lost woman.

It was perfectly clear to me that I could never cope in any book with the beauty of the State, the hospitality and culture of its people. I wish I could find a few burning words in which to chronicle the lifetime of kindness they crushed for me into a few weeks.

Later on in England I was talking to a great friend, the editor of the *Dog World* and the best-known judge of dogs in England; I said I wished she would help me to entertain some Americans who had come over and wanted some doggy talk.

"Americans!" she said. "I'll do anything in the world for them. I shall never be able to repay them for the happy time they gave me when I was in their country!"

And so there were two of us in the same predicament; we sang a long and loud duet together over the debt we had both incurred never to be repaid!

Philadelphia to me was a lode-star to which my thoughts had turned often and often during the long travel of the past months.

The blue-eyed "Worst" was to be my hostess there, and greatly did I long to renew the garden-fun of long ago with her. And Mrs. Shelton was there with her April charm, Hetty was passing through the city and Jim and Winifred Peech were due.

Philadelphia felt like home, with all these threads to draw me there. . . . It is a dreadful place to come to after Washington! The suburbs are superb, the country all

round is of a broad splendour with every beauty of glorious
trees, emerald grass, rivers, mountains and flashing dogwood
queening it over all the flowering shrubs. But the city
itself is positively drab—I do not know what has happened
to it. I suppose one will go back in a year or so and find
it utterly re-built to some beautiful harmonious plan; that
is the sort of thing the Americans do.

Philadelphia is the centre of a very close social preserve
dating from (I regret to say) the Revolution, so a good deal
of my garden-seeing there was mixed up with interesting
people; I could never quite disentangle them, and every
now and then got myself very well mixed up. It was in
Philadelphia I found the answer to a question which had been
puzzling me and that was the correct possessive national
adjective to use for the United States. "America" embraces
both North and South America . . . and yet I could not
talk about United Statesian gardens; and one day when I
said "U.S.A.," the man I spoke to thought I meant the
Union of South Africa!

The obvious word, to me, is "American," but I wondered
if they had a better. I asked Mr. Randolph Hearst at
San Simeon but he could not tell me, nor could anyone
until I met Mr. Roland Morris, one time American Ambassador to Japan. He told me that the English Foreign
Office gives the U.S.A. the right "by long use" to the
words American Ambassador. It is only the Latin countries
who object. So at last I knew.

Mr. Morris was a delightful man, as was also his witty
sister, Mrs. Russell Duane. They are descended from
Benjamin Franklin, the scientist, man of letters, and statesman, whose policy if he had not been overridden would
have made the break between England and America a
bloodless, easy transition into a new relationship. . . .

A very delightful evening was that I spent observing
the elusive John Wister. He is a recluse, but also a distinguished gardener; and so I was very happy when Mrs.
James Starr, his sister, asked me to dine at her house and
meet him. It is a lovely old house and the dinner party

was to me especially delightful because some nice puss-
cats were chatting and gambolling beside my chair looking
for (surreptitious) titbits; I like cats, and the houses where
I meet them are ones to remember.

Mr. Starr took me out in the rain to look at his azalea
Mollis hybrids; and then I found him lamenting in a
gentle grieved sort of way about his moccasin-flowers.
Something had nipped them off; all but one—a nice fat,
lonely one; it was a good-looking moccasin-flower (or
ladies' slipper, as we call it over here), rather beaten by
the rain. Mr. Wister was with us, and I was interested
to see how keen he and his brother-in-law were to find
three or four seedling rhododendrons coming up. To me
the ladies' slipper was a rarer flower.

There were long wavy lines of well-grown old English
box, and then Mr. Wister and I set forth to see his tree-
peony seedlings . . . dinner was at that moment announced
and the vile body called us back! He has an arboretum
to lay out,—and I wanted to talk to him very much, but
I was sufficiently fortunate, it appears, to meet him. He
knows a very great deal but never was man more congealed.
During dinner he became almost talkative when we discussed a pet idea I have of an international garden magazine.
Not a botanists' text-book, but a readable, accurate, lively,
world-ranging garden magazine—which we will read as
we fly from one country to another by way of killing time
in the air, and preparing us for the gardens we shall see
when we land.

Other drifts of conversation came our way. Mrs. Nixon
was busy talking about her peony "bulbs" and Mrs.
Warrender telling of Alaska. Over the table roved the
genial glance of our most attractive hostess, thoughtfully
watching her fortunate guests. She is a very distinguished
woman of Philadelphia, once President of the Colonial
Dames, the blue blood of America; and it was she who is
responsible for the replica of Sulgrave Manor.

Mr. Harvey Watts, a journalist and writer of the city
whom I met in Sally Greene's house, told me how an

English Duchess whom he was taking in to dinner said to him: "I am to meet Mrs. Starr.   Who is she?"

"She is a Wister," said Mr. Watts.

"What is a Wister?" asked the Duchess.

"Hush!" he said, "she might have been a Biddle."

From which it became clear to me that to bear either of those names was to be very grand in Pennsylvania.

I liked Mr. Watts because he reminded me of my soldier-sculptor friend of long ago, I do not quite know why . . . height, or colour, or manner, dark eyes, or something. Certainly not in voice, because no one ever heard my soldier speak; he is a very silent observant, short, swarthy man; while Mr. Watts was quite chatty.   He took Sally and me to see Newhope, an interesting artists' colony on the Delaware River, it is the oldest school of painting in the United States, and we found other craftsmen as well: Mr. Colts's forge for making fine wrought iron; Mrs. Davenport making beautiful "thrift" rugs under the shade of her enormous liriodendron trees; and Mrs. Taylor's remarkable tapestries.   She calls them hook rugs, but they are more suitable for mural decorations; I can still see the crystalline, almost enamel, effect of winter in one; and the movement, the *weather* in another with a large steeplechase design—the jockeys' coats bright against green grass, the blue water—the drawing of the three horses, a bay, a white and a black. . . .

Hillhouse where she works had once a grist mill on the stream.   She grows flowers from cuttings and makes her own garden, a green growing place of roses and box, the garden of a busy woman, full of energy and inspiration with never time to do all she wants!

Philadelphia is a great garden centre; the first botanical garden of America was founded there by John Bartram in 1731.   Kalm, the Swede, whose name is crystallised in the modest-mannered "mountain-laurel," travelled with him through the two Carolinas and down the Ohio.   When Bartram was seventy he went to Florida.

I met Mr. Frederick Stout, president of the Pennsyl-

vania horticultural society, later on at North-East Harbour,
Mt. Desert in Maine, and he was good enough to give
me a mighty tome containing the history of the P.H.S.
from 1827 to 1927, compiled by its twentieth President,
James Boyd, from which one may learn that it is an active
and able body.   It seems that Charles II sent out his
plant-gatherers to Pennsylvania.   It was interesting, too, to
hear of a "yard and garden contest" which offers awards
for the same reasons that our own National Gardens Guild
does in what we call "garden competitions" generally
organised for gardens in big industrial cities.

I have always loved the little town gardens.   People
are apt to think that space alone makes a garden; but they
lose, in that straitened belief, three parts of joy.   There
"is the wind on the heath, brother"; there are the many
musics of birds and insect and splashing spray; the moving
shadows; the colour of leaf-buds, the ways of the little
things that share our "out-door-room" with us,—yea,
even unto an observing of the fussy and passionate maternity
of earwigs.   The first step toward a town garden is to
liberate the mind from all big ideas and see what funds of
pleasure await discovery in a very little space, where there
is no room for borders, lawns and rockeries.

It is movement and the music of living movement which
one wants to conjure into a small garden; movement, and
a place of observation where sensitive and work-weary
humans may watch the birds, the shadows, the falling water,
the wind-sway of blossom-boughs, the moving panorama
of the sky—and also that other strange but real beauty
which clusters about town gardens:—the daffodil lights
of the city lamps as they spring into sudden bloom at
nightfall.

A seat beneath a leafy bough, and the world is ours to
watch.   The world?   No, the Universe; what time we
tune in to the rhythms of life, manifest in bird and beast
and inconsiderable insect and find there the true meaning
of "religion."   It is in a garden that one prays, with heart
and beseeching hands and watching eyes. . . .   Unself-

consciously, and therefore best; it is in a garden that is set free the hidden poet in the least likely soul!

I saw at Garth in Philadelphia one of the best small town gardens I have ever seen; it had the grandeur of simplicity; it was beautifully planned to make the most of every opportunity without any sense of effort; a remarkable and lovely place. I was very sorry to miss meeting Mrs. Arthur H. Scott of Todmorden, who is a hybridist with some beautiful flowers to her credit. She bred the dainty Rose Valley Iris and gave Swarthmore, to make a perfect arboretum in memory of her husband. I saw her terraces of peony and iris, but they lacked their soul for me, lacking her.

At the Andora Nurseries near Philadelphia, Mr. Harper's brilliant young pupil, Tom Marshall, took me over the handsome "plant." It was a happy morning for I found Mr. Harper is (like so many gardeners) essentially a poet. He speaks his sense of beauty in trees, and finds the rhythm of those tree-words in the grouping and placing of them.

There is in him a true landscape-artist; he feels the colour of massed foliage, the texture and the form of it; he plays with his medium, and makes pictures upon hill and valley and green lawn as a painter does upon a canvas. He fights with himself to get the actual one and only right tree to express his meaning in a group of trees, as a writer fights for the only word to fit a sentence, the one word with the right colour of meaning and balance of sound.

The choice of trees and shrubs in the state of Pennsylvania is very wide; the way rhododendrons and azaleas grow is wonderful. I could feel Mr. Harper's lot had fallen in a happy land. He took me to see his propagating method for "rhodies" and on the way I met Cornus Kousa for the first time. It is a valuable acquisition, greatly prolonging the lovely dogwood bloom; the flower comes quite green at first, but just about the time that the wide, white wings of Cornus Florida are passing over, to a sigh of regret from the whole Eastern American countryside, this new Japanese dogwood, Kousa, blanches to a dazzling white, and then (wherever it is known to grow) after people have resigned themselves to waiting for another whole year for their darling dogwood the dazzling loveliness comes back again to them! It will be widely planted as it gets better known; the petals are more pointed, the autumnal berries of a riper red and different shape to Cornus Florida, but the flat planes of whiteness, the wide white wings, hover in just the same lovely dogwood habit that having once seen one does not forget, and ever longs to see again.

I saw very fine trees of Cornus Kousa in full bloom at Mr. Samuel Untermeier's garden, "Greystones," at Yonkers, and also on Long Island, New York, in full bloom on July 15 in Mr. Sidney Z. Mitchell's lovely garden.

After I had lingered long enough, enchanted, over Cornus Kousa, Mr. Harper took me along to see the propagating grounds, and I found that in the Andora Nursery rhododendrons are grown on their own roots. Every garden-lover will know what that means! I wish it had always been so in England, and not only with rhododendrons, too. When I think of viburnum carlesii . . . however!

It was interesting to see the "mother-plants," with their branches pegged down all round in a neat circle to strike a large family of youngsters. The babes are fit to send out in four years, lusty rascals. The mother's roots (the top being very much shrunken in circumference) are given a rest for three or four years—put out to grass, so to speak, when they come back to their family-raising work, full of vigorous young wood again; very lively and chatty.

"It seems to rejuvenate them!" said Mr. Harper, thoughtfully.

I was unfortunate in missing at Wellesley Farms, Miss Sturtevant, whom I had much wished to meet, but I was taken to see her iris seedlings and found to my interest that she uses the mulch paper method I first saw at Washington, D.C., with "B. Y." in the government experimental grounds. I missed, too, the gardens of Carl Salbach at Berkeley, the famous plantsman and originator of new varieties in iris, gladioli and dahlias . . . but if I started to count the nurseries I missed and longed to see I should have to go on the "quota" and stay in America for ever; there are hundreds in that enormous country, with its astonishing varieties of climate; and incalculable resources in native flora for garden magics.

The Philadelphia taximen are a special race, famous for their nice manners and unfailing consideration. I was aware of this, but enchanted nevertheless when the taxi-driver who took me out to Andora Nurseries discovered a robin's nest for me,—and took me down green thickets and flowery byways to peer down upon two eggs of shrill and lovely blue. The robins in America are large birds, more like our English thrushes than what we call "robins"; they have orange-red breasts and are very tame.

In a small ladies' nursery at Ambler, Pennsylvania, the Logan Nursery, was the bluest lilac I have ever seen. It is called Decaine; I found it in a remote spot, picked a spray and clamoured for the name. It was single, fragrant, with a big truss and large pips of real clear pale blue; a most surprising definite blue.

At Ambler I met Mrs. Henry Ford, a little brown woman with a merry, round face, she is fond of a garden; and Mrs. Francis King was there speaking with her old laughter, but worn thinner since I saw her last. She has a new garden nowadays, having left Michigan and we had a happy talk over the experiences we gain by change, when she asked me to dine with her at the Acorn Club.

Life had its excitements in Philadelphia because I was never quite sure of getting anywhere when I set out with Sally! She is a joyous fellow-rover without any sense of direction, but a great sense of fun. We found the way by devious routes and much astonishment to Mrs. Pope Barney's house in Rose Valley where the bob-white whistled sweetly for us. I had never heard that bird before, and it seemed to suit the place, a compact and intimate garden, where the woods look to Ridley Creek, and frame a sweet-voiced Southern mother-in-law, with white hair and wonderful great dark eyes. . . . I could not make up my mind which to look at most . . . her beauty or the beauty of the roses. . . .

The garden is on a steep hillside under green trees with deep "dry walls" hung with curtains of arabis, aubrietia, campanula, sedums, cobweb-house-leeks, iris gracilipes and mauve and blue phlox divaricata. Iris B. Y. Morrison was blooming in great good humour, his violet velvet falls edged with lavender and globed lavender standards; there was everywhere the frank simplicity of a well-planned "home" garden about the charming little place.

I cannot remember all the company of that day, but it was full of amusement. Once when we were quite securely lost, bowling away vigorously in the wrong direction, we passed a cemetery and Sally turned her gold head and blue eyes upon it beaming:

"That," she said, "is where I shall snugly creep into my allotted space and behave like an ancestor."

When I hurriedly changed this cemetery topic, of which I had already had my full dose in Washington, the conversation drifted round to the question of ancestors and the relations between parents and children in the world of to-day. There must have been some Bright Young Thing in the party for an irritated voice burst forth:

"The trouble with your generation is you always had a Past; we don't care a damn about your Past."

No; why should the young ones care—they are busy making their own . . . and from that rather personal topic we somehow became involved in a great talk on the history of America in the last thirty years. Someone said: "We rose to heights we've never grown to," and I was digesting this aphorism when it was discovered that we must retrace some colossal mileage and start looking for the garden we were due to take tea in at some quite different point of the compass.

"No one but Marion Cran would trust me as a guide," said Sally, "and she won't much longer."

"Yes, I will," I said stoutly; "the English are very trustful."

And then we got on to place-labels. You are only a
Virginian if you come from Virginia—not a Southerner.
You are "a Bostonian" from Boston. South of the Mason-
Dixon line you are a Southerner, but you remain "a Texan"!
A North Carolina woman said she came from the valley of
humility between two mountains of conceit, i.e. South
Carolina and Virginia.

These local allusions, for some reason I have not analysed,
made America seem to become a very home-like, warm and
friendly place!

Owing to various misapprehensions about the way, it
was very late when we arrived at Mrs. Willis Martin's
house, but we were fortunate enough to find her in—and
to be taken by her personally round the garden, which I
had so much looked forward to seeing. It was exactly as
I had felt it might be that day, many moons ago, when I
had heard her speak at the dinner of welcome given to
the Garden Club of America in London.

It is an old and a loved garden. The "Harrison Yellow"
roses in it were planted by her grandfather who planned it.
He planted the jacqueminot roses and the "original Phil-
delphia" seckle pears. I looked at them with much interest
and Mrs. Willis Martin observed me.

"They are delicious little dessert pears," she said, and I
was glad to know that, for I had uprooted a contumaceous
apple in Kent to plant instead a "pickled sickle pear," as
Michael Rimmerley always called it. He was so fussy
about the loveliness of this sweet little pear when pickled
that I had got one, ordered a tree and made room for it in
the full orchard; I found it was called "Seckle" . . . and
having planted it with the utmost care, realised I had no
idea on earth how to pickle the fruits of it or where to get
a recipe. Now that I heard they were good for dessert I
was much comforted.

Mrs. Willis Martin's garden goes down the hill in a
series of green rooms walled in box. It was once a strawberry garden, but now she grows perennials there and at
wistaria time all is purple and mauve and blue in her "rooms"

under the lilac and apple blossom. An old greenhouse is now her "strawberry room";—it is kept there to steal from, and not for picking for the house!

She discussed the Japanese beetle and the sage in his office in Washington (who legislates plant pests away) with a good deal of cynical fun. The colours are carefully planned in her green-walled rooms, where the slow-growing English variety has made a good bulk of itself in its young life of a hundred years. She keeps the blue delphiniums by themselves at the bottom of the hill against a background of sloping green orchard.

She stood among her gorgeous peonies, a very direct downright American gentlewoman who had in her manner something of that wholesome bitter-sweet refreshment I used to know among the Ladies in my youth. I was very happy that I had met her again; and seen the garden where she knows every plant, and where she likes to work herself.

One night at a dinner before Sally and I went on to see Lysistrata, I met the President of the Swedish Colonial Society, Mr. Henry D. Paxson, who upset a lot of my ideas about William Penn and his Sylvania! I always believed the history—the modern American history—of that delectable State started in 1682 with the English Quaker. But now it appeared that the Swedes founded the first permanent Colony and established and maintained the first seat of government in Pennsylvania thirty-nine years before the coming of William Penn. And he gave me a copy of his book *Where Pennsylvania History Began* so that I can never more mistake this matter.

We went to see Mrs. Mary Wright of the Logan Nurseries who is a descendant of that James Logan who was Secretary to William Penn and I felt a stirring of shame in my bones, as though I guarded some guilty secret in having learned of this Swedish business, when I looked upon her. It was such a shock to me to have to dislodge Master Penn from his lofty pedestal that I felt it would be a score-times worse for Pennsylvanians and a hundred-times worse for those who can claim lineal touch with the (supposed) Founder

Mrs. Horatio G. Lloyd's "Iris Bowl" in her Philadelphia Garden

of the State.   I rather wished Dr. Paxson had left me in
my comfortable ignorance.   She was so nice to me, too . . .
I knew by correspondence Anna Lee Merritt, who used to
write me nice garden letters about Philadelphia, and the
"Logan cross." (The loganberry; which I found on
closer investigation originated in the West.)

We went to see Mrs. Charles Walcot Henry's 25,000
tulips in bloom, a river of colour, bronze, pink, purple, rose,
red, cream, gold, yellow, mauve, running down a valley
below her green hills, a marvellous planting.   It is a park-
like garden of glorious trees, and thence we went to the
races, where my Christian Science friend backed Imp.
Whisky and won the pool; then on to Miss Violet
Oakley's beautiful house to tell her the scandalous tale.

And then to Mrs. Haughton's beautiful rock garden,
beloved of Correvon, by an old mill where they still grind
wheat between stone grinders.   The house is 200 years
old, with deep rafters of smoke-stained wood and a huge
old open fireplace like my own away in Kent.

That was a very scholarly and interesting garden where
I found flower friends I had not often seen lately—a scree
garden (shades of Carmel Highlands!) Lewisias, iris tectorum, I. reticulata Cantab, crocus tomasinianus and such
small sweets.

At Mrs. Charles Lea's in the Pennsylvanian Devon, I
found the spacious manners and the identical hostess of an
English country house; also to add to this content (for
these things have a graceful charm) two large pink hawthorn
trees.   As a rule our hawthorn does not grow very freely
in America, and this was to me an event.

Among the house-party was Mrs. Smith, cousin to our
Susan Lawrence, M.P., and Dr. Jason Mixter of Boston
much interested in the Pekin skull.

Sally had a hard time tearing me away from all these
pleasant people,—but off we went to see Mrs. Woodward's
garden of formal lines overcome by rich individuality;
Kalmia, androsace, dogwood, and rhododendron grow
richly, over carpets of lily of the valley.

At Croswicks in Jenkintown I found the Davidia tree
at last!   It is a place of rare trees and shrubs; and there,
upreared to some thirty feet and quarter of a century old,
was Mrs. Palmer's dove-tree. It was nearly over, because
the green was in leaf; once the wide fluttering rags of
white inflorescence are out, the foliage bursts forth in a
mighty hurry: and then the dove-tree drops its little handkerchiefs. "Chinese" Wilson found the Davidia; and
to him I planned to make pilgrimage; for Sally was going
to drive me from New York to Maine by way of Boston.

A scholarly garden is that at Lockington not far away
from Crosswicks where Mrs. W. W. Frazier experiments
with soils, and likes to make things grow whether they think
they should or not;—we visited her neutral, alkaline, and
acid soil spots; and I learned that she had been at our London
Garden Club years ago when Mr. Dykes the famous iris
expert talked to us of his researches among tulips species.

She has many rare shrubs and plants; among them a
Franklinia tree; and the gordonia pubescens which enjoys a
medi-acid soil; she was collecting hellebores when I was
there and I told her of the way mine seed themselves and
hybridise among the species; but to no very great advantage
that I have been able to discover as my Hellebours orientalis
choose H. lividus or H. viridis, whichever it is that grows
rampantly under my hedge, for their paramour,—and the
fellow is not a Romeo. The purple and pink beauties
are very fond of him.

Around her beautiful old house she has English box
brought by a wife of the family from Wales in 1740.

"It is buxus suffructicosa," she said. "A great deal of
the Virginian box is sempervirens the quick growing tree
box; I don't believe, you know, that the Japanese box
belongs to the same genus."

The more I talk about Philadelphia the more like a
genealogical table does my book become—full of names—
lists and lists of names. I give up all hope of saying anything adequate.

There was one garden to which I wished I could bring

English iris-lovers—or any English body who believes
still that there are no gardens in America. I had heard
of Mrs. Horatio Gates Lloyd's "iris bowl," and heard her
speak at our Iris Society, so that when I met her again in
New York and she invited me to see it I was very pleased.

It is a beautiful treatment; original and very well designed,
to show the irises at their best; there is a succession of
circular terraces, one within and below the other; at the
bottom of the bowl is a blue pool like the lees of the sky.
I could not help thinking during lunch while we looked out
over her beautifully kept lawns to an enormous Pennsylvanian flowering cherry in full bloom that my neighbour
in Kent, Mr. Collingwood Ingram, should be there to see
it in all the splendour of its snowy single flowers.

Mrs. Gates Lloyd has placed her garden to look on a lake
down slopes of green through banks of trees and away
to the wooded hills beyond; it reminds one of Windermere.
She has a rose garden and swimming pool as well as a very
well-planted blue garden with a ribbon of water running
through it . . . water is used very prettily everywhere in this
garden.

She is a very real and very amusing gardener—it is
delightful to go down among the flowers with her; she
forgets the audience trotting beside her and speaks her
thoughts aloud.   We halted by a brake of vigorous green:
rather inopportunely vigorous it seemed to me. . . .

"Those cotoneasters looked so innocent in their little
pots, so I put them there. *Now* look at them!"

She turned a quarry into a rock garden, repeating in
another form of stone the "bowl" idea of the iris garden
on the green lawns above. The bottom of the stone bowl
is a flat meadow of grass—the lees of the fields;—and everywhere, on every hand—in that garden made by a woman who
loves it and plays with it and pets and scolds it like a child
—grow beautiful flowers and healthy shrubs in every
imaginable form and colour.

CHAPTER XVII

A SEA-GARDEN

SALLY was going to whisk me away in her chariot
of fire to the enchanted woods of Maine, but first
I must go to New York to broadcast, see my literary agent, and certain friends.

I dreaded New York; the friend to whom I took the
"gin" bottles on arrival had asked me to stay again in
her apartment on Park Avenue, and Sally begged me to
be her guest at the York Club, but even with all these
kindnesses I was terror-stricken at plunging once more
into those canyons of cement and steel; into that cauldron
of heat and noise, into those steaming masses of people;
I felt there as a fish must feel kicking and jumping in
panic on the dry hot sunny grass when its whole living
body is crying for the sleek touch of cool water and the
green shadows under water-lily leaves.

I am a fish out of water in a city.

Pennsylvania lay behind me, with its wealth of mines
and manufactures,—its broad plains and green valleys, its
rivers and mountains, glorious trees and sweet and pleasant
people; I was away to the North; and the dogwood was
well over.

Here was Richardson Wright!

As far as writing is concerned that famous editor and
I had little commerce with each other; I am not one of
his "regular contributors"; there is no such fear-compel-
ling bond betwixt us and so I am free to say how much
I enjoy his company. He is an alive vibrant handsome
man; he *cares* to grow flowers.

"Mrs. Marion Cran needs skirts of crane's-bill round

her knees," he said at lunch with Mrs. Beebe Wilder and me (for here in the flesh beside me was America's "rock garden God"). . . . "She is very strong and tall and beautiful. They grow her in Kansas, the city of irises."

"You'll find her very prolific!" I laughed. "You will be able to raise a lot of fine new seedlings from your plant."

"She marks a definite advance toward the long-sought pink iris," he said thoughtfully, "but she is a far way from the pink one we shall get. Wild rose and Airy Dream are two fine pinks; but Mrs. Marion is a garden acquisition."

"She is one of the first and one of the last to bloom for me in Kent," I said, "and though she is so tall she never needs staking, or bends in the fiercest rain."

We drifted away from Perry's beautiful iris, to talk of my astonished admiration of American gardens.

"The movement is bigger and stronger than you can guess, even after your tour of intensive study," he said. "We are going after horticulture here not only socially and scientifically, but it is becoming an every-day joy with us as in the small cottage and town gardens of England; soon the Garden Club of America will be taken out of the Social Register because there will be a *Federated* Garden Club of America."

I did not follow what all this meant, but I could see he was quite in earnest.

"It means," he persisted, sensing the perfunctory politeness of my murmured answer, "that all the little tiny towns will have their Garden Club; that the grocers' wives and plumbers' wives who love their gardens and do not want to climb into Society will also be Garden Club members."

"Your Garden Club in England is quite different?" said Mrs. Wilder.

"Yes," I said, "we have no Garden Club of England in the sense in which you have it in this big country with all its ramifications of interest and activity. 'The Garden

Club' is a building in London, a mixed residential Club-house, very pleasant and popular but of no importance in the world of Horticulture. It was intended to be when I started it; but the leit motif is not now that of gardening."

We talked and talked; they were two delightful people; . . . I enjoyed her generous soft charm and eager enthusiasm. Richardson Wright is full of go and right on the spot; there is quality and sincerity in all his garden-ways. We all three agreed in hating gloves and kneeling mats and everything that comes between us and the earth . . . and then he made us laugh.

"There is a new swank! Greater and more crushing at a dinner-party than wearing a new rope of pearls is it to say: 'My Kew gardener has just arrived.' "

I spent a happy day with Mrs. Beebe Wilder in her home and garden, and saw Mr. Durand's scholarly collection of wild flowers with her; but the real day to me was in her company, so cool and fresh her vision and her courage. And her books are the garden books I love to read. Quite "local" and therefore the perfect picture; full of flower recording and flower sense and feeling.

I stumbled through the days doing that which I had to do, gasping for the hour of release when Sally would take me up the North Shore. . . . Hetty had come to New York, and she was finding things difficult; I knew she was very preoccupied because she never even noticed my clothes! Generally she eyes me with disapproval; I like colour and am apt to break forth as the spring . . . she runs her blue eyes over my large frame and says:

"You should wear black, Marion!"

But I feel depressed in black.

I frisked along the blistering streets beside her, gay as a pup, because she was too subdued, poor Hetty, to scold me for being in green, shrimp, yellow, puce, scarlet or what-not—(beige, I believe it was)—but *not* black!

One day we found a speak-easy together—I needed it!

I had set out that afternoon to broadcast a "Garden

Talk" and found a lordly entrance on Fifth Avenue; I entered without astonishment; it seemed quite meet and proper that this enormous, wealthy, powerful country of America should have such portals to its National Broadcasting Company. I remembered the quiet dignity of Savoy Hill far away in London Town and suffered a little pang of homesickness . . . but that was only because I am not enamoured of splendour. . . .

I felt the manuscript crackle in my hands while I shot up in the lift. I hoped the American listeners would like it; it was about the garden of an English poet. I had allowed myself a few minutes' grace, hoping for a chat with handsome Miss Cuthbert, and a moment in which to spread my pages carefully out on the desk so that no crackle should go through the air to "deafen the world."

Again I remembered Savoy Hill, and the familiar Talks Studio—the soft deep pile of the carpet, the ample desk covered with felt so that one's paper should not slip; the glass of water, in case of a dry throat: the warning red bulb so discreetly placed to warn without alarming; the shaded reading-lamp; the clear, brave moon-face of the clock on the wall by which the speaker may time his words to the fraction of a minute. . . . I wondered, too, if they would have a "soother" to receive me, like Colonel Brand in London, a gentleman with winning ways, whose pleasing task it is to calm the nerves of frightened broadcasters.

Being a stranger in a strange land, I thought I might peradventure be treated to such an one . . . and learn how it feels to be calmed.

I had often wondered. Colonel Brand never soothes me; I suppose he thinks I am a hardy annual and do not need him. But even hardy annuals grow more sprightly, and flower more gaily with a spot of cultivation. I had often secretly longed for his ministrations. . . . I hoped very much I might be met by an American soother. The lift-boy directed me down a long corridor, where a girl at a desk sharply bade me "Wait!"

They were not paying anything for the talk.

It appears to be the custom in America not to pay wireless artists, unless you can get some commercial body like—what shall we say—Squealer's Chewing Gum or some such industry, to pay for time "on the air" and engage you as their artist to amuse the public before their own name and wares are announced.

As I was not boosting any American goods, I was to fill the air for nothing. However, it was an experience, and I am a collector of experiences.

English artists grumble at the low fees paid by our B.B.C., and tell fantastic stories of incredibly high fees paid to broadcast artists in the States. I had looked forward to some such manna. . . .

The decent non-commercialism of our British system, which pays little but pays everyone, took on a new complexion in the fierce light of this disillusion.

Suddenly I perceived the time, and looked round panic-stricken for direction. My hour was upon me, and I had no idea where to go. The thick heavy thud of my heart warned me to keep calm. "I shall never keep my voice steady," I said to my scared nerves. "It will be all emotional and horrible. Keep still, you fool!"

Someone shot out of a door and called my name. I leaped forward. We hurried through this room and that until I found myself cast into a sort of arena, a place full of chairs and drums, music-stands, 'cellos, cornets, banjos, pianos and paraphernalia of all sorts; there were windows all round where people could look through and see the broadcasting. I was pushed towards a microphone.

"Where is the desk?" I gasped.

"What desk?" said an astonished Yankee.

The fatal red light was flickering. I snatched a metal music-stand, put my papers on, and glared round for the studio clock. There was no clock. I tore the watch off my wrist, hung it on the wretched little metal stand and got the signal to "begin." They say they can hear me breathe, in England, when I talk on the microphone; but

I should think they must have heard the very gallop of my terrified heart in America—it seemed to be making a noise like hoof-beats.

After a couple of pages I steadied into something like a stride, and tried to convey the colour, the fragrance, the charm of an English garden in the frail pigment of the voice. "After all," I thought, "among the millions one or two may like to hear of it." I visualised them —rapt, attentive—and began to talk to them alone, feeling again the intimate communion of spirit with spirit, in the ether.

I was getting nearly happy when, half-way through, the whole orchestra arrived for the next number and began noisily to take its seats. A cornet fell to the ground.

I looked round, snapping my eyes for peace—knowing that the gesture and the fury that impelled it had taken the velvet off the voice already and made what was becoming a warm, sympathetic instrument into a lifeless mechanism. You can drop degrees and degrees of warmth out of the voice with even a tiny interruption to the flow of thought.

The public (the British public, anyhow) and all musicians are alive to tone; when one is broadcasting a talk nothing but the whole heart and soul, the whole concentrated essence of them both, is good enough to offer for the compliment of their ears.

I was destroyed. I went on trying to catch the 'fluence again. A man dropped his music. I flashed round with a brusque "Hush!"

No one cared.

Then the announcer came out of his earphones and held up two fingers . . . to me! . . . who for eight long years have timed my talks to a second and prided myself on that same small nimbleness! I cast my last carefully-balanced, impetuous word into the great American Void, and gathered up the dropped sheets of manuscript; longing with a sick, hurting homesickness for the decent dignity of the London Studio.

A voice said: "You look all in." Miss Cuthbert stood

beside me. I flamed my distress, and she listened with
sympathy. In the flurry of finding someone who understood, I forgot my watch . . . companion of travel all
round the world! . . . and when I went back to look for
it, it had gone.

"That's all right," I said bitterly. "It's the perfect
climax. You cast me like Daniel to the lions, you don't
pay me for my work, and then you pinch my watch!"

So they hunted about, and next day it came back.

I went out to Park Avenue, clammy with exhaustion,
and on the way met Hetty. "Oh, dear!" I said. "Oh
dear, what I would give for a glass of good wine now!
What a country!"

She looked at me doubtfully.

"I heard of a place on ——— Street round the corner
towards Fifth: I don't know what it is like; shall we dine
there and risk it?"

It was a very nice restaurant indeed;—and never in
my life have I been more thankful to sit in a cool room
with a dear friend and hear the tinkle of ice in a highball.
It was all we could get . . . iced whisky and soda . . .
but it was good whisky. I think that was the only place
and time when I ever liked the taste of it.

It was the next day that my watch was found; my nice
old shabby excellent watch! And I was amused to receive
(instead of my big English wireless-fan mail) two or three
letters only! But one was from Mr. Salbach of California
. . . he had heard me and liked the talk all those three
thousand miles away; his name was familiar and I treasured
his compliments.

With characteristic Western generosity he sent me
some of his beautiful irises to England; and here they
have bloomed in their splendid colours and form. The
Americans grow irises better than we do; they have quite
beaten us, and as to peonies, we have hardly begun to
appreciate what awaits the garden in that lovely genus;
they have us well beaten there, too! James Kelway of
Langport, Somerset, has specialised in the race and grows

them in a wonderful peony valley in the West; several times in America I wished that I could conjure him beside me to look at flowers in the States.

Next day we set forth to Yonkers, where I saw a garden of enormous wealth overlooking the Hudson, with a fine Japanese dogwood (Cornus Kousa) as the chief memory to take away other than Hetty's deep depression at "all this pretentious waste." It upset her very much; I have seen a lot of that kind of gardening all over the world and am pretty well hardened;—I can generally let it slip over my armour without penetrating; but poor Hetty was pierced.

I told her long tales of dear and real American gardeners all the way home, and she got better.

It was very nice, next day, on the way to Scarborough to see that Mr. Rockefeller shares his trails with people and his free-flowing Indian spring . . . it was nice to see the bridle trails of Sleepy Hollow and then on through Tarrytown by the Tappen Zee to Mrs. Frank Vanderlip's beautiful garden and Mrs. Hubert Rogers's great herbaceous borders at Scarborough, N.J., overlooking the Hudson River.

"Li Sun Yen" followed us round in our progress, full of wise glances and friendly remarks; but when we found some dead song-sparrows in their nest in the wild garden he stopped wagging his handsome tail and became entirely mournful; a most sympathetic fellow. I enjoyed Mrs. Rogers's garden of solace . . . it is an old-fashioned colour garden where Mrs. Rogers, slim and keen, works herself, and the mark of her loving care is plain to see in happy growth.

A green garden of lawns and shrubs is that of Mrs. Sidney Z. Mitchell at Glen Cove, Long Island; the house has an austere charm, a Queen Anne-Georgian-Lutyensish house set down among rhododendrons, azaleas, Philadelphus, special lilacs, special dogwoods, pachysandra, box, cedrus virginica, viburnums and many another goodly growth.

The sunk garden is nicely placed, and has had time,

being nine years old, to acquire the mellow look of an established feature. The wild "surround" is full of kalmia latifolia, (the "mountain laurel,") of dogwood, maples and American elms; around the sunk garden is a herbaceous border in which are planted out large well-grown specimens of fuchsia, lantana, hibiscus (shades of Mr. Evans's lovely variety at Santa Monica!) and at the lantana I had to linger, remembering the infuriated way Mr. Walter Webber spoke of his rampamt hedge of it in Johannesburg . . . it grew too fast and wide there for his taste.

Mr. and Mrs. Mitchell love birds, and take a devoted personal interest in the garden. He told me to try magnolia parviflora, with its gardenia size, texture and colour of petal, and the scarlet centre with a high, green point, because it grows in the Arctic Circle; a cold plant that likes some shade (but I am not sure if it would like our damp muggy winters!). We studied together his beautiful Kousa dogwood fruits. "They will be orange and red in due season," he said. "It is a very valuable introduction, blooming full thirty days later, and so prolonging our dogwood season. The petals are more pointed, but it is a real and lovely white dogwood." He had a double one; and liked it. But I wish he didn't. The white rose "Purity" round the sunk garden is child of the popular "silver moon," and is a much hardier frost-resistant form. Their estate is a model homestead, with its herd of pedigree Guernsey cows; beautiful dairy houses; fig, peach, grape and orchid houses, not to mention the one in which I found Cape jasmine and gloxinias, and a spider lily.

I was longing to see Mrs. Tom Robins's sea-garden in Connecticut, but I kept shirking the awfulness of getting there! And one day Susan Smit came to New York and we met again. . . .

About nine years before, in Kent, when I was in all the turmoil of salving my "ruin,"—up to the neck in work rescuing the old house from dropping back into the soil from which it grew six hundred years before . . . when everyone thought I was mad, and I was not quite sure about it myself, being much over-weighted with the task I had taken on . . . an unknown American woman sought me out because she was a friend of Hetty's. I was lodging in the village and unable to offer her any hospitality,— beyond that of trotting down a hill and up a hill into a shaggy lane and showing her the shell of a house! . . . the noble beams and generous roof were there but nothing more . . . windows and doors were gone; nettles and briars and thistles were all the garden. It was about to pass into the tale of forgotten things when I found it . . . and loved it with a passion and cast the whole of my strength into saving it.*

But I found most people thought I was plain mad; and it was with some misgiving that I took the pleasant American woman up the nightingale-haunted lane.

When she saw the rich colours of the old roof she was so touched and exalted that I knew I had found for ever and ever a friend as mad as myself. . . . She was capable of strange worships; and so I loved her.

Her brown eyes and sensitive giving heart passed along the life road, and for years we had only a memory; she of a roof, I of her.

But we met now in New York for a day . . . and she nearly made me like the place because it held her for a few hours. Meeting Susan Smit is to me like reading Keats. . . .

Our little time together refreshed me so much that I summoned all my forces to go to my friend's sea-garden; and on the way there a letter transported me to South Africa.

The elevator shot down eleven stories to the street level in the twinkling of an eye. The amiable breeze it made was grateful enough, but nothing has really ever reconciled me to a time-saving device which leaves my entrails somewhere on the roof. I stepped out of the hot cave, sick with yearning for my lost stomach, to meet the oven-blast of summer in New York.

* See *The Story of my Ruin.*

"There is some mail for you, and I had better call a taxi. It is too hot to walk," the hall-porter said.

"No. I must go in the subway. I have no time for a taxi."

The burning pavement; the stink of exhaust gases; the noise of hurrying people—the crowding, crushing people, sticky with perspiration, suffering, hurrying, nervous people —the clammy graveyard smells of the subway; a nickel slamming each wet uncomfortable body through the turn-stile, and then the intolerable pressure of bodies standing, packed close in the train—the hateful closeness of flesh about one's flesh. At last Central Station and the express to catch; not much time to spare either! I climbed into the clanging monster. . . .

Then I had time to examine the mail. A letter from England, little England isled in a northern sea: "Roses and peonies are out everywhere, and the lanes are sweet with honeysuckle; come home before they fade. We are tired of Cannes and this winter we are going to South Africa."

Going to the Cape for the winter, were they? Lucky dogs!

The train chugged on, virtuously toiling through miles of labour-saving homes, dear to the hearts of the emotional materialists of New York; the crowded Pullman whizzed its electric fans, the people wilted patiently. And I abandoned myself to dreams of the journey my friends would take, straight out of the damp and fog of an English winter to the merry-go-round of Madeira, and then the long lazy picnic days to the Cape, down what is the fair-weather journey of the world; dancing on deck in the light of tropic moons; garden-party clothes instead of tweeds; romance never far away in that illusion of eternity which ship life brings to the wariest—of time forgotten and glamour regained. Voyaging under the Southern Cross a sea-change tumbles its fairy breakers upon the hardest heart, on old and young alike.

I envied them excessively; from the moment when they

turned from the mists of the northern winter to the day when they would go swinging into the shadow of Table Mountain and meet the leisurely easy welcome of Cape Town. The very sun is different from any other in that most different land on earth. It has a crackling liveliness along the dry pure air, a tonic bracing feeling on the skin. And the stars hang close at night, close and clear as lamps in the velvet silence.

No one hurries in that country; the *tempo* is retarded so that every moment of life yields its full flavour; and Africa is full of rhythm. New York has *tempo* but no rhythm.

They will have the peculiar blue of the hills and the sudden splendour of the flowers on the veld after rain; out of the train windows they will have the Karoo wide and golden, sharpset with blue kopjes; the tumbling waters on the uplands of Sabie; the opalescent beauty of the cyanide dumps at Johannesburg in the mysterious lights of dawn. They will lean out to touch the cool sprays of Cape heather hanging from the close rocky banks in the Montague Pass on the way to Knysna; they will sniff the incomparable exciting fragrance of kat-doorn, borne across the flats of prickly pear at Addo; they will pass through vineyards, almond groves, peach and nectarine orchards.

Perhaps they will take a car . . . and learn the motorists' Paradise of a scanty population and beautiful roads; factors which make the Union of South Africa one of the few countries where it is still a pleasure to drive! They will dally along the sunny roads, past beautiful old Dutch homesteads, and modern houses of harmonious design richly influenced by the lines of the original architecture of pioneer-settlers.

They will sleep in white rondarvels thatched with silver river-reeds, and take (if they want to leave the world behind) a trek into the blue, into gold and diamond country, behind slow-moving oxen, shooting for the pot as they go, swinging down red dongas and across treeless plains and savage mountain passes—up and away to the game country which

Jock of the Bush-veld roamed.   They can learn the simple
hard life, lave in deep wells of solitude, know the rich peace
of immense silences . . . or they can be merry in the more
usual manner at country clubs and hotels—swimming and
surf-bathing, riding, dancing, tennis, yachting.   There is
no compulsion to live close to Nature!

"Going to South Africa for the winter," are they?
Lucky dogs!

With my mind still dwelling in South Africa I found
myself at Saddle Rock; and had to tell them about the
letter at once, because we had sojourned there together ten
years before.

Saddle Rock is well-named;—Mr. Robins loves the
sea and cannot get close enough to it, so he has built
his country house on a rock thrust out into the waves.
Mrs. Robins loves a garden, and if ever a woman's courage
and love were tested, hers is!   The place on which she set
forth to grow plants and trees, make hedges and walks,
is swept on *both* sides; there is only a hundred feet of rock
between the waters . . . it is beaten by south-west gales on
one side and on the other by the north-east straight
down the Sound from the Atlantic.

Sea-thrift was thrown fifty feet from east to west,
uprooted and thrown; it stayed there for three or four days
and then she planted it again . . . and it grew!   She started
with six hundred dollars' worth of evergreens, and only
one is left . . . an Austrian pine which was planted too
deep and so it was able to stand the gales;—and lived.

I listened to the story as she walked along her garden
with me . . . perceiving at last in the brilliant illumination which a garden sheds on every heart the greatness
of hers.   Winifred Robins is of pioneer stock;—and her
garden tells it. . . .   I wonder if she would have sickened,
grown neurotic and testy on rich valley land?   Maybe
this brave nature needed something rough to temper its
steel . . . I believe attrition is wholesome. . . .

There were casualties of the spray all round—a dying
locust tree, dead laurel-leaf willows, silver moon and grape-

THE SEA GARDEN IS ON A ROCK THRUST OUT INTO THE WAVES

THE BROWN SAIL IS THEIR SHADE-PLACE IN THE FLAGGED GARDEN

vine. But she has made a garden! . . . out of her great courage. In the ten years that she has struggled there since the days I met them on the Sea-that-never-was she has learned a score of lessons, priceless to any who want to grow flowers under the same conditions.

She had said to me, long ago, on that englamoured ship: "There is no knowledge; no one can help me." . . .

But I wish she would keep a record, because *now*, out of the years and out of the toil . . . out of disappointment and rebuffs . . . out of the measure of the valour of her heart she has learned a great deal that would shorten the way for others.

"If I started again," she said, "I would make my garden of rosa rugosa, privet, tamarisk, beach-pea, sea-thrift, dusty miller and beach-grass."

Rosa rugosa certainly grows well! It made winding walks for her with its dark, deep green leaves and wide, white flowers,—and tamarisk was out in pink sprays against the stone wall of ochre and grey; it was rose pink against a misty blue-grey sea under a pale blue sky; the colour of her garden picture was exquisite.

In everything she does she shows that sense of colour, and expounds the precious craft and wisdom of the famed "New England housewife." I never cease to admire a woman who is a good housewife. . . . I feel, like the old man did about the pansies at San Simeon, "the mettle that is in them!"

I had the wrong hat! I saw Hetty looking at me with the warlight in her eyes and felt virtuous because the dress I had was dark enough, heaven knew! It was navy blue and much too hot a colour for my taste;—but then I saw I was really all wrong . . . the others had black hats! —Winifred's was a shady black straw of beautiful line against her proud, fine face; Hetty had a nutty black affair with a jewel in it; the daughter-in-law of the house wore a black beret, and they all had light dresses . . . even Hetty wore grey, and here was I in a lime-coloured Tappé hat and a dark ensemble. I tried to parry the shaft of Hetty's eye.

R

"Do you like period rooms?" I asked.

"Do you mean rooms that look as if you had no ancestors?" she snapped, and I realised this was not my good day. I wish there were sumptuary laws, or we all wore uniforms.

After lunch we went out into the blinding light of the sea,—the clam-smelling sea, so delicious and so clean,— to see the picking garden. There it was! Two dozen zinnias, two dozen calendulas, two dozen ageratums, one dozen salpiglossis, one dozen cosmos, two lemon verbena and two sweet geraniums,—in a sheltered precious place. . . !

"You've no idea what a lot of decoration I get from them," she said.

We drove over to see Jessica Cosgrave's garden of vistas (she is Mrs. O'Hara in private life) and I learned from her the excellent beauty of Oriental poppies against the sea. . . .

"If it is true, as many people hold, that the value of a life is to be judged by its moments of ecstasy, then surely we should all be gardeners," she writes. "I know of no other occupation, to which almost anyone can aspire, which offers so many of these higher moments." . . . She gave me her book *Gardens,*—and in it I find constant happy contact with a virile and charming woman.

There was a morning when I breakfasted alone on Mrs. Robins's porch and tasted the essential courage of her again, —and more strongly for being alone. The grass was dewy under the sea-mist of early morning and among it the bosses of pale rose sea-thrift shone in an exquisite pastel harmony. The airs swung by, sea airs smelling of ozone which is what clams taste like;—a song-sparrow sat on a rose bush and shouted his sweet sharp song at me; a bell-buoy clanged away at sea.

The marble baby held out his arms, asking to be lifted up;—the brown sail which is their shade-place in the flagged garden cleaves its sharp and moving line against the sky. . . . Mr. Robins is an inventor and a sea lover,—it was

natural for him to make a shade in just some such way!
The "dusty miller" was coming now into soft yellow
bloom, a misty indeterminate yellow among the grey leaf;
it makes her a carpet, and has spread a coloured rug on
her arid wind-whipped sand . . . tamarisks in pink feather,
irises, rambler roses, ivy, virginian creeper . . . a stone arch
here, a wrought-iron gate there . . . the great-heart has
made a garden and never known defeat.

Of all the gardens I saw in America, none stirred me
to a keener pride or left me so near to tears.

fiery stem and break at last in high heaven into a shower of
falling streamers.

"Is there anywhere you particularly want to go?" said
Sally.

"Only to Hartford, if it is convenient," I answered.
"Mrs. Francis King lives there: she has a new garden and
she asked me to come.   I would like very much to see her
again."

So we went to Hartford—and it was the wrong one.
We went to Hartford, Connecticut, and it should have
been the Hartford in New York State!   So I did not see the
nice garden-writer again, or her garden, for which I am sorry.
But we did see, near our wrong Hartford, the largest
American elm in the whole of the States!   It is ninety-
seven feet high, has a circumference of twenty-eight feet
and a diameter spread of 147 feet.   It is two hundred
and fifty years old.   A noble and gigantic tree.

The New England houses and farmhouses have much
charm.   There were old-fashioned roses on the front lawns
of the houses of wood and stone.   Tall mulleins grow wild
by the roadside in their silver-velvet with golden spikes.

It was a lovely day of sun and cloud.   There were wild
grapes growing everywhere and Sally said they made good
jelly!

"Since prohibition a great many more grape-vines of all
sorts are grown," she said thoughtfully.

We came to "Deep River" and I remembered Paul
Robeson singing of the Mississippi.   This Connecticut
River was lovely indeed—but I had seen the other, and
my passion for rivers was assuaged . . . there were lawns
and gardens everywhere—spacious, emerald spaces set with
comely white houses, and round them grew mock-orange,
moon-daisies, elder, Kalmia, peonies, roses, irises . . .
guelder roses . . . all sparkling out of the rich valley land.
There were sheets of wild iris like Sibirica in swampy
reaches of fern.

Then we passed a place called "Cromwell," but it did
not warn us!   We came next to a seemly village of wide

streets planted with avenues of the graceful elms, and under their shade spread fair green lawns with the pretty low white wooden houses facing them.

"I begin to think this is a typical old New England village," I began when we saw the name Saybrook. The same thought seized us both—and the next moment we were passing the "Saye and Sele Inn."

Sally stopped the car, and we wandered about fascinated, transported in memory to the long ago day when we stood in a moated castle and heard the lord of it tell us about his ancestor who went to "the Americas" with Lord Brook—and made a town there. . . .

The Saye and Sele Inn knitted up for us a skein of memories; we went in to lunch and were made right welcome by Master and Mistress Hubble, who fed us on clam chowder and lobster and cutlets and lemon pie with wonderful sweet water out of a deep well, at a red table, where we sat on little red settles and toasted our good host in his crystal well-water, not forgetting the name of Lord Saye and Sele (and wishing his lilies well, on the moat by his castle wall).

The Saye and Sele Inn is a charming old place two hundred and five years old, with wide, open fireplaces, and flooring of broad oak planks; it has green shutters, and neat lawns set with lilacs and elms. George Washington was there in 1775; John Hancock in 1776; John Quincey Adams in 1796; Benjamin Franklin in 1790; and Charles Dickens in 1868. We heard the feet of the dead Great pass across those broad oak boards as we sat in the sun by the little red table and talked of the linked past.

There were miles of rambler roses by the roads trained on low arches after we left Saybrook to go on toward New London. It was still amazing to me, even after all I had seen of their land and ways to realise how big this people can think—and can do. I like bigness.

And then came the munch houses. They may be a convenience for motorists, but no one can say the signs are attractive! All along the Boston Post Road, "Jane's Waffle Shoppe"—"Aunt Bett's Pantry"—"Captain Jimmy's

Jamestown, Virginia.   English yew, cryptomeria, sequoia
gigantea, eighty years old apple trees and weeping birch . . .
all fine and pleasant things, but I think the loveliest was the
beautiful figure of her daughter playing tennis,—perfect
in grace and proportion,—with the supple movement of a
young wild animal.

As we journeyed on the catalpa trees now began to take
the place of pawlonias and I could not be sure which were
the most beautiful;—at Wellesley I saw the first out-
and-out topiary garden yet—at what is generally called the
Hunnewell place.   But I saw another garden owned by
a Mr. and Mrs. Henry Hunnewell which had to me a
far warmer appeal.   A garden of lawns, shrubs, great trees
and a fine rose-garden on land that rolls away up and down
looking on to splendid views.   There were many pretty
gardens in Wellesley where the wonderful paper birches
grow to which Mrs. Joe Snell took me; she lectures on
trees for the Garden Club there.

At Concord I found myself touching history of a more
sympathetic nature than "minute" men;—for one thing
here was the home of the Concord grape which marked the
beginning of the table grape commerce in America; a very
far-reaching fruit!   The original vine is protected, and on
a carved board beside it is written the following, autographed
by Ephraim Bull:

"I looked about to see what I could find among our wildlings. The
next thing to do was to find the best and earliest grape for seed; and this
I found in an accidental seedling at the foot of the hill. The crop was
abundant and ripe in August, and of very good quality for a wild grape.
I sowed the seed in the Autumn of 1843. Among them the Concord was
the only one worth saving."

It took him three grape generations to get his Concord;
it "became in the garden in September, 1849, the Concord
grape."   Mrs. Russell Robb believes that the grape was
actually found on her hillside, where she has a charming
informal garden full of beauty and of feeling.

There was more than a famous grape at Concord.   It is
a place of many memories of men of letters.   Thoreau,

Waldo Emerson, Nathaniel Hawthorne and L. M. Alcott wrote in this peaceful New England village where two rivers meet to make the beautiful little Concord River, beloved of Thoreau the man who "indulged in fine renouncements"; a creature moulded and marked by Nature more than most of her lovers,—and therefore to them always of her essential Wonder.

The fires of Emerson and Hawthorne shine bright in Concord . . . I made my bow of the heart to them; and then paid my respects to the home of Louisa M. Alcott, the author of *Little Women*. For here was a little talent worked to the uttermost; a small orchard tilled to a full harvest by a very brave woman.

Boston is a nice city. It has a great dignity and its people have pleasant manners; one has the sense of *decency* there—and its women do not suffer so much from the national female disease of verbal diarrhœa.

The very next day after we arrived I went off to see the Arnold Arboretum, a garden in the front rank of the great collections of living trees and shrubs in the world.

It began with an endowment upon his death "for the promotion of agricultural or horticultural improvements" by one James Arnold. Professor Sargent was made Director of the Arboretum which was the form it was decided the bequest should benefit, the President and Fellows of Harvard College became the trustees of the Fund. Then began the great work of a tree lover's life. For all time the name of Charles Sprague Sargent will be associated with the Arnold Arboretum,—the famous Boston "tree-garden"; for he spilled every drop of life force, of enthusiasm, obstinacy, vision and will into its creation. He organised the collection of woody plants from all parts of the Northern Hemisphere. He selected assistants, officers and agents far and wide to collect seeds and specimens and transmit information about trees and shrubs in their native habitats.

His most successful plant collector was E. H. Wilson, who made four trips to Asia, visiting China and the far inland mountains in the neighbourhood of the Thibetan plateau—Japan, Korea, Formosa—also Australasia, Indo-Malaysia and Africa from the Equator South. He was Assistant Director of the Arboretum under Professor Sargent, and upon his death became the "Keeper of the Arboretum," a new title, with a careful pleasant sound to it.

I had heard tales far and wide of the lilacs at Boston,— and they were on the list of my important "dates"—but I missed them . . . I was too late to see them in bloom now; and I lamented that fact when I wrote to Dr. Wilson asking if I might see him as well as the famous garden.

He was reproachful. . . .

"You must come again, Mrs. Cran; you miss more than you know when you miss the bloom-time here."

I looked at him with keen interest. A man not tall nor short—with brave, brown eyes, bronzed—vital—an earth-man. I liked him.

We set off on one of the happy memorable mornings of life. He was like a boy among his playthings, and wherever we went he was pulling up, and pruning—with those ever-watchful gardener hands of his—a plantsman's hands——

"Who have you seen and where have you been?" he asked.

I reeled off a list of names and places, commenting here and there on what I had felt.

He was pleased. His brown eyes smiled. "Well, you have paid us the compliment of taking some trouble, anyway! You won't go away judging all America by New York, Boston and Philadelphia."

He went over many of the people I had seen, repeating names. Of Mr. Fairchild and Mr. Swingle, he said: "They did the date and the fig." He asked me what I thought of Luther Burbank and I told him about that simple grave at Santa Rosa. . . . "He was very good to his mother," said Wilson. He said of John Wister: "He is a gentleman";—of Ben Morrison: "He is a good lad."

Now and again he hit shrewd and hard.   He had no use
for humbugs.

"The best rule is still to plant thick and thin quick,"
he laughed.   "Now look at this grove of virgin hemlocks
and tell me if it isn't a possession worth having?"

He was a tree-lover.   There was no mistake about that.
We went to and fro and round and about, while I garnered
spots of wisdom.

"Hopa crab-apple (species and first hybrids) is better
than Pyrus Eleyi."

"President Lincoln is the best lilac,—it is a wedgwood
blue," he said, lingering by the noble syringas.

"I used to doubt the Garden Club movement, but I have
seen those who came to swank and stayed to pray.   It is
all right," he remarked later.

And then again:—"*Look* at this Chinese larch!"

We had a long look at the blue pickerel weed in the water
(pontederia cordata) and rosa Virginiana out in a tide of
pink bloom. . . .

Then suddenly . . .

"Have you a Siamese cat still, and how is your daughter?"
asked Dr. Wilson.

I faltered.

"I like your books," he said.   "A garden is not all
botany."

"If my books please you, I have won my crown," I said
in the purest sincerity.

The dark brave shade of hemlocks towered over him.
"Stand still," I begged, and I took his picture.

"Now about this daughter business?" I said.   "She is
well and I miss her sore.   Why did you ask?"

"I thought you would be missing her!   I miss my
daughter.   She is married and happy, but I miss her.   I
never had to tell her how to spell a word.   She was a wonderful Secretary."

Presently we were in a small, sunny garden under
towers of "Regal" lilies.

His lilies!   They stood up high,—the most glorious

planting of them I suppose I shall ever see. They shone satin fine in the sun,—pouring out fragrance,—their petals stroked with rose. . . .

His lilies. He brought them from the border-lands of Tibet, to be grown in their millions now from the Atlantic to the Pacific, around the world.

"This is their sixth year," he said. "How long will that bed continue? Last year there were nine hundred and thirty-seven blooms." . . .

And then I told him of the dove-tree trail, and how I had promised to find out the Davidia for Mrs. Palmer. We went to look at his Davidia and I took his picture under *that*, too,—for I would have my friend in distant Vancouver Island to know that I kept my promise and not only traced the tree, but found the man who introduced it as well.

He told me to go to Cape Cod and notice the character of the country . . . to Hyannis and Province, if possible . . .

I did not go. Some day I must because he told me to; poor man. Three months later he had passed on. . . .

Yet I wonder why I call him "poor"? He rendered great service to the world and was widely loved; he was not called upon to suffer the agony of loneliness which so often waits upon old age, for his wife was with him when the accident happened which took them both, still active in middle-age, into the larger life which men call death.

It is we who are left who are poorer in the whole world by the loss of his inexhaustible energy, driving power of sympathy, force of understanding and extraordinary knowledge.

Sally and I went to see the little Town Gardens of Beacon Hill. They were truly delightful. I gathered that most of the owners were architects or artists, so I suppose they ought to be good! Mrs. Bourne-Wheeler gave us lunch in her pretty, formal "out-door-room," where I found myself more excited by Harry than anything, though the wall fountain she modelled had its claim, and the staddle-stones from our own English Cotswolds, and the bull's trough which is now a sink garden! . . . There was a

A Wall Fountain in one of the little Town Gardens of
Beacon Hill, Boston

sweet bay from Belgium; an ivy that had wintered; native white rhododendron, snowberries, zinnias, sweet williams, lilium auratum in decorative majesty; and a topping dove cote made out of a butter barrel and champagne straws for thatch . . . but all these were nothing beside Harry. He is an Australian.

Very jealous and upset at our merrymaking, he screamed and clambered in and out of his cage, and yelled for attention and gossiped . . . his yellow crest spread high over his head, his white body gleaming like satin, his wicked beak ever open to utter noise.

At last Harry was smacked,—and then hosed; and that calmed his transports.

Mr. Leslie Hastings built his town garden during a perid of convalescence; he began with no scheme on a sloping ground. One year he made the terrace, the arch, balcony and pillars; and then, when troubled by the way his soil packed and sooted and soured he saw an English Town Garden book; and found out how to build up a small "dry-wall" surround, on the top of which he now grows his flowers sucessfully because in that way the soil can aerate. In August his leaves are black with soot from the oil furnaces,—all sticky and horrible. Yet they grow phlox and red-berried bug-bane, centaurea, hepatica, lilies, climbers, pachysandra ground cover, arabis, irises, sedums, bleeding heart, may-apples, ferns, trilliums, ladies' slippers and other pink and yellow heuchera and in spring a fine show of the bulbs, all in that tree-shaded town garden.

"It is not finished yet," he said mournfully.

"How dreadful if it were!" said his wife, wisely.

They are neighbourly people, there on the hill! They encourage window-boxes and "stage" competitions (or as we would say, organise them), and teach children the fun of growing flowers.

There was beautiful iron scroll work in many of those Beacon Hill courts; a shapely green garden was that designed by Miss Eleanor Raymond, with not too much statuary . . . I wondered how the privet edging to the

I like that word "gave." The poor Indian.

In Mr. Crane's lilac garden are 125 varieties and 1,000 plants. I wished I could see them in bloom;—but that collection still has to rank below my friend Mr. Roland Taylor's lilac collection in Philadelphia, where at Treweryn he has 175 varieties, many of them very rarely found in gardens.

A home to remember was that of Mrs. Keith Merrill who sent us forth with masses of sweet mock orange saying: "We aim never to have anyone leave Avalon without a flower."

In Judge Moore's garden I saw the "Lambertiana" roses so exceeding like my late friend Mr. Pemberton's race of hybrid-musk roses that I longed very much to meet the originator of the "Lambertianas" and ask how his were bred.

At the garden of the Misses Hunt of Beverley (Mass.) I saw another of Mrs. Foote's rose gardens. It was she who designed and carried out the new one for Mrs. Curtis James at Newport. This was in the Italian manner and I gathered that Mrs. Foote must be a rosarian as well as a maker of plans. I wished we had met.

"My garden," said Mrs. William Coolidge (with a basket of the lovely roses in her hand), "is put down to Dr. Van Fleet because no bugs will eat it."

I made a note to find out why this lovely climber is not "put down" more in England since its habits sounded so useful. When we went to Crowhurst, lovely as the garden was, we were overtaken by familiar names and sat talking to Mr. and Mrs. Whitehouse under their fine old oak carving from Stow-in-the-Wold about Brede and Brickwall and the Frewen family of my own far-off Wealden land. And then there were the gardens of the Chimneys and Mrs. McGinley's, the gay, tender, laughing soul, and more gardens, and more lovely . . . each with its dominant note of personality . . . each telling its tale. I was snowed-under: exhausted with gardens: I could feel no longer . . . hardly see them when I looked. . . .

*   *   *   *   *

"Blanche is waiting to take care of us," said Sally comfortably.

Nice Blanche . . . how I longed for her clever, quick sympathy: she was unhappy, she wrote, because Ginger had eaten the canary—and we hated to think how she must feel with the yellow fur walking about the house purring, with yellow feathers inside him . . . and never another high, sweet song from the little yellow throat. . . .

"Tell me more about Blue Hill," I begged, sitting back in the car; and Sally told me more of her wood, where there was no interference by axe or saw, and of her house built without a plan.

We were travelling New England through lovely little villages of white houses with green shutters, passing under avenues of the incomparable American elms; and along the hedges the wild vine changes the contour of the roadside, throwing massive piles of greenery hither and yon,—rough modelling,—effective and vigorous.

Sally's voice drifted from her wood to tales about Christopher Wren churches and Bullfinch staircases.

A girl sat on a low stone wall in the sun; it shone through her pink dress making her sweet drawn as a flower . . . Catalpas in bloom, and huge wayside trees of lilac; the ditches full of tawny lilies; growth everywhere abundant, rich, luxurious; some of the white houses had vines *painted* on them! The landscape was lovely—we were bowling along through a natural colour scheme of deep pink clover and purple vetch among goldy-brown grasses . . . and lamb-kill—the little kalmia.

"That is Blue Hill," said Sally, pointing to a small blue mound on the skyline.

CHAPTER XIX

STEVE'S MEADOW

I HAVE flowery indigestion and have turned to the wild woods. I am englutted of made pleasaunces. I feel like the coloured chauffeur-gardener after he had been taken to the New York flower show to spur him to further efforts in the home backyard—"a bit discouraged!"

I am drowned in magnificence. What limitless money, fine taste and great natural resources can do now I know, and I am utterly swamped. . . . Never again let anyone say there are "no gardens in America"!

In the beautiful sea and woodland country of Maine my stunned senses are slowly regaining their poise. I am recovering in a garden where nobody walks but me. Abandoned to the seasons, deserted by the absentee landlord, it is a sanctuary to which I escape every morning before the dew is up and before breakfast makes gay coffee-smells upon the ledge, to wander among the spontaneous beauty of nature's plantings and review in that grand simplicity the marvels of this America.

The empty house with its pretty dormers, grey shingled roof and wired stoep, stands wistfully among the unpruned maiden blush roses which are thrusting up, and blooming even through the floor-boards. Across what might once have been a lawn some fine red peonies are in full bloom, the only garden flowers left; a thicket of blue-tufted vetch is creeping toward even these to engulf them in the wild; the grass is dewy with the misty bloom of blueberries so stout and fine that they look like small grapes in their heavy bunches; the berries are of every

276

colour and size among tiny green glossy leaves on slender
nodding stalks . . . they are like gems, like many-coloured
pearls, from purple to pale eau-de-nil. After the blueberries will come cranberries, they are already confidently
nodding, elliptically rounded, among the grasses.

There are wild harebells; and scarlet pimpernel; and
maianthemum canadense—a most delightful little flower
—growing like lily-of-the-valley; it has a delicious scent
and the tall spikes are about the size of muscari. In the
white cups are long lady pistils, peering slinkily round for
admirers and also a huddle of staminate youths bunched all
on one side, retreating from the virgin's advances. Scared.

American flowers are so nervous. That Kalmia! The
day I saw it first was after Sally and I had lunched at the
White Turkey in a loggia in a garden where there were
hollyhocks painted on the Quimper ware, and a red-
winged blackbird sat close to us on a fence. We had
iced tea with mint and lemon in it, and fried chicken and
sweet potatoes and asparagus. There were old-fashioned
cabbage-roses on the table in a bulbous glass bottle; and
hot corn bread and white curds of cottage cheese in a
lordly bowl, with fresh cool lettuce leaves . . . and strawberry ice-cream and home-made butter . . . my weight
went up frightfully in New England. There were peonies
everywhere, there was one I longed to take home to Kent,
a semi-single of darkest richest red with a fat golden heart.

It was after that pleasant lunch that we got to the Berk-
shire Hills beyond Canaan . . . and saw Kalmia growing
wild . . . that petted shrub of our English grandee gardens. . . .   They call it "mountain laurel" in New England; the gophered buds, so tidy and prim, are very New
English; in the open cups of dimity china a queer phenomenon is toward . . . ten chaste impassioned stamens
hiding their heads, each in a secret closet, each gentlemanly
head turned away from the tall rosy lady pistil, and only
ten slender backs for her to look upon. At a touch, however, the anther flies out and flees temptation, tossing his
treasure of pollen—his manhood—away from him. . . .

Queer chaste Kalmia! I never tired of touching those anthers tucked away in little pouches of the corolla, and seeing them shoot out in a panic and lose their heads; standing at last upright headless gallants before their startled queen.

The maianthemums remind me of Kalmias as I walk among Steve's flowers between the house and the sea; his wharf shoots out over the rocks a long way into the sea, a motor-boat, a row-boat and two canoes bob on the shining water looking up to the little grey house—forlorn without its master.

I walk through the fragrant sweet fern, and wintergreen which smells like rather nice tooth-powder;—there are tall huckleberries, wild roses, crab-apples, laden thick with fruit by the brim of the sea,—clintonias with their navy-blue marbles in shady places, scarlet bunchberries, pretty wild orchids, "ladies' tresses," self-heal and moon-daisies —and here is a large colony of hawk-weed.

I suppose a lot of people would call Steve's garden a plaguehouse of weeds and "B.Y." would find no end of his pests there. But to me it is a place where one need not fear to be alone with oneself. In a loud-speaker age this sunny meadow unriven by spade, uncoerced by scythe or shears, offers the physical gain of silence. To-day meditation is nearly a lost art.

For the sick, and the old, it is vital. Multitudes with ragged nerves, on the edge of a nervous breakdown, are forgetting this wonderful medicine. There is healing in the hush that soothes and rests the heart. Need of it was never greater, as an antidote to the noisy lives most of us live.

It is perhaps the unconscious reason why so many and ever so many more turn to gardening. . . .

That hawkweed! It makes me remember. . . . I sit down on the top step of Steve's stoep, and look out to the shining sea; where there is the white sail of a cat-boat. . . . Frederick de Wolf Pingree coming to breakfast perhaps? . . . I fall into a dream of my own garden in Kent

... I am reminded of the way people who come to see it are hypnotised by long names!

There are two plants in my garden which bring into it a great deal of interest; pleasant, quiet, personal interest, because the plants are in no wise showy or exciting things, and because the people who come visiting my garden, and are pleased with these two pretty subjects, always dismiss them as "weeds" when I call them by their country names and make respectful notes about them when I call them by their grand names. Which is really rather funny.

They are both good-hearted happy groundlings, truly not far removed from the wild, very well able to shift for themselves when established in any place; and of the two I far prefer linaria alpina. It is a small thing, with glabrous lanceolate leaves of a tender milky green, growing about six inches high and with a preference for rooting among stones. It gaily finds out an ash path, or a crazy path, and makes there its appealing mats, sowing itself industriously year after year, in the nooks of its preference. In early summer it starts sending out its enchanting flowers which, borne in short racemes, soon cover the ground with myriads of tiny "bunny-mouths" or snapdragon-shaped flowers, each with a long sharp spur as long as the corolla, delicately curved, each splashed with orange upon the purple lip.

A description of this sort is anatomically accurate, but I prefer the impressionistic form which would tell me of "linaria alpina," that it makes soft grey carpets among the stones and covers itself the summer through with a haze of amethyst, through which come definite spots of orange!

The earlier flowers ripen their small black seeds very unobtrusively in green ruffed capsules under the glowing purple of succeeding flowers; the plant does not fall away into a dishevelled abandon, making a great fuss about the exhaustion of seed-bearing as so many do.

The common name of my pretty friend is alpine toad-flax, and it has a delightful sister in "mother of millions," the trailing ivy-leafed toad-flax, linaria cymbalaria, which loves a damp shady place and makes an admirable basket plant for poorly-lighted places. Its tiny flowers are lilac with a yellowish throat; they lack the rich softness of the other variety, having a different value in the garden economy, and a very special one, with a clearly defined sphere of usefulness.

The other plant which I find interests people a good deal is hieracium aurantiacum: it grows in close green mats of herbage sending up slender hairy stems upon which are carried cymes of brilliant orange-red flowers. They make a fine showing in the light of noon, and few guess the peril which lurks in them unless I happen to mention the country name "hawkweed." The spreading habit of hieracium aurantiacum is then generally unmasked, but it is still possible to earn it a measure of respect by using the other less notorious folk-name "twelve apostles."

The orange hawkweed does and does not deserve its bad reputation. Planted in the border in full sun it will speedily form a dense mat, over-running and crowding out more desirable plants. Nothing it offers in colour makes up for the room it takes if planted in the wrong place, and it has nothing else of value, being scentless, short-lived, and of no delicacy of form. But it has its proper place in the high and dry part of the rockery; there it will make a splendour of rich colour, clothing and beautifying a spot where few other plants will grow.

When it drops its flaming furs, and goes to seed, it has a new beauty to many eyes in the pure white fluff of the tiny what-o'clocks it carries. The small oblong seeds, crowded together, have each a parachute of gossamer fluff, so that when the wind blows, these what-o'clocks are broken from the parent head and take flight on the exciting adventurous winds, each tiny black seed hanging tight on to his glistening parachute and travelling high overhead till a lull in the wind drops him down again somewhere, where he may find himself on stones, or water, doomed to destruction, or snug on the good earth with all the ups and downs of life in front of him.

The "shaggy hawkweed" or hieracium villosum is claimed to be a better garden plant, easily kept from spreading, but I have never personally grown it. It has showy bright golden flowers and silvery foliage; hieracium nivale is, I believe, the only white-flowered species in the genus; it is found on the Tyrolean Alps and has somewhat leathery leaves of a nice glaucous green; for those who like white flowers this variety has its attractions.

With all my desire to be fair to hawkweed and give it a chance on this pleasant round earth, I have my misgivings when I see it flourishing so bravely in Steve's garden! There are places in New England where it would certainly be called a noxious weed. . . .

I believe I have a disorderly mind towards weeds; I am not able to hate them enough . . . there is that teazle. . . .

In Kent, England, on the bank over my larger pond are many delightful wildlings, things that are welcome to any garden—bluebells, orchids, anemones, foxgloves, primroses, violets—and in the hedges are spurge laurel and the red periwinkle. These come and go in their seasons and are accepted as treasures by the most sophisticated, but here and there among them are some plants that I treasure, for one reason or another, which seem to be a cause of stumbling among the weaker brethren.

One day a party of members of the National Gardens Guild were going round the place with me, and presently I heard a man say, "There seem to be a few teazles here!" He spoke kindly, as one would refer delicately to a scandal.

But I love my teazles, and when the rougher plants are weeded out from what is, after all, a semi-wild spot, these are always carefully left. They are, for one thing, beautiful, both in the stage of green leaf and in the mauve blooming. And for another, they are very interesting, being a part of the history of the English countryside.

On one side of nearly all the lovely old fourteenth-century

houses of my part of Kent one finds a rather muddy pond, muddy because of its clay bottom—a sensible deep, fish-loved pond, the marl-pit of the cloth-workers who built up fortunes there, long ago.

It would seem that before the fourteenth century the people of England wore very rough woollens. Edward the Third, an enterprising monarch, learned that the Flemings had found a way of fulling and of carding the coarse wool into a richer cloth, and he invited them, or enticed them or imported them, I am not very sure which, to come and teach the English their trade secrets.

And they did come.

And they made the part of Kent in which my old house stands (with its deep, muddy ponds adjacent) exceedingly rich and prosperous. They fulled the cloth—that is to say, milled it—and used the marl, or fuller's earth, to absorb the grease and oil of the wool.

It is queer stuff, that fuller's earth, which made us so many little ponds in Kent —a kind of clay, difficult to define. In colour it is generally a greeny-grey and turns to brown or white under the weather. When we dig up streaks of it in the gardening operations and try to model it into shapes, it falls to pieces, for it is not really plastic; but it has the distinguishing characteristic of absorbing grease and clarifying oil. It is used nowadays in many ways besides in fulling—in soap-making, in filtering mineral oils, and so on.

But it is the teazles which interest me most, despised by those modern gardeners who cannot perceive how seemly a herb it is, flourishing by my pond and telling its story of the centuries foregone.

In spring it sends up its tall, stout, rigid stem; bearing large, spreading, opposite leaves of a good wholesome living green; and presently the bases of them make their cups. They are strong cups, always full of water, and I wish I knew whether it is rain or dew, caught and stored, or some sweet secretion like those mysterious tears in the great fritillaries, the Crown Imperials. Whichever

The Woods of Maine come down to the Sea

it is the liquor has a fatal attraction for flies, little beetles and small winged creatures. It is crystal clear at first, but very soon becomes stained with their tiny bodies.

I have a suspicion that the teazle feeds on this witch's broth, but I do not know for certain. The botanical name of the genus, Dipsacus, means "to thirst," and the variety I like to watch by my pond is Dipsacus Fullonum, the fuller's teazle;—the scabious family is related to it.

The tall stems grow on and on, bearing at last conspicuously beautiful heads of purple flowers. The time of the blooming of these self-sown teazles is pretty, and they have other admirers than this unfashionable soul . . . earwigs love them too! The purple flowers are subtended by long, stiff, hooked bracts. They poured great wealth into the Weald of Kent in ancient England, for the Flemings knew how to "teaze" or raise the nap on woollen cloth with them—and that was one of the mysteries they brought across the sea six hundred years ago.

I like to see the fuller's teazles telling their tale of industry to the initiate, and scandalising fashionable visitors who expect to find in my garden only "exhibition" flowers!

This hawkweed . . . those coy Kalmias . . . the dear rough teazles . . . personalities which companion our days, if we will admit them;—amusing, rugged creatures in every form of life, manifest . . . sometimes I think we harden for ourselves the arteries of happiness in our half-terrified selectiveness.

The sun pours down more strongly: I hear Walter by the well, in Sally's garden next door. . . . I must go over the warm flowery grass of Steve's enchanted meadow to breakfast in a few minutes. . . . This is a lovely place, I love it all. Sally has made her home in the wood most cleverly,—you can't see it from the sea, but from the cool, great music room you can look straight to the sea through a cool green shade. . . . Walter is probably taking water to the roses . . . he is a Maine fisherman and that means so much,—fine clear small features, a compact, well-knit frame, a rigid honesty, an unalienable loyalty to any he and-ready instinct; he is a good woodman and ditcher, and they say he made good bricks; in the garden he has often driven me to the extreme edge of exasperation with his dreadful mistakes . . . but there are always the crumbs. . . .

He taught me a lot about mushrooms; that clever old brain would in easier circumstances have belonged to a *bon viveur*; he has a passion for the delicate leaf-mouldy taste of mushrooms, and as the fields are raided by all and sundry for the common varieties known to the multitude with their button or their umbrella shapes, their pink or their brown gills underneath, he early set himself to learn the rare edible fungi; and now I have learned, too, from him how to find the delicious honeycombed morels, that look like bits of pale rubber sponge, and the amethyst agarics, and those long bomb-shaped agarics which are of an exceedingly pearly white beneath, and a rich nutty flavour, as well as the big ivory puff balls and yellow funnel mushrooms that are invariably called toadstools by people who have not had the advantage of learning the old man's unusual lore. I feast on his wisdom and share my fields with him.

I once acquired merit with those long agarics. Two ladies from Pittsburgh, Miss Edwards and Miss Stoney, have a beautiful old house at Pevensey, not fifty miles from mine. They are friends I cherish; it is pleasant to see their car at my garden gate. One day they came unexpectedly with a basket full of the beautifully pearly fungi. . . . They wanted to know if they were good to eat. I did not know then that they were; we sat round the terrifying things and wondered! They ended by leaving them with me;—and I consulted Morphett.

The fungi made a wonderful breakfast dish next morning. I wired, "Have eaten the lot, am still alive," and earned an easy reputation for dash and daring.

Morphett learns things from me, very slowly and generally with but a grudging grace. He has a truly Moslem contempt for women, and keeps me well in my place.

But there is one thing he has learned which enchants him so much that it has become a sort of refrain, and that is the advantage of using chemical fertilisers in most of their forms. There is one form he dislikes.

At times I have found myself wishing I had not let loose this concentrated fiend in the garden, for I have a profound and obstinate affection for farm-yard manure when I can get it . . . not an everyday matter in this era of motor-power.

I like to have my soil rich in the humus farm-yard manure supplies, and well cultivated; and *then* use upon it the invaluable artificials which come in the artificial manure bags.

Since farm manure means heavy barrowing and digging, I have had to fight every year with my old woodpecker to get it dug into the soil, but it was always done after a tussle and it was followed by reinforcements of a chemical nature at various times which I attended to myself, not daring to trust the Primitive with the delicate matter of the balancing of my plant menus. I prefer to struggle in the half-light of my own small knowledge of chemistry.

One year I found that H. H. Thomas was recommending Norco fertilisers—and his word I accept in garden affairs with the blindest faith. He has never misled me yet.

So the bags of Norco soon arrived, each labelled clearly for its special purpose; perfectly balanced and thoroughly well-mixed fertilisers. I surveyed them with approval and decided Morphett might be instructed in the way of using them in their proper places and times, since they were almost fool-proof.

He accepted his lesson with quiet glee; I did not immediately perceive the reason and rejoiced to see how carefully he was following instructions—forking his powder lightly into the damp earth and using the right fertiliser for each place,—one for the roses, one for the kitchen garden, one for sweet peas, and so on.

I must say the result staggered the old chap; the good

supplies of nitrogen phosphate and potash washed down to my well-cultivated soil gave us rich and abundant growth. He was genuinely astonished; but sophistication speedily followed that naïve and sincere emotion. Nothing will now induce him to use the heavy farm-yard manure barrow; he is prepared to lavish Norco for the rest of his days !

"Look at these 'taters," he says; "and what be wrong with they roses? Farm muck ain't no manner of use when you can get this 'ere stuff."

But he dislikes the Norco lawn sand! Intensely. It makes the grass grow green and strong; and that means more mowing.

True, he found that mowing is shorn of much labour now that he has inveigled Tom the Postman into wearing a sort of harness and acting as a draught-horse while Morphett guides the machine from the back. He ambles along on his crescent legs up and down the not inconsiderable lawns, and Tom strains in front, a willing amiable little man.

*   *   *   *   *

Back to Sally's cool house on the rocky ledges. Blanche is setting out breakfast; and as usual Gertrude has made hot cakes that offer a perilous heavenly temptation!

CHAPTER XX

MAINE FIREFLIES

I OBSERVED with astonishment when I walked on the sands among the rocks below Sally's house that streams of water spouted up here and there; slender jets of water shot up with force and made my legs wet as I went by.

"That," said Walter, "is clams."

"Can I get some?" I asked, thrilled to the core to think I might come close to these delectable fish in their native pastures, and perhaps even gather enough to take to Gertrude, the coloured cook, to wreak her magic upon. Gertrude did not know it, but I had for her a very real affection in spite of the way she led me into the cruellest temptations at every meal with the wonderful things she sent to table. I loved to hear her talk in her soft voice, about the sea and the flowers and the sky. She noticed all the beauty round her, and was very handsome in a big, old, splendid way. She could feel—and could make me feel, too, by the changing colour in her emotional speaking voice.

Walter said I could get clams—and he would show me how. So off we set at low tide with a queer short clam-fork, like a short-handled deep-tined rake, and a bucket. In New York I had grown used to the delicious taste and rather hard texture of "little Neck" and "Cherrystone" clams, preferring them to any American oyster, always excepting the marvellous Bay St. Louis oyster! I did not know then that Little Necks are the young of the *hard* clam, a deep-water shellfish; so I was much frustrated to find myself digging out, on Sally's beach, long, blue mussel-shaped shells, spouting vigorously, and to learn that these accessible delights were another variety—they were soft clams with a thin shell and long siphon.   I dug industriously, to Walter's great amusement, for I soon found out how the biggest and fattest grew under the seaweed by the rocks in black sand; and we went back up the rocks with a good bucketful and gave them to Gertrude who was not very pleased because her carefully-thought-out menu was all ready for the day.

She learned in time that this odd English guest had a passion for harvesting things—and bringing in the fruits of land or sea to her clever hands. . . .   I would come in every morning with baskets of blueberries from the meadow next door,—"Steve's Meadow"—(clever, handsome, debonair Steve, away in Paris forgetting Maine) . . . and sometimes we would come in from the boat with buckets of flounders flapping uncomfortably.   Gertrude grew to associate me with sudden offerings and even the yellow cat learned to greet me with a fishy leer when we met under the pines.   And as to Rigoletto.—Rigoletto adored clams.

There was mud as well as rock and clam-sand on the shore, too; mud that made one's limbs tingle if you rubbed it on them at bathing-time.   Dr. Moorhead said that the water was full of radium and that was why everyone felt so well on that coast.   His wife had been over in England studying our wireless methods, and she had met a good many of the people of the London Studio whom I knew; we had some merry conversations together, and I told her what I thought of broadcasting in New York: she retaliated with a tale of British ignorance and told me how Lord Robert Cecil had said, while his wife was giving her some lithospermum: "I thought America had no gardens, only road signs and tin cans!"   So I expounded the tale of my own liberation from a network of similar misapprehension.

We spent our time fishing, bathing, roaming the woods; in picnics and sailing . . . it was no wonder people's faces

had grown sick with longing when they heard the word
"Maine" in New York!   And now here was the opening
of a Theatre Season thrust into all these simple, pleasant
things.

Sally had kept on talking about a Theatre . . . the
"Little Theatre" . . . the "Surry Theatre" . . . words that
meant nothing to me until they crystallised one night soon
after we arrived at Ledgewood Clippings with the remark:

"We go to the Surry Theatre to-night; it is the opening
of the Summer Season."

It sounded rather grand.   I knew, of course, that the
"Summer people" of Blue Hill, of Bar Harbour, of Mount
Desert and all that part of the Maine coast are of the
fashionable world, but I had somehow abandoned myself
to the joyful fancy that this house freed itself from all
the accustomed trammels and obligations of the social
treadmill and enjoyed the marvels of these enchanted woods
upon the shores of a crystal sea in admired simplicity.

We set off in the car after dinner along the dark, winding roads smelling of green woods and meadow hay, of
ozone from the rocks and salt sea winds . . . the darkness crackled with sharp lights as we went, flashes of
brilliance where the fireflies danced.   They made the
darkness snap at us.

As had become quite usual with me in America by
now, I had to undo a preconceived opinion.   I soon
learned that the Surry Theatre gives its own peculiar
flavour to life in that favoured countryside.   It is in
the nature of a school of acting because there the young
artists from Philadelphia and New York, etc., find the
opportunity for playing bigger parts under fine direction
than they have had a chance to play before in larger
companies, and they live in the cool sea-breezes for the
summer, so they can go back to their autumn, winter
and spring engagements in the big cities refreshed in
body as well as further accomplished in their Art.   It is
a fine idea in which the advantage is much to the "summer
people."   The company is made up of nice young men

and women of Vassar, Yale and Harvard, keen with the
ideals of youth ; ambitious; poor; and very pleasant to
look upon. They have a zeal for their art and do not
care how hard they work to learn more about it.

If that "Little Theatre" were only run for the wealthy
summer holiday-makers it would still be worth recording; but it is more than that. Leighton Rollings who
founded it has to his credit in it the establishment of the
first Summer Repertory Theatre and watching him about
his business I perceived that he is a man who follows a
star—he knows how to pick people, and while I might
surmise that in the matter of vile pence he has the tradi-
tional bewilderment of genius in the face of clogging
material, in matters of inspiration he is not at fault. The
Summer Theatre was to him a child; I beheld in him indeed the "pelican vulning" when finance committees were
toward; his fine, soft, rather scanty hair swept back in a
startled candour from his earnest brow, no one was too
mighty to approach, no one too busy to waylay if some
matter of the Theatre must be decided. Only one thing
mattered: the well-being and future security of his dream.

Sally used to shake her golden head. . . . "I believe
I shall end by owning that theatre," she would say. She
was a stalwart patron of the project: and by this time I
believe she has indeed shouldered most of the burden!

In that little theatre, set on a hill looking toward the
mountains of Mount Desert Island, we had good plays and
good acting. Leighton had been literary manager of the
Boston Repertory Theatre and closely associated with Mr.
and Mrs. Charles Coburn at the Coburn Theatre, New
York, so he was able to make the wise choice of Leo
Bulgakov to train his young company. He and Madame
Bulgakov,—a lovely and most accomplished actress,—had
been with the famous Moscow Arts Theatre where the
whole school of training is based on sincerity and hard
work. Bulgakov will work hours to get one single inflection right in his productions,—he always made his cast
dig their presentations out of themselves. He never told

them how to say a line. . . . He would explain how the character was thinking or how it felt and from that they must give out the action and the voice inflection.

I have often sat in a great theatre and been bored, and offended, too, with stale mechanical gestures with false unconvincing voices . . . it was fascinating to see this utterly sincere and brilliant artist teaching these young people how to win the truth out of themselves and to realise that only the truth was fit to give. He was piercingly shrewd, too. In some who seemed quite likely he detected the vanity or the stupidity which would ever stand between them and the truth.

Every week the young company gave us a new play; and sometimes they would fill Sally's beautiful house with their youth and their laughter . . . Harry Green with his fine head, his slow gibes and his quick wit; Judith Elder with her clever brain and dilettante ways, her broad face and exquisite profile; George Cotton, the tall Spartan soldier who rolled so convincingly down the steps in Lysistrata and who, for some jest I have now forgotten, was known as my Peach-Pie Paramount; Sylvia Wade with her sensitive brilliance; Fred Daly, the musician, with his curly head thrown back, his blue eyes sparkling, an ever-ready Troubadour who for his many arrows we called "Sebastian"; Shepperd Strudwick, the young Southerner with his warm voice and fiery heart; Henry Peirce, looking like the heir of an English duke; and Chase Adams, the young St. Francis of Assisi—and more, and more . . . charming, merry children in their firefly youth.

Sebastian and I got shipwrecked once; we went on the rocks and were cast on the shore because we were looking at the sunset and the moonrise instead of where we were going; that was after Frederick de Wolf Pingree's picnic. . . . Sebastian was rowing—we were lost in waters of pearl among the isles.

But Frederick de Wolf Pingree,—the author,—he of the picnic, and I, had a more watery adventure still, on another occasion. His picnic was great fun; Shura Bulgakov and I dug clams for it all the morning and got so hot that we had to swim; Rigoletto, the silver tabby Manx kitten, pursued us from rock to rock like an elf, —being mightily enamoured of clams which it ate with intense earnestness, like some old epicure his caviare;—and later Walter took us in the motor-boat to Freddy's Island, where we sang and had eggs and sandwiches and watermelons and doughnuts and peppermints and marshmallows, and Rigoletto went half mad with thirst after his clams . . . we came home by moonlight to Sally's wonderful house of bewitchment in the enchanted woods, where we sat round a leaping log fire and heard Bulgakov and Bulgakova talk of Duse and Ysaye; of Isadora and Mordkin; of Rasputin, of Moscow, of the Czar—before 1914 . . . and then Sally sang Rigoletto.

She was going to be a great singer; only Dr. Greene caught his nightingale and caged it for himself; but she always keeps up her singing though it never became her profession.

At breakfast on the Ledge where humming birds hovered over the purple petunias and red fuchsias, where I tried to resist Gertrude's blueberry muffins,—came Frederick de Wolf Pingree.

"Would I go sailing with him?"

I would. Some day.

Shura, son of Leo and Madame Bulgakov, is a very delightful boy, sturdy, and clever; I liked fishing with him, he did not talk too much; we would sit in our little boat enisled in the grey, lost in a world of sea and mist; of barking seals and flying herons; of laughing gulls and noisy terns and lobster pots,—the shore and the spruce-clad hills hidden in a sea-fog. We would haul in bright blue cunners with yellow mouths; and "scalpens" (which I think are John Dorys) and hope for flounder.

The roads of my morning walks were gay with evening primroses, bunchberries, red yarrow, blueberries, clintonia, roses, fireweed, spiræas in many forms, and the starry Michaelmas daisies; but it was hard to walk, for cars kept coming by and offering me a lift. No one could believe I *wanted* to walk! So at last I took to the woods and never found my way at all to the pitcher-plant bogs where Mr. Kurrie had promised to show me a lot of the queer flowers in bloom. And presently I could not go anyway to see him and his blue delphiniums and gay humming birds and merry wife and all, because he was unhappy. His close friend, that distinguished and most attractive sailor, Admiral Rousseau, died very suddenly; and my gay, delightful garden-friend, Gladys, was a widow. It was a shock to us all;—I could not forget her laughing eyes among the tall blue flowers of her Maine garden as I had seen her but a few days before . . . by her charming old New England cottage. . . .

Suddenly Sally and I were on the road again! We were off to a fishing camp at Rangeley.

"We will go to the pool of the nymphs," said Sally, and as usual I was lit up into strange, impossible fires by a word. "The pool of the nymphs"—"A fishing camp in Maine." . . .

I saw slim marble maidens by the side of a deep dark pool . . . and rough log cabins by a flowing river, where we fishermen would sleep on beds of balsam boughs, catching our fish for sustenance and cooking it in the open.

But no. I must say the "wild" is well bitted in America. I begin to believe that a *real* rough simplicity will soon be the most expensive thing left on earth. . . . The houses in the camp were made of sawn logs; with plumbing, hot and cold; there were made roads through the woods where I had hoped to plunge into ferny deeps. And our hostess was not a bronzed, open-air, weather-bitten, rough old sport but a slender, lovely woman of fashion from Boston, about to remove to New York! The realist things in all this fantasy of "simplicity" were the guide and the beaver dam.

Perhaps one might also say the biting flies.

Frank Nile, the guide, was a dear; he took me through the woods,—and paid me the compliment of saying I saw more than he did. But then he was not so young as he had been and he had grown used to sawn log houses and made roads! There were white-throated sparrows singing in the woods, where green clintonia berries were turning blue and the brakes were thick with wild raspberries; we looked for humming-birds' nests and traces of black bears, but found instead the bright red berries of Solomon's Seal.

We had a great talk about swallows, some of which he persists in declaring hibernate through the winter. I believed that Hudson and others had quashed that thought known to Gilbert White. He told me he knew a man who had cut down a decayed pine tree in January and found hundreds of chimney swifts hibernating there, many years ago.

"John Bubier is very old now: he saw them: and Frank Philbrick who was 75 or so and died last year saw barn swallows go in the mud——" he said. I wished I could have talked to these men myself!

We got back to Mrs. Marion Chapin's bungalow, full of fresh air and bites, and found Sally and her full of that replete and satisfied air which old friends have when they have met again for a real good gossip.

I liked Mrs. Chapin, apart from her beauty; for she loves animals and her house was full of pets. The little creatures show the quality of the personality they live with in a score of ways to another animal-lover.

Koko was very indiscreet; he whistled and sang and sneezed and that was all right: but when he kept saying: "Hullo, Marion!" in a rich expectant voice and then giving loud kisses I felt that he was betraying poor Mr. Chapin's devotion in a shameless way. Even a grey parrot *with* a red tail might have some reticences.

It was my birthday. I kept thinking of Mother all those long years ago in a small room in a South African rectory surveying this newly arrived visage with passionate joy while her young husband hung over her . . . protective . . . thankful. Poor mothers of all the world . . . they are so glad when the hair-shirt materialises!

Bunny, the Chu-Erh Peke, had something to say about it. He was jealous. He did not care for the way the other Marion laid a parcel by this Marion's cup at breakfast . . . or the gay chat that followed the opening.

He would be upset if he saw that beautiful little basket of coloured porcupine quills beside me now. . . . A very jealous little dog of surprising beauty, but not so surprising seeing his pedigree. . . .

The fish are land-locked salmon, and of those Mrs. Chapin caught the nine-pound one; brook trout go into the lakes here (the place is a chain of lakes), and grow very big ; it is the only place in the world that they do, says Agassiz.

Frank the guide got us our breakfast, boiling the coffee and making toast for us with slow quiet movements; and then he took Sally and me on to the Kenebego stream where we clambered out of the canoe and up the gnawed logs of the beaver dam.

One needs to see the real thing to realise how these little creatures can alter the geography of a country; they had made an enormous lake and on it grew yellow water-lilies—Frank called them "mud lilies." They were like golden incurved kingcups lying on the water among flat floating nymphœa leaves.

Mrs. Chapin's garden was one of the smallest I did see, bar none, in America. But she loves it dearly. She grows the meadow lily with its lovely hanging bells on slender stems (lilium Canadense). Its gracefully pendant swaying bells like even swamps before they will forego moisture; but the red, or wood, or flame lily (lily Philadelphicum) likes dry places and full sun in open sandy spaces. Tiger lilies (lilium tigrinum) and day lilies (hemerocallis fulva) seem to love Indian Rock or Blue Hill equally.

On the way back to the clams and the sea and clever

Blanche and dangerous Gertrude and good Walter, we
passed *forests* of Joe-pye weed. It is a handsome com-
posite with pink heads of tubular florets; it has thin rough
saw-edged foliage in whorls and grows three to ten feet
high in moist soil of meadows and woods. Butterflies
adore Joe-pye weed. Now I had touched and seen it,
"Wychwood," of my unknown gardener's book in Wisconsin, shone for me in a fresh illumination.

To get back to Blue Hill we had to pass through
Bangor. When we were children long ago we used to sing
a lot of odd chantys in the winter evenings . . . a bunch
of fat babes and school lads and lassies . . . we sang loudly
with great pleasure ditties which had no meaning to us
at all. . . . There was one:

> Riding down from Bangor, in an Eastern train
> After weeks of hunting in the woods of Maine
> Sat a student fellow. . . .

I forget how it goes on . . . but interminable verses disclosed the story of a tunnel, and "a tiny little ear-ring
in that horrid student's beard" . . . a line which was
always sung with great expression by Alice the chubby,
the blue-eyed, who seemed to know exactly how the ear-
ring got there; which I didn't—though I was two years
older. Father's dark eyes would rest upon her thoughtfully while she raised her cherub face to shrill out the
tale . . . Alice, away in Vancouver, grey-haired and widowed
now. . . .

Suddenly I realised we, Sally and I, were "riding down
from Bangor" . . . that the song we children had sung
by the English fireside had been an American student
song. However did we come by it?

And did students ever wear beards?

I sang it aloud in my excitement at remembering all
this so suddenly, to Walter's extreme alarm. He hurried
the car along. He was used to Sally's elegant soprano,
and this peculiar growling was unlike any sound she ever
made. I should like to be a singer. . . .

There are many beautiful gardens in Maine, but I was
very particularly happy in two . . . at North East Harbour
after we had made merry with our friends at Thrushwoods
we went to see Mrs. Arnold Wood's garden, a space in
the pines, where everything grows with a sweet will.
"Having no money, I try to get the best results for the least
labour and the least cash, and do it all myself," she laughed
gaily.   It was a garden precious to me because of the loving
cleverness which had made it.   The house is of the New
England farmhouse type and Mrs. Wood has used vines to
soften any hard lines.   Good hedges protect the garden from
North winds; there were clouds of spiræas and masses of
day lilies, huge delphiniums (which grow marvellous well
in Maine), fuchsias; the native pines and birches were
used with a sense of decoration to frame views of the sea;
sedums and campanulas, thalictrum, and polemonium, irises,
lobelia and a lily-pool with no hard rim, for there were
grasses and flowers flowing over to soften it.   She had
mandarin hats hanging from the trees to hold seeds for
the birds!   And in every way one looked it was plain to
see that energy and affection and fine taste walked with
all this gardener did. . . .

At Castine I found again the lady of April charm.   She
and her good-looking daughter took me to Mrs. Hutchins's
garden at Penobscot Bay.   There I sojourned with a
new-old friend,—new in time, but old from everlasting
in communion of spirit, for she has made her garden
out of the rough.   It was a sheep pasture, where everything
was grazed off but juniper, a place which her husband
acquired only as headquarters for sailing.

Patiently year by year she has learned the earth-lessons,
making her soil with much haulage of sand and farm-
yard manure by scow across the bay, by farmhorses with
meadow-soil up the hill, and by little boys with burlap
bags full of leaf-mould from the woods.

"My garden," she said, "does not live up to modern
standards; it simply grows flowers.   It lacks colour-schemes
and design.   When a plant seeds itself I leave it to grow

where it has chosen to,—in the soil that owes its existence
to so many efforts . . . to scow and beaches, barnyards
and horses, a meadow and woods,—and chiefly willing
hands to remove weeds and stones from and constantly
turn it over and spade it deep!"

In her tool-shed is a text;—I am not given to these
spiritual cocktails as a rule—but I record hers:

"He who sows the ground with care and diligence acquires a greater
stock of religious merit than he could gain by the repetition of ten thousand
prayers."

This my friend Mrs. Hutchins, like my friend Mrs. Keen
in England, loves to grow things from seed (a gardener's high
caste mark). Unlike many Americans she grows her *trees*
from seed; the pink Japanese cherries are now very tall
with big trunks, though they are only seventeen years
old,—and maples, also from seed. She grows named
bearded irises in great number, and wonderful delphiniums
and verbascum, as well as some of the dear old friends I
seldom seem to find in gardens; *real* tarragon,—viburnum
Davidii, with its turquoise berries, and that other David
—clematis Davidia, the bush clematis, with whorls of pale
blue velvet flowers that smell like hyacinth,—snake-root,
—and a large bush of lemon verbena which is taken in
its tub to the root-cellar for the winters. . . . Impulsively,
as we parted, she pressed a little picture into my hand,
a photograph of a lonely road . . . a New England road,
. . . empty of people, winding along to a distant sky.
And now, every morning when I wake up to the English
dawns, that road in America is the first call of the open that
greets me . . . it lives over the window in front of my bed.

Frederick de Wolf Pingree chose a lull in a day of
sudden storms and pelting rain to take his English lady
for her sail.

I lowered myself gingerly into the cat-boat, reflecting
on the glare of warning that had shone in Walter's eye
when I got out of the car.

"You ought not to go," he said.

"It's all right," said Frederick.

I could not possibly show a white feather in face of his assurance, and so off we went.

I sat on a soap-box and asked if I could help.

"You can hold that," said he, snappily, being much overtaken with ropes and things,—and so I held the centre-board down.

The boat sulked and flew by turns; every now and then the wind blew hard and it turned on its side. We were out in a waste of gloomy dark waters; Freddy told me to run up the hill quick and sit on the edge of the boat to tip it straight again. I did it several times; weight has its uses. In between these pastimes I studied my gallant's absorbed face,—and held the centre-board,— which suddenly began to feel peculiar and jerk under my hand. I mentioned it to F. de W. P., who was entirely absorbed in the sail; he was looking up, like a boy flying a kite, staring at it and holding the string. When I told him about the bumping he changed completely and got very excited. His phlegm departed;—he let his string go and the sail flew out like a great angry bird.

I gathered up the rope reproachfully, letting go of the centre-board, now quite unmanageable . . . I gathered the rope in and pulled the sail taut. I felt thrifty and useful.

But Fred had turned into a demon. He snatched at my hands and flung the rope all over the place,—and then jumped overboard and pushed the cat-boat off the rocks.

That was where we were; the bay is full of hidden ledges and rocks.

I did not like seeing Freddy in the sea; it was lonely in the boat, with all that rope lying about and a swinging boom. I was glad when he scrambled in again—wet and dripping.

After that we were lost in the bay for hours, tearing up and down in the wind and pelting rain,—round buoys and things. I did not care for the way we were sailing at all.

Whenever we got near the landing-float at Harpers

Point the boat shot by it, and Freddy said it was a "difficult night to make a landing."

I reviewed my past life and found out that I regretted
not the things I had done, but those which I hadn't.

It is not adventure which is sin, but being afraid of
adventure. . . . Anyway, I had had a fuller life than most
women.

 *   *   *   *   *

And I gather I kept an appearance of stolidity, because
I heard afterwards that Mr. Pingree's chief cause of thanks-
giving was "at any rate Mrs. Cran had no idea of the
danger we were in."

Silly ass.

 *   *   *   *   *

It was good-bye to Steve's meadow; to the blueberries
and sweet fern,—to Frederick de W. and his perilous
delights; to Sebastian and his music; to the rich lustre
of summer evenings; to the unbelievable dawns; to my
walks in the early hour of crystal clear perceptions; to
swimming in sharp, cold waters,—good-bye to Maine.

The Surry Theatre Company, having given a Special
Matinee at Bar Harbour, and played their evening bill
at Surry, came over all the seventeen miles to Ledgewood
Clippings to serenade Sally the night before we left for
New York.

They sang in the midnight dusk of her woods,—a
lovely gesture of farewell from those weary young bodies.
They looked beautiful, offering their tribute of love out
of the shadows . . . in their young, empty hands the
riches of Heaven.

Sally stood by her open doorway framed in light,—the
small, fair woman with the heart to feel and the ear to
hear.

And then she and I were away, away, to the open seas
. . . and Europe. . . .

The last garden I saw in America was Mrs. Samuel
Sloan's.

There was a day or two to spare in New York before

the *Leviathan* sailed; I went to Garrison near West Point, and saw her stately green garden, where her father-in-law planted every tree sixty-five years ago. In 1873 there was not a tree at Lisburne Grange; only crinolines!

"Everybody seems to think a garden must mean flowers!" she said, "but this is a green room full of the outdoor sense. I prefer trees to herbaceous borders; I find flowers restless and too exciting!

The trees are magnificent, one gingko is eighty feet high and eighty feet in girth,—and there are magnificent chestnuts, white maple, and larches, great American elms, copper beech . . . Canadian spruce on the wide green lawns. It was interesting to meet a gardener after all my long and varied garden travel in America who was able to give me at the very last gasp the fillip of something different to others.

Mrs. Sloan has definite tastes—and in the result she has one of the most reposeful gardens imaginable. The balustrades and banisters of stone stairways and terraces are clothed in green ivy.

"I have learned the secret of wintering ivy here," she said. "We lay the strands flat on the ground, unhook the ropes and lay them down, and they do not get frozen." . . .

I remembered the same trick with canes of loganberry in Vancouver Island. . . . It is fun getting the better of frost!

Lisburne Grange is well placed,—it has a constant current of air; from the library window one looks on deep after deep of green; no colour at all;—one could feel the courage and the vision of the brave old Mr. Sloan who planted for the views,—the majestic views; framing them in young trees which, not he, but the next generation would enjoy in their splendour. We went over the farm and saw a fine herd of Guernseys with their neat bull,—saw pigs and ducks and squab pigeons,—admired the new swimming-pool, designed in the Italian manner; the avenue of magnolia glauca; and the sweet-scented pot plants on the terrace.

We talked, laughing, of the time Mrs. Sloan came to speak at the Garden Club in London, years ago, and disclosed to each other our mutual tremors; we spoke with love and admiration of Mrs. Tom Robins's great-hearted "garden" on harsh sea rocks.

When I left the sun was setting in glory . . . the Hudson a river of gold under great green hills.

* * * * *

The first thing I saw when I got to our rooms in the *Leviathan* was a large basket of "Marion Cran" roses from Pete and Lucia . . . the gracious dears!

Phillip Runciman was on board, a mournful shipmate, I think he missed his wife, so gay and kind . . . She knows how to find a bird's nest better than anyone . . . and she loves her garden, where I have pottered about full oft watching her work—lively and laughing—with Whiskers and Jenny barking around her feet for tennis balls to play with. Dogs are not very good for tennis balls. . . .

CHAPTER XXI

BACK IN KENT

AND my book should end here.

But it had to adventure along a fiery road with me before I might put down for English garden-lovers what they may see if they go to America. To get the book I had travelled a long way—it went out in unsubstantial hope and came back in four fat little note-books, and whatever it costs people to read, it cost me more to write, for the Scotch editor of the magazine, that "bought" me in America cutting out all the other papers who wanted my work, went back on his obligation. They tell me it is a common business method in the States. I know Americans best as friends, thank God!—for in friendship they do not let you down.

Well, I was back.

Loud bells rang in a new year over hills and pastureland; we raised our glasses to it; we held hands and touched the eternal sad-sweetness of the old and the lost year, while we smiled and well-wished upon the new.

And now even New Year's Day was gone, the week-end, hard on its tail, had prolonged the merry crew, but here was Sunday night and to-morrow my party would break up, and go. Once more I should be left to the fruitful silences, to my desk, to the strange unseen company of that mysterious cloud of witnesses every writer knows, which is called "the public."

I sat back in the shadows of the big music-room and looked at the faces of my friends;—sorry the hard-worn dear-valued Christmas holiday was over. They looked mysterious and beautiful in that mediæval room, where a lofty king-post soared up to the peak of the ancient roof, and great oak beams supported the span of tiles holding up the roof like a tent.

The lovely old house I adore and have won back from ruin by the sweat of brain and brow, gave each person there an added grace; they were listening to Lambert's "Rio Grande"; there were a young soprano; a dark-eyed professor of music—both attractive, delightful people; Michael Rimmerley and Jane with her abominable knight. I was sorry he had caught her at last, vain, good-looking brute that he was, and of a granite selfishness. He had dogged her long and persistently. Their engagement had been announced just before Christmas, and so, of course, I had had to ask him when I renewed to her the yearly invitation.

"It will be a squash," I said grudgingly, waiting for tea in her studio.

"Poor Betham! How you do hate him," laughed Jane, washing her brushes, while I scraped a palette.

They said of her that her eyes were too large, her nose too short, her skin too pale; but I loved her small, quick-moving body, the strength in the sensitive hands which painted those beautiful flower-studies for which she is famous. I loved to watch the changing lights of thought upon her pale face.

"How's Hug?" I asked abruptly.

"How do I know?" she said serenely, and I wondered if that old, wild, mad fever were truly stilled at last;—if she would be able to meet Hugh when she was Betham's wife, and not turn faint and sick as the bare sound of his name had made her for years after she divorced him.

This "being faithful" business is very difficult to dog-matise about. Hugh had been technically untrue, there was no getting out of it because he himself admitted it. I can hear to this day and ever shall, his steady fury of truthfulness.

"Yes, I embraced the woman carnally. What of it? It means no more than last night's dinner. She doesn't

count as much as your little finger-nail to me. We can't
break for a silly hour's rough play, Jane, not you and I."

But they could. She saw to it they could. In the white
heat of her jealous agony, reason was gone—nothing but
unbearable pain was there. It was pain to be near the
child—for she was little else in 1920. Hugh must suffer,
the more the better. She was pitiless, and suffer he did—
a very hell. I had a merry time between the two, loving
both. And even now I was the only person in the world
who dared use to her the old absurd pet name—no one but
me—not even Jane ever spoke of "Hug."

After eleven years she was going to marry Sir Betham
Wing;—good-looking; rich; but not good enough for her.
She had kept her pride inviolate;—flung herself into the
arena, fought and won. The friends who knew her
struggle rejoiced in her success. To the rest of the world
she was the popular, well-dressed young woman who
painted expensive and lovely flower pictures. Jane and
Betham were photographed in all the smart journals.

"Rio Grande" poured over me unnoticed while I watched
her and this man who had won her at last. It was a "scoop"
for him, and he knew it. Betham had political leanings
and with that went a way of playing to the gallery. He was
sprawling now on a very wide and majestic hook-rug, the
pride of my life, at Jane's feet; but he was watching the
beautiful adventurous profile of the young soprano who
with hair streaming back like the figure-head of a ship
was lost in the music . . . rapt and transported. He
would be faithless, too, of that I felt perfectly sure; only he
would probably intrigue and lie, and Jane would never
know . . . unless he got tired and meant her to.

I twisted on the divan and sighed. Life is a muddle—
there is no denying men are polygamous. It sometimes
seemed to me that Jane in grasping at the shadow of the
body of the man she loved had lost the substance of his
soul.

"Let me compose you a cocktail," said the young Don, as
the record ended—and my sigh made itself unduly heard

in the silence. "We all feel like you, it's the end of a jolly party."

So off we went to the kitchen. The others streamed out of the music-room to the dining-room downstairs.

"See we have a jolly fire," I shouted.

"Right-o—we'll put on a faggot," they said.

And so they did.

I never saw the start of the business. Michael Rimmerley and I were in the kitchen, mighty merry; being the Sabbath the maid was out, and so we were squeezing lemons and hunting for a tray and glasses while I told him the tale of Hetty and me and our speakeasy in New York, when suddenly the dark, leaded windows sprang into roseate light. The lawns, the pond, even the distant orchard were lit with a ruddy effulgence like some of those miraculous desert sunsets.

"By Jove," I said fatuously cheerful, "they *are* making a bright fire!"

Michael stared at the light and then at me; and the next thing I saw was a man's form racing in the bright light to the garage where the pigeons cooed sleepily, surmising an unexpected dawn.

"Now whoever is that, and what's the matter with *him*?" I thought, gathering up the tray of glasses hospitably.

In the passage I met Betham, furiously shaking a fire-extinguisher.

"How does the damned thing work?" he said.

Now I have two very elegant fire-extinguishers which I cherish, they were given to me by Bertie Jacobs, a nice Johannesburg engineer of high degree, years ago, to mark his appreciation of my old oak house; and they had hung where he put them ever since. I looked upon them as more or less sacred, as things to respect;—jewels;—precious gifts of love hanging on my walls. To find Betham rudely banging one about and swearing at it was a very great astonishment.

I put the tray back in the kitchen and went to the dining-room to see what it was all about. A noise like a squadron

of aeroplanes in flight met me;—and the great open fireplace where we burn mighty logs, where the troth-settle had
held Jane and Betham crowned with mistletoe only the night
before, was a roaring torrent of fire.

"Shut the door! Stop the draught," said the soprano,
her hair flown back, her bright eyes gleaming in the glare.

"You look like a Valkyrie," said Betham.

"Where are the fire-extinguishers!" cried the girl.

"There's another in the study, and one in the garage,"
I said, "but I don't know how they work—you stamp on
them or spit on them or wring their necks or something."

She pushed past me, and I followed, much confused to
see all this energy. Everything was suddenly out of my
hands. I had been ministering in a mood of benignant
sentiment to a parcel of placid guests—and now all in a
minute they were doing strange upsetting things; being
masterful and competent.

There was Jane at my desk calling out the Fire Brigade.
They are sacred people who have shrines and tokens
behind glass windows in streets, which you must not smash
under great penalties:—the *Fire Brigade*!

Everything was all wrong. In the clamour of my senses I
even thought I saw Hug looking at his lost wife through the
dark window-pane! A cold stream of foam struck me on
the cheek.

"I've done it! I've done it!" said the Valkyrie, running
back to the roaring flames with the extinguisher grown
vastly active, spurting out stuff like soap-suds.

Suddenly there shot into my veins, into my whole being
a violent apprehension. Was my house about to be burned
down? My beautiful little old house, six hundred years
of England—my last, best, dearest possession?—Not so
much a possession as a trust; the "long, low, white house"
of a soldier-sculptor's dreams . . . the house where I
waited till he should come again,—and recognise it for the
fantasy of long ago come true . . . waited while he barged
about the world getting into scrapes, the silly—the blind
—the dear. Anyone can build a house, but no one can

build an *old* house. Was this faithful, generous roof presently going to crash in—the great king-post outlined red in fire?—Had the little old house come to ashes? Was this the end of all dreams?

A hand on my shoulder, and there was Jane, so sweet. "Darling, have you any manuscripts lying about? You ought to take them out."

Of course! Of course! When houses catch fire things must be saved:—what must be saved? Everything. How could I get everything out . . .?

People pile furniture and things up on lawns: I had seen pictures of them in the daily press when houses were burned down; futile, pathetic heaps; piled anyhow.

I ran to the study and found four fat little books, thickly scribbled with names and names, of flowers and people, of a wonderful, lovely country—my American notes!

Out of doors, as in another existence the cold, brightness of a full moon shone on green lawns; the sweet, clean, night wind was edged with North . . . the village policeman was propping his bicycle by the front gate and a man ran under the shadow of a yew tree toward the house.

The little books looked very tiny on the lawn.

"Has the Fire Brigade come? Is that one of the men?" I asked. I longed for them passionately now—fire or no fire.

"They're coming; the maroon went off," said the guardian of the peace. "What was it you said, ma'am?"

"That man," I said, "is he one?"

"That was one of the gen'l'men in your 'ouse-party."

"No," said Michael's voice, "he's an advance fireman; he's been locating the water supply and he got the garage extinguisher to work and he's put out the lower part of the fire. Awful good chap. He knows his job. But, my dear, do come to Jane—she fell down some steps, and she's been sick; and Betham says it's a woman's job to help her; he's an ass!"

No one can say it is romantic to be sick, but when Betham saw poor little Jane stretched out like a rag, I did feel he might have bent his broad shoulders in her service and carried her to a bed.

"Bit of a mess, eh?" he said in a silly, conventional voice.

"Oh, get out of the way, you fool!" I said, "lend me a hand, Michael."

But before we could do a thing a man had swooped down and lifted her; all wet and bedraggled as she was, and was carrying her upstairs

Michael's round dark eyes goggled.

"It's the fireman," he said, "stout fellow!"

And just then with hooting and clamour and brazen regalia the Fire Brigade swept up. In a moment the house was swarming with men;—little ones and big ones;—familiar, homely faces from the country town near by, all dressed up in knives and hatchets and beautiful brass hats. . . .

"I say, you others, will you cope with the fire—I'll go to Jane," said I, and crept pitifully upstairs after those two.

She was lying very still; he was washing her face.

"Help me off with her dress," he said, "I'll roll her in a blanket."

"Is she hurt?" I asked.

"I don't think so. She saw me and crashed. Got any brandy?"

I went over to the medicine chest.

"How did you get here?" I said.

"I was driving back to London from Dymchurch and we ran out of petrol up the hill here. While they filled us up I heard someone say Coggers was alight, so I asked my friend to come round this way and drop me. He had to be back in Town by ten—or he'd have stayed, too . . . that's better . . . that's better, kid. . . ." Jane was moving. His bitter, passionate face was bent over her cold hands, chafing them. I went out softly and shut them in.

The firemen were perfectly wonderful. They swarmed up and down, on the lawns, up ladders, in every room but the blue one (where they were told there was a sick lady).

"She's asleep," I told the others, "leave her alone."

Whenever the brass helmets saw me, they offered kind words. "Leave it to us, ma'am; we'll soon have it out.— Good thing you called us, ma'am. These 'ere wood fires make a soot what sticks like cement and burns like tar . . . all these old beams o' yourn! . . . We'll soon put you right!"

And so they did.

And when Betham saw the house looking horribly cold and blank with no merry blaze left in it and the fireman mopping up flooded floors with pails and shovels and old dust sheets, he had one of his selfish brain-waves.

"Look here," he said, "I'll run the rest up to London to-night. Jane will want looking after, Marion,—you don't want a party as well."

The singer and the musician and Michael protested violently; they wanted to stay and help; but I snatched at the idea.

"That's a real kindness," I said heartily. "It really is a good idea. Jane needs sleep more than anything."

"We'll telephone first thing in the morning, and we'll fly back if we can help," said the Valkyrie anxiously.

*   *   *   *   *

The house was very quiet at last . . . I opened the blue-room door.

"You little fool," he was saying, "I want more than your barbaric physical integrity:—I give you more than mine!"

And Jane was saying "Hug!"

*   *   *   *   *

I crept out into the moonlit garden and retrieved four fat, damp books crammed full of untidy writing. . . .

And again that should be the end of the book!

But it is not. At breakfast next morning Hugh said, "I met Fergus last week, Marion; he's got an inferiority complex and won't ring you up. I told him he was a fool."

The world swam back . . . I was waltzing again with a swarthy, swash-buckling Troubador . . . I was sitting to be sculped . . . I was seeing a soldier off to France . . . visiting him in hospital . . . and then I was trying to forget him through long, desperate years.

"I hope he'll ring up," I said politely.

There came a midsummer eve when Gladys Rousseau bade us to Wassall Court in Kent, where dear people of both her land and mine smiled on him and on me.

THE BEGINNING

INDEX